Life Painted Red

Life Painted Red

The True Story of Corabelle Fellows and How Her Life on the Dakota Frontier Became a National Scandal

Chuck Raasch

TWODOT®

Essex, Connecticut
Helena, Montana

A · TWODOT® · BOOK

An imprint of Globe Pequot, the trade division of
The Rowman & Littlefield Publishing Group, Inc.
4501 Forbes Blvd., Ste. 200
Lanham, MD 20706
www.rowman.com

Distributed by NATIONAL BOOK NETWORK

British Library Cataloguing in Publication Information available

Library of Congress Cataloging-in-Publication Data
Names: Raasch, Chuck, author.
Title: Life painted red : the true story of Corabelle Fellows and how her life on the Dakota frontier became a national scandal / Chuck Raasch.
Other titles: True story of Corabelle Fellows and how her life on the Dakota frontier became a national scandal
Description: Essex, Connecticut : TwoDot, [2023] | Includes bibliographical references and index.
Identifiers: LCCN 2023008854 (print) | LCCN 2023008855 (ebook) | ISBN 9781493074136 (paperback) | ISBN 9781493074143 (epub)
Subjects: LCSH: Fellows, Corabelle. | Dakota Indians—Education. | Teachers—South Dakota—Biography. | Women—South Dakota—Social conditions—19th century. | Dakota Indians—Missions. | Dakota Indians—Social life and customs. | Interracial marriage—United States—History—19th century | Cheyenne River Indian Reservation (S.D.) | South Dakota—History.
Classification: LCC E97.65.S8 R33 2023 (print) | LCC E97.65.S8 (ebook) | DDC 978.004/975243092 [B]—dc23/eng/20230517
LC record available at https://lccn.loc.gov/2023008854
LC ebook record available at https://lccn.loc.gov/2023008855

∞™ The paper used in this publication meets the minimum requirements of American National Standard for Information Sciences—Permanence of Paper for Printed Library Materials, ANSI/NISO Z39.48-1992.

To Sandy, Will, Sam, Tessa, and Reena; family now, family forever.

Contents

Preface

Boundless, Limitless

It was high noon on the Great Plains. A gentle breeze tempered midday heat and coaxed into flowing motion a dreamy landscape of bromegrass and sagebrush. From a bluff on the rolling shoulders of the Missouri River a boundless lap of prairie expanded into 360-degree infinity. Cedar trees stood sentry over the breaks and ravines that ascended from the river. A meadowlark sang its story over a symphony of insects whose melody rose and fell with the wind. Overhead, a hawk perched on a power line, eyes darting for the next careless field mouse. Pillows of clouds, feathery white, blue on the bottom, played shade and shine games on the grassy ocean. Taken together, this canvas hinted at the naked power and mystical appeal of this place: comforting and inviting in its serenity, overwhelming and intimidating in its limitlessness.

The late-nineteenth-century teacher and author, Massachusetts-born Elaine Goodale became mesmerized with the deep mysteries of these plains. She had spent a single year traveling by horse and wagon across 2,400 miles of this place called Dakota, opening and inspecting government schools for Native children. Mocking maps that then called it the "Great American Desert," she quoted poet William Cullen Bryant in describing the allure: "These 'gardens of the desert,' these 'unshorn fields boundless and beautiful,'" she wrote, "enjoy the keen thrill of an exhilarating, truly intoxicating climate. Body and spirit are keyed to the pitch of that dry, clear atmosphere and dazzling sunlight."

Goodale marveled at the "subtle variety of the prairie landscape," an "undeveloped taste that complains of monotony in a scene that possesses the grandeur of ocean, with a mellow softness peculiarly its own."[1]

Forever, humans standing on this land would have felt the same overwhelming pull between connectedness and aloneness as I felt that warm July day in 2022. Along with its lonesomeness, this place emanated a soft, yet powerful reassurance. I had come, and I would go, but this place has been like this for a long time, and it shall continue into the infinite mysteries of tomorrow. One man-made change submerged part of it but retained the mystery in the deep-blue reservoirs from massive US government dam-building programs of the mid-twentieth century. Yes, Goodale was right—there is much more to the plains than monotonous expanse. Standing there, it was impossible to escape feeling that there were far greater things than I at work.

The Great Plains make you feel intimately alone yet innately connected in a way no other environment on the planet does. The open seas can produce a greater sense of aloneness, but they lack the reassurance, for beneath their roiling waters lie deep and foreboding dangers. Here on the plains, even when swept by the fiercest wind and snow, firmness lies beneath. Here, Heaven and Earth embrace. When the sinking sun paints brilliant splashes of red and orange and yellow across the entire horizon, you stand with the same awe the nomads who called this place home did thousands of years ago.

I had come to see the country around the tiny settlement of Swift Bird on South Dakota's Cheyenne River Indian Reservation. To say the village is hardscrabble is to understate hard and scrabble. A few dozen late-twentieth-century government Housing and Urban Development homes huddled in ravines and breaks on the rolling plateau overlooking the once wild Missouri. The Big Muddy has become more lake than river—the reservoir the Oahe Dam formed is actually now the ninth largest lake in the nation—after the US Corps of Engineers, in quest of flood control, irrigation, and recreation, dammed the Missouri six times over three states, from Montana to South Dakota. These gigantic dams, some of the biggest in the world, represent white civilization's grandest attempt to "civilize" the plains since the frontier was settled.

Swift Bird is so out of the way that some of its neighbors don't know it exists. There's a lot of that in this country. A guy in a South Dakota Transportation Department pickup scarcely thirty miles down the road and off the reservation told me he'd never heard of it. It's there if you want to find it, perched on a grassland just west of a quarter-mile-long bridge over the Missouri and scarcely a half mile south of Highway 212, the concrete slash that connects eastern and western South Dakota and dissects the Cheyenne Reservation. A young man in an old pickup assured me I was in the right place when I turned off Highway 212 on a rutted gravel-dirt road to approach the village.

Kids and teenagers lolled and played outside a few of the houses. Basketball hoops loomed over driveways. Bikes were strewn about. Three middle-aged guys, one wearing a Raiders football shirt, talked casually around an idling truck. Political signs for a tribal chair election were impaled in the hard earth. Virtually all the homes could use repair. Swift Bird displays the kind of naked poverty that has long denoted reservation life for many people of the Sioux nations.

The 2020 Census recorded 8,588 souls on 4,259 square miles of the Cheyenne River Indian Reservation. Three out of four were people of Native heritage. The poverty rate of almost 38 percent was three times the national average, the per capita income of $17,841 was half the national average. Half of the children under eighteen lived in poverty. But it is a stable population. Cheyenne River's "geographical mobility"—those who had moved in the previous year—was a fifth the national average, and almost all of them moved within the reservation.[2]

Although I left the state in the early 1980s, I was born and raised in South Dakota, about two hundred miles east of the Cheyenne River Reservation in the fertile glacial lakes of the Sioux River Valley carved by glaciers two million years ago. Dutch, English, and German ancestors worked hard and prospered in farm life on rich bottomland bought from the ever-westward pushing railroads or homesteaded from the government. Swedes, Norwegians, Irish, Russians, and others from that great nineteenth-century flood out of Europe also set down roots here.

They were pioneers of the so-called Manifest Destiny, that "go West" doctrine of eastern promoters and politicians who declared the settlement of North America to be pre-ordained, blessed by cultural superiority and Christian beliefs, and essential for the growth of a new nation. Scarcely, over the decades since, have my people interacted with the descendants of the Indigenous people—Dakota and Lakota Sioux—who had been pushed westward before my family arrived. Today, eastern South Dakota is a bountiful breadbasket of 640-acre squares of wheat, oats, corn, and soybeans. Native people, Dakota and Lakota, live on nine reservations that cover roughly five million acres of the state, much of it west of the Missouri—an area bigger than Connecticut and Rhode Island combined. Almost one in ten current South Dakotans has Indigenous blood.[3]

The 1973 occupation of the village of Wounded Knee on the Pine Ridge Reservation in southwestern South Dakota came when I was eighteen and just beginning to look at the world from the outside in. It was the first time I remember truly confronting the idea that my family's roots in that land, deep and unquestioned as they were by the time my fourth generation of white settlement came along, would always come with a caveat that others had come long before.

Although I had spent a fair amount of time as a journalist reporting on South Dakota's reservations as a young man, I had never viewed these lands like I did that day at Swift Bird years later as an old one. I was trying to look through another person's eyes, through those of a young white woman in the 1880s who had come to this boundless, limitless, challenging place. She had come in faith that her cause was righteous and her works that of a higher power. Her name was Corabelle Fellows. Her last posting as a teacher and Christian missionary in Dakota Territory in 1888 had been at Swift Bird. As I discovered on a long and winding research path, the original site of the village is a short distance, perhaps no more than a couple of miles, from where the current Swift Bird is located. We will return to the reasons why it was moved later.

Corabelle had written vividly and lovingly in late-in-life memoirs about her time teaching and preaching in Nebraska and Dakota Territory. She arrived when Dakota was a territory and left after Congress created South and North Dakota in 1889. Here at Swift Bird, Corabelle's life took a dramatic turn, an experience that personified the deeply embedded biases in the popular culture at the time, a life scarred on the sharp edge of conflict between white settlers and Native populations on the American frontier. Although she came with an aura of superiority, she eventually admired and even practiced many Native customs that her government had resolved to drown in waves of assimilation. Most significantly, she flaunted marital customs that looked askance at marriage between Indigenous people and those of other races—so much so that newspapers sneered that "painted red would be a good title" for a novel she was reported to want to write.[4]

The frontier that Corabelle saw is ostensibly gone, but its fissures have persisted despite repeated attempts at reconciliation.

In this third decade of the twenty-first century, statues of the past are being torn down, language is being re-thought, and whole genres of literature and the arts are devoted to racial and cultural identity. Sports teams are shedding mascots objectifying Native peoples. The highest peak in South Dakota's mysterious granite-and-pine-covered Black Hills, once named for a ruthless nineteenth-century army officer William Harney who commanded troops during wars against the Sioux, was changed in 2016 to Black Elk Peak after a famous Oglala Lakota elder. The US Department of Interior, in September of 2022, removed "squaw," a derisive term widely used in the nineteenth century, from about 650 geographical names around the country.[5]

Yet, conflicts over Native vs. Christian religion persist. As if on cue, the day I visited Swift Bird a news story illustrative of that point came out of the Pine Ridge Reservation along South Dakota's southwestern border with Nebraska. The chair of the Oglala Sioux Tribe was demanding that a Christian missionary leave the reservation for preaching "that Jesus, not Tunkasila (a Lakota word for Creator), is the 'true God.'"[6]

Politicians, some catering to the backlash of a "woke" culture they see as tearing down the very ideals of America, have determined they can decide what our history should tell us. To them, I say: Tell all of it. Tell it without bias or reservation or scrubbing to hide the ignorance and shortcomings of our past. The founders recognized their flaws and shortcomings. Many, including two whose giant likenesses are carved into South Dakota's Mount Rushmore, were slaveholders. Yet, intrinsically recognizing their failings, they called for a pursuit of a more perfect union, not the preservation of a perfect one.

The tide of white civilization long ago submerged the American frontier, but in the twenty-first century we have not reached settlement on how the past should be remembered. For every tale of a missionary's benevolent intentions to "civilize," a la Corabelle's, for every hearty tale of hardy immigrants populating the plains with sod huts and straight furrows, we have the shame of abuse in Native boarding schools and the massacre at Wounded Knee to remember. For every attempt at reconciliation between Natives and non-Natives, we live with persistent tension between tribal nations and the United States.

The Christian missionaries who believed they were introducing religion to an uncivilized people were actually attempting to supplant one religion for another. For Dakota and Lakota, faith was a central strand of life: Faith that the great herds of tatanka (buffalo) would appear and sustain. Faith that the rivers would flow and the rains would come. Faith in endurance, faith in neighbors, faith that in these infinite surroundings, there was something greater at work than any single soul. Faith in a Great Spirit that presided over it all.

Earth, sky, humans, animals, plants, and the cosmos were inseparable. Place itself was spiritual. The Great Plains "is also part of the He Sapa (Black Hills), or *the best of everything that is*," writes the Sioux author and historian Nick Estes, the italics his. "He Sapa is the beating heart of the Lakota cosmos, where we emerged from red earth, took our first breath, and gained our humanity as Oyate Luta; the 'Red People,' or the 'Red Nation.' During the last ice age, massive glaciers carved up the land. After the ice retreated, it left rolling hills and tunneling valleys that became buffalo roads, which herds that once blackened the plains traveled during seasonal migrations to and from water. The buffalo followed the stars, and the people followed the buffalo."[7]

That nomadic, harsh physical life of the Dakota people was softened by dances, rituals, and feasts. "Religion permeated every aspect of the Dakotas' life," observed famed Dakota author Virginia Driving Hawk Sneve. "It was impossible to differentiate between the social, economic, and religious phases of the Dakota culture.

"Religion was inextricably interwoven with every pattern of individual behavior," she continued. "Thus, the Dakota held a special reverence and respect for all religions. The early missionaries were welcomed and their message reverently heard. It was only later when the Indians saw that not all white men followed the doctrines of Christianity, that the motives of the missionaries were questioned."[8]

For the Natives who hunted buffalo and gathered in settlements along the Missouri River long before the Europeans arrived, the gaze of history goes back over the horizon at least 12,000 years to the Pleistocene Age. Mound builders built impressive civilizations along the meandering river. For centuries, the Big Muddy was a vital and busy transportation and trade route for a vast swath of North America. As deeply as I feel connected to this land, I must always remember that my rootedness is shallow compared to the history of the Native people who still live on it, and even to the other tribes and bands of Indigenous people they went to war with, and themselves pushed out.

The story I am about to tell is primarily about women. Women whose frontier lives were every bit as adventuresome and challenging as those of their male counterparts, but whose stories are often relegated to secondary roles in the literature and press of the age. In dime novels and newspaper pages, women were often portrayed as sidekicks and victims. The explorers and trappers and soldiers and warriors and villains were almost always male, the politicians even more so. The frontier tome *Little House on the Prairie* became popular when it was published in 1935 in large part because it was centered on a little girl on the nineteenth-century frontier. Laura Ingalls Wilder's story wouldn't have seemed such an anomaly if a more complete narrative of the frontier had been told in the first place.

White women taught and preached and nursed and trailblazed on the frontier, and in this part of the world it was Dakota and Lakota Sioux women with whom they most often bonded and held community together. And, as we will see with Corabelle and Elizabeth Winyan, the latter a selfless Dakota servant, they learned from one another.

As their triumphs and tragedies unfold, fair warning to the reader. Words and phrases that may be considered racially injurious under a modern light will be included as expressions of their times. They must remain to retain the authenticity of the story, to show the racism, sexism, and classism of the world surrounding the American frontier.

In that spirit, the reader should also keep in mind that reservations are part of a system of Indigenous nations within the geography of a nation, the United States. The Native people known as Sioux are often known as one, but individually they are as diverse as the earth's infinite variety.

Traditionally known as Oceti Sakowin, which translates into "The Seven Council Fires," their tribal governments, villages, and communities today are spread out over reservations and individual lands, from south central Canada to Nebraska. South and North Dakota are named for one band, the Dakota. The Great Sioux Nation is comprised of Dakota, or Santee; Nakota, the Yankton-Yanktonai; and the Lakota, or Teton, who are often called "the dwellers on the prairie."

The Dakota consist of Mdewkanton, Wahpekute, Wahpeton, and Sisseton. By the mid-nineteenth century they generally resided among the lakes and rivers of Minnesota, Nebraska, and eastern South Dakota. The Nakota include the Yankton and Yanktonai, and they primarily resided in the far northern and northwestern regions of Montana and North Dakota, and in several Canadian provinces. The Lakota subdivisions include Hunkpapa and Oglala.

As the Minnesota Historical Society explains, "each group is a distinct but similar culture." And within all groupings, family—held together for centuries in oral traditions and constant pursuit of survival—is the organizing center of it all.[9]

A day before that July visit to the Cheyenne River Reservation I received word that a pioneering Lakota journalist, Tim Giago, had died at the age of eighty-eight. The *New York Times* obituary heralded this fellow South Dakotan, whom I had known for five decades, for challenging "discriminatory government policies, American Indian stereotypes in popular culture and, at times, tribal leaders themselves."

Like Corabelle Fellows, Tim was fearless and passionate. Like her, he gravitated to remote places and focused on people in need. He was unafraid to challenge authority and as a result he was threatened with violence for printing uncomfortable things, once surviving an assassination attempt when a bullet pierced his pickup windshield. He confronted biases inside and outside his profession that his white counterparts could never fully comprehend.[10]

Tim saw one world of different peoples, with good to encourage and bad to overcome. He wrote with blunt clarity of the challenges of Native people. He challenged authority from within, and he did not spare tribal leadership in his critiques. Yet in his first gaze across a river, he most always looked for the bridge.

I have faith Tim spoke to me that day at Swift Bird. When I returned to my pickup to leave, Tim's voice was on the radio. The Native station, KLND, was replaying a thirty-two-year-old interview Tim had given to South Dakota Public Broadcasting. There was Tim talking about reconciliation in his familiar soft clip. I knew right then that I had taken the correct path to this beautiful country, into this story.

"You know there is an old saying that if you care about someone, take them out to dinner," Tim said. "I'd like to see that happen in South Dakota. I'd like to see the non-Indian people of South Dakota feel that they can be friends with the Indian people. Because I think it could be mutual."

A compelling, yet sad, plea, because the reality of distant neighbors still abounds in this boundless place. As Corabelle eventually discovered, life's best intentions can be overwhelmed by ignorance. Love alone is not always enough. Faith in something greater than oneself can sustain through it all. Corabelle came to preach and teach. She left this land having learned far more than she ever could have imagined.

Chapter 1

A Blind Woman Wants Us to See

She was in her seventies, diminutive in stature but grandiose in spirit. Corabelle Fellows was blind and, at times, living alone or with relatives in Wichita, Kansas. The world was in the stranglehold of the long, hard 1930s Depression and Dust Bowl, a decade that its survivors would label the "Dirty 30s." Disruption, displacement, and suffering had been unleashed on America and on the rest of the world.

Tough times were familiar to this old woman and had been ever since her days as a young adventurer on the Dakota frontier in the 1880s. She was looking back on a life of wanderlust, of love gained and love lost, of friendships that transcended warring cultures, and of a marriage that had eventually been smothered by racism and exploitation. This tiny old woman began writing down all the memories, line by line.

Then known as Corabelle Fellows Tillman, she was living sparsely, fending off poverty. She had eagerly sought some challenges, others had been thrust on her by fate, ignorance, even the powerful vagaries of nature on the Plains. A life that could have hardened her, that could have pushed her to bitterness and regret, had done just the opposite. In her handwritten memoirs—contained on crumbling, fading, and disordered pages handed through generations to a great-great granddaughter—she expressed faith in optimism. These handwritten memoirs, which will be referred to often in the coming narrative, tell of a lifetime of overcoming much more than the blindness that had descended on her in her twilight years.

Corabelle's first marriage more than forty years before, to a man of Dakota Sioux and European heritage in the previous century's wild Dakota Territory, had fallen apart, but only after their union had gained national fame and notoriety. The marriage to Sam Campbell had been mocked and ridiculed in crude, racist terms in the sensationalist, yellow press. A second husband, a Civil War veteran almost two decades older than Corabelle, a stoic and purportedly abusive man, had died in the decade before she began writing her life's story. A troubled son from the first marriage—one of her five children—sometimes came to live with her, and he was alleged to have sometimes stolen his mother's pension for the blind. But despite the abuse, Corabelle protected him and defended him. "He needed me the most," she told Flora Isely, an author who went by the pen name of Kunigunde Duncan.[1] To the end, Corabelle's stubborn resolve and selflessness sustained her.

She had embraced the challenge of spending her final years by learning Braille, reading classics, and helping to record Native Sioux songs she'd learned. As a young woman, Corabelle had taught children and adults of the Dakota and Lakota Sioux in Nebraska and Dakota Territory. Her time in the territory was in that tenuous transition between the 1876 defeat of Custer at Little Big Horn and the 1890 massacre of nearly 300 Sioux and Cheyenne people at Wounded Knee, South Dakota. She had learned much from these Native people, especially the women and their customs, their resiliency, and their reverence for the mysteries of the hosts of earth and sky. She had told her "lively accounts" many times at events hosted by the Wichita Association of the Blind.[2] Now she was trying to put the best memories down on paper.

Rebellious and adventurous, a twenty-three-year-old Corabelle had ventured west in 1884 from her home in Washington, DC, after spending six years preparing in divinity school and teaching in a school she had started barely out of her teens. Upon arriving on the frontier, Corabelle initially was a teacher in a Christian boarding school for Native children in Nebraska. She came filled with expectations and preconceptions that would soon be challenged. Later, she taught in various locations in Dakota Territory, and she experienced all the natural fury of the mighty host. She nearly died in a blizzard and survived a monstrous prairie windstorm that decimated the village where she was living. She cut her own wood and built her own fires, learned to break horses, raised cattle, evaded snakes and wolves, forded icy rivers, and learned from Sioux women how to glean wild beans, berries, and potatoes. In one dramatic act that forever changed her, she fought off an insistent Dakota suitor who literally carried her off in the middle of a cold Dakota night for an intended forced marriage. Only the intervention of a bold and insistent friend, a Native Dakota woman of equally selfless spirit and resolve as Corabelle's, a woman who herself had overcome soul-searing tragedies and loss, saved her from forced matrimony. Elizabeth Winyan's own rich life tapestry became intricately woven with Corabelle's.

How these two women came together on the harsh plains of the American West in the late nineteenth century, how each tried in their own way to round the cutting edges of a white civilization that was encroaching rapidly and inexorably onto lands long traversed by Sioux

Young Corabelle
COURTESY OF CARRIE LINDSEY

and other tribes, tells as much of the lived and authentic history of the American frontier as anything in Buffalo Bill's shoot-'em-up shows of the day ever did.

In the end, Corabelle embraced Elizabeth as her mother—"Ina" in Dakota—after Corabelle's biological mother disowned her.

Through Winyan and other Natives, Corabelle became enraptured by Dakota Territory's subtle, complex mysteries, mesmerized by its expanses, taken in by its emerald and blue oases of ravines, ponds, rivers, and lakes. The sunrises and sunsets became masterpieces in the sky for a young woman who at one time aspired to be a painter. Trees, preciously few, grew like stout stewards of hope. Clear night skies cascaded from horizon to horizon and shimmering diamond clusters of stars could coax the spirit into self-reflective moments of wonder. The bitter cold winters, the blizzards, and ice-locked rivers presented challenges many would have walked away from. She reveled in enduring them. Under this canopy, Corabelle became awestruck by the perseverance of the Dakota and Lakota Sioux with whom she lived, the wanderers who were now being asked to settle on lands that ultimately could not support them.

In truth, the Sioux also were no strangers to conflict and displacement, having roamed for centuries in search of the life-sustaining tatanka (buffalo) and having over the arc of time fought with other Native people over land and resources. Their oral traditions traveled with them. By the time Corabelle arrived that Thanksgiving of 1884, the recent, written history of the brutal Indian Wars and the broken promises by the US government were just the newest acts in the Oceti Sakowin's constantly moving story.

The yellow press of the East had made Corabelle and her first husband, Samuel Campbell, a man of white and Native parentage, both famous and notorious. Newspapers simultaneously mocked and praised Corabelle's spirit and independence, even while vilifying and dehumanizing Sam without ever bothering to really know him. Corabelle's father, a gentle man from whom she inherited her wandering spirit and empathy, worried about her constantly, and had at least attempted rapprochement after her marriage to Sam. Corabelle's mother, sister, and aunt, all social climbers in Washington, DC, had disowned her in the harshest of terms.

But in her journey away from the life they thought she should have lived, Corabelle had found another mother in Winyan. In a tiny log cabin along the Cheyenne River in the wildest expanse of Dakota Territory, their brief time together left a legacy of understanding.

Five decades later in Wichita, as Corabelle patiently wrote her life story in longhand, the memories of those Sioux Indians inspired her.

"As I look back at those days now, a gray-haired woman of seventy years, I can see now how those days of roughing it gave health and vigor to these present years of my life and no doubt preserved my good health for the remaining years of my life," Corabelle wrote in memoirs scrawled over dozens and dozens of pages.

Her story, though filled with danger and daring, had been largely overlooked and certainly undervalued. By the 1930s, many of the Christian missions or boarding schools that Corabelle had come to serve had vanished or were on their way out, faded with the frontier. Yet as the mid-twentieth century approached and Corabelle sat writing her memoirs, the American West was still being mythologized in books and memorialized on film largely by men, about men. On big screens in big cities and small towns, Natives were still being portrayed as obstinate, ignorant, bloodthirsty, and in the way, as inferior beings either to be corralled or eliminated altogether. Women—white and Native—were almost always supporting actors. Women in distress, women as sexual objects, women as followers. Women as bit players and afterthoughts.

When Corabelle decided to write her own story, whether she intended it or not, women became the central characters of an entirely different frontier narrative. The prose and imagery poured forth as if the scenes were as fresh as yesterday. There were thrilling stories, touching tales, harrowing episodes.

Corabelle's then-middle-school-aged granddaughter, Rose Staunton Kirkbright, became her physical guide as the story flowed from one memory to another in a scrawling, messy manner. During the day, while Rose was in school, her grandmother would position rubber bands to guide her hand evenly across the page. When one line was done, Corabelle moved the rubber band down to the next. She marked pages by poking pins into the upper corners; one pin prick meant page one, and so on. The pages piled up and were handed down through family through the years.

She had remained fiercely independent even after her sight began failing in the mid-1920s, and total blindness had set in by the early '30s. Corabelle often insisted on living as independently as she could, but offspring from both husbands congregated nearby. Sometimes her son, Claude, would be there with her; at times she would live with others. She had counted the steps from one Wichita apartment to the streetcar that would take her to and from the state School for the Blind, where she learned Braille. Afraid of fire, she sometimes turned down offers to live with relatives who smoked. She learned her vegetable garden by heart and valued the experience of bringing life from the ground as well as the sustenance it provided, a feeling she carried forth from her time gleaning on the prairie with Dakota and Lakota women a half century earlier.

"She had a way of marking money so that she could tell the difference in the denomination of bills," recalled Rose years later. "She loved to do her own cooking and gardening."[3]

Day after day, teenaged Rose would come from school and read her grandmother's thrilling and mysterious life as it unrolled like a living play. The writing was often messy, like memory itself. Sometimes young Rose would arrive to find words scrawled over others, with thoughts jumbled and intermingled as Corabelle had mistakenly started over on a filled page she thought was blank. Some words survived clearly and boldly, but the overwritten and jumbled ones became an apt metaphor for how memory itself often presses and comingles and obscures. To augment, Corabelle provided an oral history for her grandchildren, teaching them to sing in Dakota and to dance to melodies she had learned among the Sioux.

"I spent many hours with my grandmother, listening to her wonderful stories, singing Indian songs and even dancing Indian dances, circling from the living room through the dining room and kitchen and back to the living room," Rose wrote Bruce David Forbes, a religious professor at Iowa's Morningside College. "She had many intriguing examples of beadwork, moccasins, pin cushions, clothing and toys, especially a doll that had been made for her."[4]

That doll, made of cotton with a deerskin face, remained with descendants in Corabelle's family, eventually landing with her great-great-granddaughter, Carrie Lindsey. It speaks of resourcefulness, of making do, of the strength to hold onto something of meaning in the bleakest of times and places. The manuscript has faded, but the memories remain.

"[She] was an amazing woman," Rose said simply of her grandmother.

In 1938 the amazing woman's story became the basis for a book. But someone else had appropriated the experiences, told it incompletely and sometimes incorrectly, and shaped the story line around the societal biases and prejudices of that age. Flora Isely, a freelancer from Wichita who went by the pen name of Kunigunde Duncan, read Corabelle's memoirs and letters, spent hours interviewing her, but published only a part of Corabelle's life story. And she put her own pen name on it, describing it as "told from the life of Corabelle Fellows."

Isely/Duncan, as she will be referred to in the coming narrative, was a successful poet and writer in Wichita. The book was called *Blue Star, The Story of Corabelle Fellows, Teacher at Dakota Missions, 1884–1888*.

In correspondence after the book came out, Isely/Duncan said she had helped Corabelle financially with proceeds from the book. But there is no evidence Corabelle received money from the publishers of *Blue Star*. In truth, it most likely didn't make much money. The book had modest sales of about 1,800 by the mid-1940s, and Corabelle's descendants wondered through successive generations how the book had all come together. Shortly after publication, her relatives contacted a well-known Wichita lawyer to see if Corabelle had been treated fairly, but nothing came of it. In a letter to an associate of Corabelle's, Isely/Duncan said she wrote the book, in part, to help Corabelle financially. The truth of that part of *Blue Star* may never be known, but the records of the publisher, still kept nearly a century later, showed that all of the proceeds had gone to Isely/Duncan and her husband, Bliss.[5]

One of Corabelle's mentors in the Dakota missions also questioned key parts of the book, including and especially how it depicted Corabelle's relationship with Winyan.

Blue Star—the name given Corabelle for the color of her eyes by Dakota children at the Santee Agency in Nebraska—came out after

Corabelle died. Wichita Girl Scout chapters put the book on their must-read list as a tribute to strong, Christian, white women. At a time when American Indians had been confined to reservations for more than a half century and were still routinely portrayed in press and film as inferior beings and threats to civilization, the book was favorably reviewed as a story of a white woman trying to bring Christian civilization to Native people along the Missouri River.

"Girl teacher is heroine of Indian book," headlined one review, in the Ogden, Utah, *Standard-Examiner*. "The girl had an indominable spirit, combined with real sympathy for the red people to whom she was offering the first taste of the white men's knowledge," the reviewer wrote. "And the Indians, who valued above all things a brave heart, gave her an affectionate title—Blue Star. Personalities like hers are fast disappearing as the frontiers of the west become past history."

Corabelle, the reviewer wrote, "remained at her post while other women teachers fled from Indian scares, the cold, and privations."[6]

The Sioux Falls, South Dakota, *Argus-Leader* described Blue Star as "a really fascinating story that is an important contribution to the early history of the Dakotas."[7] By Dakotas, it meant the states, not the people who had inhabited it. For the early history of the Dakota people went back long, long before it.

Blue Star did weave many of Corabelle's words into its pages, but not nearly all of them, and what it did not tell forms the basis of this attempt at a more complete narrative of her exhilarating, tragic, and eventually come-to-peace life. In particular, *Blue Star's* misportrayal of the relationship between Corabelle and Elizabeth Winyan is a testament to the damage of presenting contrived narrative over true history, of the distortions when the predominant memories come from a culture seeking dominance, and of the traps all humans fall into when broad brushes are applied to relationships, and to history.

Most frustrating in hindsight, the book ended just when Corabelle's story was becoming a national sensation. What it omitted is a testament to the utter destructiveness of prejudice and mythmaking in popular culture, then and now. Corabelle's story is certainly one of defiance, service, survival, acceptance, and enlightenment, and that is all told in her voice, often quite eloquently, by Isely/Duncan in *Blue Star*. But Corabelle's life after her marriage to Sam Campbell, a man of Native and white ancestry, was wracked by appalling racism and sexism, detonated in the public sphere by predatory hucksters in the nineteenth-century press, and by an American culture approaching the twentieth century that was fascinated with the freakish, mysterious, and unfamiliar. Corabelle's journey eventually coursed through everything from national politics to Buffalo Bill's Wild West show. She became a celebrity against her will just as celebrity was becoming a staple of mass-produced Americana.

Yet as she looked back five decades later, she had few regrets.

"I gave myself to God's keeping at seventeen years, and although I have made many serious mistakes, I have been blessed," she wrote in her memoirs. "And whatever you do, do all for the glory of God."

Her experience in Dakota Territory bracketed two seminal events of the Indian Wars. Just eight years before Corabelle arrived in Dakota Territory, a large Lakota, Arapahoe, and Northern Cheyenne force had wiped out George Armstrong Custer and his Seventh Cavalry at Little Big Horn in Montana, four hundred miles to the northwest from where Corabelle first stepped off the train in Dakota Territory. Sioux leaders and survivors of that battle, which Natives called the Battle of Greasy Grass, including the legendary Sitting Bull, were living on or near the reservations Corabelle would soon serve.

Corabelle's marriage to Sam Campbell and the end of her mission work came a little more than two years before the 1890 slaughter of Native men, women, and children by that same Seventh Cavalry at Wounded Knee. In between, epic political battles over the survival of Native language and religion were raging in government and in the newspapers. Fights over land and Native sovereignty were an undercurrent and swirl through events even today.

Yet, for her entire life, Corabelle had an ever-firming belief that she had not been hardened but had been transformed in the warmth of memory of the people who, in the end, had given her at least as much as she had given them. She would be changed in ways she was still grasping to understand fifty years later.

Chapter 2

The Most Penetrating Cold

It was only November, but it was the coldest Corabelle Fellows had ever been when she stepped onto the railroad platform near Springfield, Dakota Territory, three days before Thanksgiving, 1884. Born in Illinois, her childhood had been filled with movement and adventure. She had lived her formative years in rural New York, the Midwest, and then in and around Washington, DC, as her father followed wanderlust and jobs, and her mother sought high-society connections almost as fast as they could unpack. But this place was different from anything she had ever encountered.

She felt immediately how Dakota cold forced one to snap to attention. Corabelle remembered stepping off the train into "the most penetrating cold I had ever experienced."[1] It immediately clarifies one's predicament, a stark demarcation between past and present.

Corabelle had arrived after a four-day train trip through the heart of late-nineteenth-century America, interrupted by a short stay in Chicago at an uncle's home. Even as she arrived in Dakota Territory, her destination at a mission school for Santee children in Nebraska was still several miles distant by boat and then wagon, on the opposite side of the Missouri River.

Standing just five-feet-tall and weighing 105 pounds—her self-description in her memoirs—Corabelle would have been an unimposing figure in such vastness. She had seen a growing nation on her way west. On that last stretch out of Chicago, towns were growing every few miles along busy rail lines bustling with commerce and fresh settlement.

But as she approached Dakota Territory, the settlements spread out, and the emptiness began taking back. Though it would be almost a decade before the historian Frederick Jackson Turner famously declared the end of the American frontier, and Corabelle had seen with her own eyes how rapidly that end was approaching.

Fresh, orderly grids of immigrant farms and communities in Wisconsin and Minnesota had made Corabelle realize the change she was stepping into was ordered, real, and irreversible. Harvested fields of corn, wheat, and oats stretched mile upon mile, homesteads often abounded four to one square mile, their houses plump with white settlers in big families pouring into what was becoming the world's most abundant breadbasket. The promise of free or cheap land and fresh opportunity was part of this great "Manifest Destiny" the talkers and writers of the period extolled like a God-given birthright. Five years before statehood, new waves of immigrants were crashing into Dakota Territory, urged on by railroads whose public relations mavens promised that rain followed the plow, even in places accustomed to a fraction of the precipitation of that a few hundred miles east.

Existing at the edge of this final frontier were the Dakota Sioux whom Corabelle had come to teach. Scattered for years by the force of the American military, they were being pressed and pushed into ever-more hardscrabble landscapes, continually viewed as in the way on land they had long traversed. Some of them, by force or by their own doing, had sent their children to boarding schools run by the federal government or churches, or both.

Springfield, on the northern banks of the wide and wild Missouri River, was a mile from the railroad station. It had been incorporated only three years before, but it had long served as a trading post. Before the Sioux, the Arikara, Cheyenne, and other Native tribes had occupied this prime spot astride the river. Corabelle spent her first night in her new life in that new town with an ancient history. Her final destination was the Santee agency on the other side of the Missouri River in Nebraska, at a boarding school for Sioux children run by a member of an already famous Christian missionary family, the Reverend Alfred Longley Riggs, and his wife, Mary Buel Riggs.

In *Blue Star*, Isely/Duncan wrote that Corabelle was helped that first night after her arrival by two young Native boys who, upon the recommendation of the train conductor, guided her to a rustic boarding house. She had cried most of the way out on the train, the book said, and she was experiencing serious doubts and regret. The two boys were sullen and standoffish until she was able to communicate that she was a friend of a mutual friend. Then, "they thawed as suddenly as they had frozen," Duncan/Isely wrote. "How, my friend," they were said to have exclaimed—the "how" a stereotype expression that would have been familiar to filmgoers and readers of Wild West novels of the mid-twentieth century. The next day, the book reports, the two boys rowed Corabelle across the Missouri River on their own canoe. It was, Corabelle said, "the muddiest river I have ever seen," one "choked with dirty ice."

The night before, she had "cried until morning under the smelly bedclothes," Corabelle said. "How glad I was that Mother and Marian [her sister] could not see me."[2]

But this account is wider than the river they called the Big Muddy apart from what Corabelle herself wrote a month after her arrival. In the January 1885 edition of the *Word Carrier*, a missionary newspaper produced by Riggs's organization, the two boys are not mentioned at all, nor are they mentioned in her handwritten memoirs. The actual story Corabelle told in the *Word Carrier* is equally as harrowing: The air was piercingly cold, the river town was isolated, but almost everything else was different from the *Blue Star* description.

"I left [Washington, DC] on a beautiful warm morning, with my heart full of doubts and misgivings as to whether I should reach Santee in safety, or do the good upon my arrival that I had it in my heart to do," she wrote in the opening paragraph of the *Word Carrier* account.

Entering Dakota Territory, Corabelle had "looked with curiosity at the strange Russian houses I saw, built so far apart from each other. The dwelling part of the house, with the one or two tiny windows, was built adjoining the barn, and the roofs were covered with straw and mud to make them warm enough to live in. I wondered much what could have brought these people so far from their own country to live in this desolate style."

Some early white settlers in Dakota Territory were identified as German-Russian, the descendants of Germans who had emigrated to Russia in the eighteenth century at the invitation of Catherine the Great.[3]

Corabelle recounted that, as the train approached Springfield, the only other person in her railroad car was a man named Clarence Dick. He also was heading to Santee to become the assistant principal and superintendent of the Young Men's Hall at Santee. He was fresh out of the Minnesota State Normal School at Winona, and the two young people bonded on the train as it approached Springfield.[4]

"So we, as a matter of course, seemed to have a fellow feeling and sympathy for one another, traveling alone and upon a like mission," Corabelle wrote in the *Word Carrier*. Kindred spirits, on identical missions, they linked up in that frigid air. It was 9 p.m. when they arrived in Springfield.

She wrote that they took an "omnibus"—a horse-drawn carriage—to a hotel called the Mead House in Springfield, where they stayed until 2 p.m. the next day. There was no mention of a harrowing canoe ride across the muddy Missouri under the two boys' guidance. But it wasn't smooth sailing, either.

"The river was very much frozen," Corabelle told readers of the *Word Carrier*, "and we were told that in all probability we could not cross in safety for some days. But Mr. Dick and myself were determined not to remain longer at Springfield, and found at last a boatsman who was willing to row us over. We clambered in, satchel, shawl-strap, books, maps and all, and were safely carried across, only twice striking a sand bar, which for crossing the Missouri, was doing very well."

It was only the first of many harrowing crossings of the Big Muddy or other Dakota Territory rivers Corabelle would experience over the next few years. The ordinary dangers of travel in a country without roads and bridges would accompany her for the rest of her time in Nebraska and, later, in Dakota Territory. But Corabelle's focus was mainly on her new home, at Santee, two miles from the river, where 135 Dakota Sioux children were boarded.

After the crossing, she and Mr. Dick were met at the river by Alfred Riggs, Corabelle's new employer and soon-to-be mentor. Santee Normal Training School was "a pleasant little settlement, with grounds laid off and fenced, the buildings neat and pretty finished," Corabelle recounted. "There are four large buildings for pupils and teachers—'Young Men's Hall,' 'Boys Cottage,' 'Dakota Home' (for the older girls) and the 'Bird's Nest,' (for little girls). Then there is the school house, also used as the chapel, Rev. A.L. Riggs' cottage, stables, etc. Also, blacksmith shop, shoe shop and carpenter shop."

She declared the mission boarding school "a wonder to me . . . so neat, quiet and orderly. Everything that is done is like clockwork. And when I think of the one hundred and thirty-five pupils who attend this school, with their wild, free, youthful, Indian spirits, I marvel more and more at the prompt obedience with which each pupil who has an allotted task performs it, not always quickly, but as I have heard people say, very well *for an Indian*."[5] The italics were hers, an abrupt testament to the Colonial attitude toward Natives she had carried from back East.

Corabelle would be challenged to shed that arrogance of cultural superiority. But in her first days at the mission, she very much believed that assimilating Native people into her white culture was their only road to survival, a simple choice between inevitable change or irreversible loss.

Corabelle wrote often in the *Word Carrier* during the next three and a half years as a teacher and missionary. The Riggs-established publication, based out of Santee, was institutionally bold in its declarations, often taking sides in heated debates over Indian policy in Congress, and weighing in on presidential elections and candidates' stances on issues related to that policy. Its platform, printed boldly in every edition, read: "For Indians we want American Education! We want American homes! We want American rights! The result of which is American citizenship."[6]

It was a declaration of assimilation. With proper teaching and religious instruction, Natives would acquire American citizenship that had been denied them. Yet there was wiggle room in that declaration, for the *Word Carrier* often expressed sympathy for the need to retain Native languages and for a halt in the relentless stripping of land holdings and other rights from Dakota and Lakota. There was also frequent pushback on the most egregious racism expressed toward Indigenous people. But the pages of the *Word Carrier* also often carried calls for harsh treatment of Natives who resisted assimilation. After the slaughter at Wounded Knee, for instance, the *Word Carrier* did not drape itself in mercy or understanding in an article justifying the killing of women and children.[7]

But Reverend and Mrs. Riggs also resisted imposing certain practices and customs of white civilization, which they deemed inappropriate, on Natives. Two months before Corabelle arrived at Santee, the *Word Carrier* had reported on a new government agent in Yankton who was encouraging dancing for students in schools across the border. Not Native dance, which soon enough would stir fresh conflict, but that of "the polite arts of civil society."

The *Word Carrier* was not enthused, and its front-page article ended with an admonition. "Now the Indians themselves ought to know about things in the Indian community, and they say that though it may be all right in white society for the young men and women to hug and whirl each other about promiscuously, but as Indians are not used to that kind of thing yet, it is not conducive to good morals for them to do it."[8]

In successive editions, the *Word Carrier* was filled with articles debating the revival of Native dancing, and Corabelle would eventually witness a Sun Dance, a multiday pageant of endurance, sacrifice, self-denial, and vision-seeking. At the end of that decade, however, government and white settler fear over the emergence of the purportedly prophetic Ghost Dance would lead directly to the massacre at Wounded Knee.

The Riggs family left an indelible imprint on the march of white civilization in the land of the Sioux, first in Minnesota, then later in Nebraska and Dakota Territory. Alfred's parents, Stephen Return Riggs and Mary Ann Clark Longley Riggs, began their mission in 1837 at Lac Qui Parle, in present-day Minnesota. Several of their eight children would follow them in mission. Alfred Riggs and his brother Thomas Riggs would have many interactions with Corabelle, who taught both in Riggs mission schools and separate government day schools during her time in Nebraska and Dakota Territory.

While believing that Natives' fates rested with accepting Christianity, perhaps more than any white person, Stephen Return Riggs fought to retain the Native languages of the Sioux. But he also forbade his children, at early ages at least, from learning to speak Dakota to stop them from being exposed to "impure thoughts and impure words."[9]

The *Word Carrier* to which Corabelle frequently contributed was the Riggs's clarion call to the world. Founded by Stephen Riggs and fellow missionary J.P. Williamson, it was printed in English and Dakota, the latter edition called *Iapi Oaye* (carrying the word) in Dakota. The *Word Carrier* published until 1939, the year after Corabelle died, the year *Blue Star* was published. The broad citizenship for Indigenous people called for in the publication's platform declaration would not be granted by Congress until 1924, forty years after Corabelle had arrived at Santee. And even that ideal got wrapped in conflict: Citizenship was not sought by some Dakota and Lakota, who saw the designation in direct conflict to their citizenship in the Great Sioux Nation.[10]

The *Word Carrier* had announced Corabelle's arrival in its November 1884 edition: "Miss Corabelle Fellows comes as a missionary of the Women's Indian Rights Association," the notice said. "She will assist in various capacities and at the same time be pursuing her studies in the native language and become initiated into the practical part of mission work."[11]

The Women's National Indian Association (WNIA) had been recently founded in Philadelphia by activists Mary Lucinda Bonney and Amelia Stone Quinton of the Home Mission Circle of the First Baptist Church of Philadelphia. It initially focused on holding the government to promises it had made in treaties, but its primary goal shifted to establishing missionaries and teachers among Indigenous people. It was aligned with the Indian Rights Association, which had also been formed in Philadelphia in 1882. And it had important allies in Dakota Territory, starting with a prominent Episcopal bishop.

"While the women's group focused primarily on religious matters, on December 15, 1882, thirty or forty wealthy reform-minded gentlemen gathered at the Philadelphia home of the Honorable John Welsh to hear from the judge's sons, Herbert and Henry S. Pancoast," a history of the organization said. "They had just returned from a visit to the Dakota Territory as guests of Episcopal missionary Bishop William Hobart

Hare. Concerned about the living conditions of the Sioux and US Indian Bureau corruption, the men created the Indian Rights Association."[12]

Dubbed "an apostle to the Sioux," Bishop Hare was presiding bishop of Niobrara in Nebraska when Corabelle arrived; he was later named bishop of Dakota Territory.

When Corabelle arrived at the Riggs's mission, she soon discovered that the students were children of a Native nation under immense pressure. Boarded far from their parents in many circumstances, they came from tribes that were being forced onto reservations in some of the most desolate and economically precarious locales in North America.

In the years immediately after Custer's defeat at Little Big Horn, groups of Lakota and Dakota Sioux, spread across what are now the states of Minnesota, South Dakota, North Dakota, and Nebraska, had been, in the words of religious scholar Bruce David Forbes, "pushed into jarring transition" onto reservations or allotted federal lands, much of it not suitable for subsistence farming in the semi-arid Northern Plains. The Indian Wars had raged in the region most harshly since the Civil War, and although it had been eight years since the destruction of the Seventh Cavalry at Little Bighorn, tension still abounded.

A little over two decades before Corabelle came to Santee, the 1862 Sioux uprising in Minnesota had resulted in the killing of more than 300 white settlers, some tortured, when bands of Sioux men began attacking white settlers after promised federal government support did not come through. An unknown number of Natives were also killed.

A quickly arranged trial resulted in thirty-eight Sioux men being hanged in Mankato, Minnesota. Stephen Return Riggs assisted a commission that conducted the trial. The Mankato executions remain the biggest single act of capital punishment handed down by the US government. Hundreds more would have died without clemency from then-President Abraham Lincoln. The hangings had drawn thousands of spectators in a carnival-like atmosphere.

The 1862 uprising launched decades of roiling warfare, flawed attempts at justice, and genocide. Later investigations proved that some of the men hanged that day were not guilty of the crimes for which they were put to death. When Corabelle arrived twenty-two years later, the threat of such violence had abated but was still portrayed as possible in the press.

Elizabeth Winyan, a Dakota woman born in Minnesota near where the violence began, had become a hero by helping to save lives during the 1862 uprising. But in the aftermath, the government cited the threat of more violence to justify the removal of her and her family from their homes along the Minnesota River to wilder lands north and west, first near the border of present-day Minnesota and northeastern South Dakota, then eventually to the Missouri River Valley a couple hundred miles west. Living a life of service for the next three decades in the more arid, tree-scarce prairies of Dakota Territory, Winyan longed for her lush, picturesque Minnesota River birthplace for the rest of her life.

In an introduction to a later edition of *Blue Star*, Forbes, the former department chair and professor of religious studies at Morningside College, explained what had happened to Winyan's Dakota in the half century before Corabelle arrived.

"The Dakota people had lost most of their land in Minnesota through treaties in 1837, 1851, and 1858. After 1851, they were restricted, at least in theory, to land along both sides of the Minnesota River, about 140 miles long and 20 miles wide. In 1858, they lost the northern half of the reserve. Unable in this limited area to maintain their traditional lifestyle, they were encouraged by missionaries and government agents to adopt many features of white culture."

But, as Forbes pointed out, the missions' goals were often antithetical to the history and culture of the people who had roamed and subsisted for centuries on the resources-rich landscape of the Northern Plains.

Writing through a twentieth-century lens, Forbes observed that "what missionaries saw as God's reward for their long, sacrificial labor, most anthropologists explain as a result of cultural disruption, where persons in turmoil look for a new organizing center for their lives."

Forbes quoted Big Eagle, a Dakota leader, who said: "The whites were always trying to make the Indians give up their life, and live like white men—go to farming, work hard and do as they did—and the Indians did not know how to do that, and did not want to, anyway. It seemed too sudden to make a change. If the Indians had tried to make the whites live like them, the whites would have resisted, and it was the same way with many Indians."[13]

In this chaos, Dakota, Lakota, and other bands of Sioux searched for any organizing center, oscillating between resigned dependency upon government allotments and defiantly clinging to old ways. By the time Corabelle had arrived, Sitting Bull—the great Sioux Leader who had led refugees into Canada after the Little Big Horn victory—was living peacefully on what would become the Standing Rock Reservation, a few days' horse ride from where Corabelle would eventually teach in one of the Riggs's mission's most remote outposts. But his legacy of resistance would eventually cost him his life.

Young, idealistically attuned to her Christianity, and half a continent from her family, Corabelle at first leaned heavily into the belief that Natives needed a new organizing center imported from white Christendom. Her stereotypes and cultural biases were continuously stoked by sensationalist streams in American press and literature that routinely portrayed Native populations as heathens, savages, and obstacles. An edition of the *Word Carrier* published a few months before Corabelle arrived at Santee in late 1884 included a copy of a letter written by Gen. Charles Howard, then a government inspector of Indian agencies under President Chester A. Arthur, rebuking a white Presbyterian elder in Illinois who had declared that he "had no use for Indians except as rifle targets."

"But I have lately seen a Presbyterian elder, who was himself a Sioux Indian," wrote Howard, whose devout Christian brother, Oliver Otis Howard, was, for a few frantic hours, the senior Union commander on the first day of the 1863 Battle of Gettysburg. "He said nothing about making a target of his white brother."[14]

In the 1880s, the federal government and missionary societies were engaged in fierce debates about whether the Sioux should be taught in their Native dialects, or whether their language and customs should be banned altogether. There were relentless attempts to deny age-old traditions and religious rituals that had been passed on through innumerable Lakota and Dakota generations. Dancing and other cultural expressions were seen as acts of war by some presidential administrations and Indian agents.

On March 13, 1884, eight months before Corabelle arrived, former Indian Service Agent V.T. McGillycuddy, the former agent at Pine Ridge in southwestern Dakota Territory, had declared the "aboriginal ceremony, known as the Sun Dance, is discontinued" at the Santee Agency, and others. The missionary Alfred Riggs, writing in that June's *Word Carrier*, declared that the ban "shows progress in the Indian himself, that such an order can be made without a riot, and a war."

The Sun Dance had been a purifying, unifying practice for the Dakota and Lakota, an elaborate ritual that brought bands together for an annual rite of sacrifice and introspection. A cottonwood tree placed in the middle of a wide circle would typically be the focal point. Dancers, tethered to the tree by ropes tied to piercings in their chests, would go on for hours, even days. It was widely seen as the most important ceremony practiced by Plains Indians. And for a half century, until 1934, it was banned by the US government. Alfred Riggs and many of his missionaries were all for its banning. Grass dancing, another elaborate Sioux ritual where participants were festooned with intricately sewn costumes, was next on Riggs's list.

The Sun Dance ban "shows progress in the Indian Department, and it gives some ground for hope, that the next thing will be, to break up the indecent and demoralizing Grass Dance," the missionary Riggs wrote. Civilization, at least as he saw it, could not include the dance, for it was tethered to a belief system antithetical to the Christian doctrine, the "true religion" of the time. Or so the missionaries thought.[15]

In *Blue Star*, Corabelle said she attended a Sun Dance near present-day Sisseton, South Dakota, and she expressed horror at seeing blood from the exhausted male dancers, witnessing women self-mutilate and tear out their hair. The book depicts her as leaving the dance, where she "rode furiously away, in what direction I neither knew nor cared."

This account does not appear in her handwritten memoirs and must have come from interviews conducted by the author. Isely/Duncan also included an explanation of the dance's importance by a man named Gray Hawk. Corabelle had helped care for a grandson of Gray Hawk who had been scalded by hot soup. Their conversation soon turned to the banned dances. In recounting it, Isely/Duncan drew a subtle, yet undeniable connection between the meaning of the dance and a core belief of Christianity: through the suffering of the selfless, others could be saved.

Not only were the dancers showing power over suffering, but they were also doing it in memory of all those who had suffered before them, Gray Hawk explained. "Only through suffering might the living hope to please the all-brave, all enduring Great Spirit," Gray Hawk told Corabelle.

"I was unable to bring any comfort with my story of my Great Spirit, who asked only kindliness among all men together to be pleased," Corabelle said.[16]

By the end of the 1880s, the emergence of the Ghost Dance—a prophetic expression forecasting the return of the buffalo and the demise of white civilization—would increase tensions. But even then, a special government commission sent to Dakota Territory to encourage Native men to sign onto a new land allotment decried federal crackdowns on all Native dances. "It, of course, can not be questioned that the savage ordeals like the sun dance have been properly interdicted, but other forms of amusement, such as corn dances, squaw dances, and the Omahas, are innocent," the commissioners reported to the US Senate. "Pastimes are a necessity to all people, and perhaps more necessary to the Indians whose conditions afford so few opportunities for diversion, than to the whites whose lives contain so much more of variety."[17]

By the 1880s, the wave of farmers and merchants and speculators had included scores of teachers and missionaries flooding into Dakota Territory, and to other areas of the country where Native people had been pushed onto reservations and forced into foreign lifestyles. At Santee Normal Training School, Corabelle was one of twenty-six teachers or administrators for the 135 boarded students. Censuses often listed the students with both their English name and their Dakota name.

"Advanced scholars," including three in 1885—Charles Eastman, Angelique Cordier, and Mary Mani—were routinely sent away to boarding schools in Illinois, New Hampshire, Pennsylvania, Iowa, and other states. Eastman would later marry the aforementioned Elaine Goodale in one of the most celebrated marriages between a Native woman and white man in the late nineteenth century. Six months before Corabelle's arrival at Santee, the *Word Carrier* had contained news that twenty-five children from the Yankton Agency, across the Missouri River from Santee, had been transferred to government boarding schools elsewhere. "Much feeling was shown by teachers and parents," the author, Nancy Hunter, described.[18]

Through the years, allegations of widespread abuse and genocide were made against some of these schools, allegations that have recoiled through generations of dislocation and trauma. In July of 2022, Pope Francis offered an official Vatican apology for the Catholic Church's treatment of Native children in boarding schools. "Sorry for the ways in which, regrettably, many Christians supported the colonizing mentality of the powers that oppressed the Indigenous peoples," he said on an official visit to Canada.[19]

In 2022 the US Department of the Interior reported it had documented hundreds of deaths at boarding schools for Native children over the previous two centuries, although it did not name specific cases in specific locations, declaring it a matter of privacy.

"The United States directly targeted American Indian, Alaska Native, and Native Hawaiian children in the pursuit of a policy of cultural assimilation that coincided with Indian territorial dispossession," that Department of the Interior report concluded by May of 2022. It said that federal boarding schools for Indigenous students "were used as a means for these ends" and that there were "at least fifty-three burial sites for children across the system with more site discoveries and data expected as we continue our research."

Santee and Fort Bennett, a Dakota Territory industrial trade boarding school for boys where Corabelle briefly taught, were among thirty identified in the Interior Department's report. About a fifth of the 408 Native boarding schools across thirty-seven states that operated between 1819 and 1969 were in Oklahoma, making it the highest concentration.

"Despite differences in operation, management, and funding, the United States recognized that the Federal Indian boarding school system was central to Indian territorial dispossession and Indian assimilation," the federal report concluded.

It quoted William A. Jones, US commissioner of Indian Affairs in 1902, comparing Native children to wild birds. "The young of the wild bird, though born in captivity, naturally retains the instincts of freedom so strong in the parent and beats the bars to secure it, while after several generations of captivity the young bird will return to the cage after a brief period of freedom. So with the Indian child."

Over many generations, he predicted, those "instincts of freedom" would eventually fade. A child, Jones wrote, "chafes at the loss of freedom and longs to return to his wildwood home. His offspring retains some of the habits acquired by the parent. These habits receive fresh development in each successive generation, fixing new rules of conduct, different aspirations, and greater desires to be in touch with the dominant race."[20]

This government report identified Santee as established by Alfred Riggs in 1870 and operating until 1937. Over those sixty-seven years, it boarded and educated 2,398 mostly Sioux children. The Pilgrim Congregational Church and Manse, associated with the school, remains on the National Register of Historic Places.

When Corabelle arrived, children were boarded there from as far away as Montana Territory and the Manitoba province in Canada.[21]

In 1893 the Riggses turned the operation of the school over to the American Missionary Association, an arm of the Congregational Church in the United States, after "the strain of trying to accommodate the school and the government proved too great." The Riggs may have lost federal funding, the Department of Interior report suggested, because Alfred Riggs insisted on continuing to teach Dakota and Lakota children in their Native language and to publish teaching and religious material in Native languages.

Fort Bennett, where Corabelle later briefly taught, was a school on the Missouri River about fifty miles north of present-day Pierre, South Dakota. It was for boys only and was in operation from 1880 until about 1894.[22]

There was no evidence of abuse or death in any of the Riggs's schools at the time of Corabelle's arrival at Santee. But there was tacit recognition of fatalities of Indian children at other schools around the country. The April 15, 1884, edition of the *Word Carrier* (it was published sporadically;

there were two editions that month) reprinted an *Omaha Bee* newspaper account of the work of an Episcopal Day School at Pine Ridge. It said Native children had died in eastern boarding schools because of a change in climate and exposure to malaria for children who were accustomed to "the clear, light atmosphere of this prairie country." Therefore, the paper maintained, day schools like the one at Pine Ridge were better than sending kids to far-away boarding schools.[23]

The Riggs family of missionaries had lofty goals, some of them adhering to shifting government edicts through the years, many of them not. The Santee school had been established in 1870 "for the purpose of raising up teachers, preachers, interpreters, and business men for the Dakota or Sioux nation," Alfred Riggs wrote.[24]

He, his father, and his siblings and their spouses, were respectful of aspects of Sioux heritage and culture, but realistic about the pressures arriving with legions of white settlers and their powerful, distant government in Washington, DC. Despite insisting that Sioux students retain their Native language while also learning English, Alfred Riggs was clear in his intent toward a Christianized education. And he had a dim view of Native religions.

The Dakota, Riggs declared, "are so thoroughly controlled in all their ideas and customs by a heathen religion that no change in life is possible except through a change in religion. Their religious philosophy makes their ideas of life so wrong that nothing but the true religion can set them right. Hence the hope of their regeneration does not lie in education or in civilization, but in the gospel and Spirit of Jesus Christ. Education and civilization are of use only as instruments of this gospel. Our aim, therefore, is to bring everything into a religious atmosphere, and make Christianity the ruling power of life. And we confidently expect our pupils to become, in one way and another, missionaries of the new life they find."[25]

In other words, education was a means to Christian conversion, the primary goal. The *Word Carrier* called it "the work that has to be done."

"This is the missionary age," Alfred Riggs declared in the March 1886 edition. "At no time since the beginning of the Christian era, have missions been more widely projected and thoroughly prosecuted than now. And the characteristic of missionary work of this age is organization. Spontaneous and individual work is not lacking, but it quickly links itself in with other work and workers, crystallizing into a new combination, and speedily adjusting its operations to some plan or line of regular work."[26]

At their best, missions did soften the harshest and cruelest edges of the rapid changes coming to the Plains. They fed and they clothed when lifestyles and livelihoods were abruptly taken from the Native people, often after violence or the threats thereof. Missionaries in Corabelle's orbit frequently spoke up for the rights of the Dakota, responded in fierce defense against the assimilation-or-extinction headlines, and even scolded those "back East" who exhibited the racist, stereotypical images painted of Native populations in the late-nineteenth-century press and literature. Corabelle's own handwritten memories are abundant with tender mercies, both given and received. The progression of her articles in the *Word Carrier* shows an increasing frustration with a misunderstanding of the people she had come to teach.

As she soon discovered, and as she reflected later in life, the human heart has a great capacity to expel reckless preconceptions and feckless dogma when confronted with real faces, real relationships, and true hearts. The unexpected intervened. Love poured forth from the unlikeliest places. Faith and devotion would eventually acquire new, deeper, meaning, far beyond the status-craving orbit of Corabelle's mother, sister, and aunt, far beyond even her own understanding of Christianity at twenty-three years old.

Intermarriage between white missionaries and Dakota men and women was a big story line in Corabelle's first winter in Nebraska. While interracial marriages were outlawed and socially taboo in large swaths of the country, they were gaining qualified acceptance on the Dakota frontier, where they were not specifically outlawed.

"The intermarrying of white people and half-breed Indians seems to be growing into popularity," the *Word Carrier* reported in March 1884. The headline read, "Discreditable Marriages," and it told of the union of "Miss Rebeca Hobbs, matron in the government school at Santee Agency," and "a young Santee-American as a husband." It also reported that Rev. S. D. Hinman also "takes to his bed and board" a young Native woman named Mary Merrick, who was reported to be "heir to a goodly slice of the Santee Indian reservation when it shall be parceled out." That reservation in northern Nebraska had been established in 1863, more than a quarter century before the breakup of the Great Sioux Nation and establishment of separate reservations in Dakota Territory.

The article, a reprint from the *Springfield Times,* went on: "We are not afraid to say that we have no objection to the marriage of whites and Indians, provided they are properly mated. We have known several marriages of both white men and white women with women and men of Indian blood, that have been very happy and good in every way.

"But the conditions for such mating are as yet rare, though they will increase, and such marriages become more frequent. But generally, such unions have no basis in any rational or moral sentiment. They are merely for the gratification of the animal passions, and such unions make the first parties to them more animal than before, and their offspring is brutalized from the very start. This is the reason of so many worthless half-bloods."

"Animal passions" and its crude description of love among people of different cultures and the children they bore aside, sentiment like that conflicted with other challenges of the missionaries. Part of their work quickly became trying to assure friends and donors back East that the people they had come to live among were peace-seeking, that a missionary was not in constant danger, that the stereotypes of the popular press—which routinely referred to Natives as "dusky," "bucks," and "squaws"—were cruelly incorrect, themselves contrary to civilized behavior.[27]

Writing also that month in the *Word Carrier*, Mary Buel Hatch Riggs addressed "eastern friends" who "say to us, 'tell us about your work—are you not afraid of the Indians?'

"How I wish I could transplant some of those kind solicitous friends to our mode of living for six months, and let them see for themselves," the leading female missionary at Santee declared. "Why! Those who come here to help us, many of them, more than half expect to pass sleepless nights in fear of massacre or something dreadful and are almost disappointed to find Indians living in houses like people and using cook stoves and doing things very much as white people do.

"We have nothing to fear," she wrote, "unless it may be that we get too tame, in some way, not the Indian, but we."[28]

Corabelle's second impressions and those that followed challenge almost everything she had been led to expect. Her evolution, her conversion, began soon after she arrived.

"These Indian pupils I have become very much interested in," Corabelle wrote two months after her arrival. "I must confess, I did not expect to find them such bright boys and girls, but with the training they have had here, are quite as advanced as some white girls I know of their age, who have had many more advantages.

"I will speak of my class of six Indian girls, who are studying in fractions, and seem about as quick to comprehend as any class I ever had. But they do not like to review or go over old ground. That is a peculiarity of all Indian pupils; they are not inclined to be thorough. But when one bears in mind their early training, their homes, their peculiar shy natures, and that their own race has always tried to keep the girls degraded and the inferior of the boys, I think they do remarkably well."[29]

A little over a year later, Corabelle told readers of the *Word Carrier* that she had become friends with many Native women, that she had learned from them. By then, she had been transferred to one of the Riggs's most remote outstations on the Cheyenne River roughly two hundred miles north of Santee, one she shared with Winyan. Corabelle's report was headlined: "Among the Wild Indians."

The story alternated between affection and scolding. She said Sioux women needed to focus more on cleanliness, although she did not explain how that could be accomplished in portable tepees or dirt-floor log homes, where much time was spent on the ground, sleeping, eating, or resting, and where water supplies were almost always what one hauled from rivers or lakes. She also chided Native women for spoiling their children.

"These Dakota women seem very fond of their children; watch them as affectionately as I ever saw a white mother; they are so fond that they do not make them obey, or control them one bit, for fear that they will not love them."[30]

But she had become a great defender of Dakota women, a frontier feminist. Corabelle was not sanguine about gender roles in the Sioux culture, and she expressed her disapproval of the expectations made of women. In her handwritten memoirs, Corabelle wrote that the division of labor in the Dakota culture she encountered had put too much of a burden on women, who in her observation did much of the hard, physical work, even after just giving birth.

"I wanted to make their lives as cheerful as possible, for women's lives are dull and hard," she wrote in her handwritten memoirs five decades later. "Among Indians they have been taught to be drudges by their mothers, and do most all the wood chopping, water carrying, meat cutting, and putting up of their tents as tipis are done by the Indian women. The men paint and dance, herd the cows and ponies, go hunting and trapping, so they have no time for other things, but smoke and relate Indian traditions."

She expressed the same sentiment about gender roles publicly while in Dakota Territory. Halfway through her teaching there, she declared to the readers of the *Word Carrier*: "I hope the day will come when these heathen customs will be done away with, and the man will learn that his first Christian duty is to his wife and children; to shield them from these things and be noble enough to do the hard work."[31]

But simultaneously, Corabelle was embracing the beauty, loyalty, and individuality of the people, including the men. She wrote lovingly of her relationships with several men and boys. In the "Among the Wild Indians" article, Corabelle described an encounter with a Native man, Good Dog. He had helped her conduct worship one Sunday. Four women, two babies, two children, and a young man joined in singing hymns in Dakota. By her second year in Dakota Territory, Corabelle was singing and praying in Dakota. Fifty years later, she sang those songs to her grandchildren.

Chapter 3
Restless Heart, Defiant Spirit

Corabelle Fellows was born on March 3, 1861, in Princeton, Illinois, a small town west of Chicago, where her father was postmaster. As it happened, it was the day after Dakota Territory was organized. Destiny seemed to be on the calendar. Corabelle was also born the day before Abraham Lincoln was sworn in as the nation's sixteenth president, and five weeks before the cannonading of Fort Sumter, South Carolina, by separatist Southern rebels set the spark for the Civil War.

Corabelle's father, Homer Fellows, worked many professions in his life beyond delivering the mail: He was a surveyor, photographer, prospector, farmer, government employee, including a stint as a doorman at the US Capitol. Working for the war department later in his life, he survived one of the biggest tragedies ever in a federal workplace, one that killed nearly two dozen of his co-workers. He was, Corabelle wrote in her memoirs, "of New Hampshire stock and loved the country."

But mostly Homer Fellows was a wanderer, a dreamer, never content in the moment, never anchored to one place, always looking for the next thrill over the horizon. His oldest daughter inherited his wanderlust and ability to adapt, and she also held his trait of any confronting challenge as an opportunity for grand, new adventure. Homer Fellows was immensely proud of his daughter for most of her time teaching in Dakota Territory.

In *Blue Star* Corabelle recalled a brief visit to her parents' home in Washington, DC in 1886 during which she thought her father was "so proud of me he was simply ridiculous. I was feted and entertained and taken the rounds of Washington, and Father and I stole off for a week together at Deer Park in the Allegheny Mountains west of Washington."[1]

Corabelle's mother, Cornelia Haight Fellows, was a socialite who had attended seminary at Glens Falls, New York, and, according to her daughter, was "educated in music, French, needlework and fine cookery."[2] Cornelia was permanently anchored to tradition and status, an inveterate social climber who sought the company of the rich and influential no matter where she called home. She was shattered when her son, Clement, died of scarlet fever as a toddler while the family was moving to Washington, DC.[3] Isely/Duncan's *Blue Star* also portrayed Cornelia as a racist who would not even touch a Black child, and who would use the crudest terms of the age to refer to people of color.[4]

Her daughter, Corabelle, despised the high-society circuit. "I thought these Washington society women a set of silly ninnies to spend their lives in a round of pretty parties,"[5] she said.

After the Civil War broke out, Homer Fellows, dejected and humiliated by rejection from the Union Army because of a childhood hip injury, left Cornelia and Corabelle in Glens Falls, New York, while he and a man named Charles Tupper went in search of gold. For eighteen months, Homer was trapped in Mexico, and as the Civil War raged, he lost all contact with his family. That family eventually would include Corabelle's younger sister, Marian.

By 1863, as the war approached a killing crescendo, Homer Fellows returned from the West virtually penniless and entered the emerging field of professional photography. It was a booming enterprise that employed new technology that was literally reshaping how people viewed themselves and their world. Homer, like many Civil War–era photographers, capitalized on the sudden demand for images that allowed people to remember loved ones as soldiers headed off to war. He set up shop to take photos of Union men heading for the front.

As the war dragged on, the Fellowses lived in the small Missouri towns of Glasgow and Chillicothe, and eventually St. Louis, where they were on April 15, 1865, the day Lincoln was assassinated in Ford's Theater. Corabelle, who had just turned four, remembered in her memoirs that all the adults were talking in hushed tones.

This was one of several notable traumas that helped shape her view of herself and the larger world, traumas that helped propel her to a life looking outward. She was inquisitive and adventurous, testing boundaries and flouting conventions. From the beginning, the two sisters were opposites. Marian "was demure and conventional," Corabelle recalled. "I was eternally doing what wasn't the thing to do. Marian accepted. I inquired as long as no one checked my path."[6]

They were groomed in a society of debutante balls and status. As they grew older, the sisters sewed an hour each day, memorized catechism for Sunday school, and took lessons in language, math, and the arts. Wherever the family lived, the sisters were educated so that "we might marry in a higher walk,"[7] Corabelle recalled in her handwritten memoirs decades later. There was a perpetual tug, she recalled, between her father's "urge of the outdoor life," versus her mother's interest in high society.

When the war was over, the Fellowses moved to a farm in Richmond, Missouri, forty miles east of Kansas City. Homer raised hogs and sheep, and Corabelle delighted in riding to the market with wagons loaded with protesting pigs that gave her a "fine chill of delight."

"The farm home at Richmond is clear in my mind: a large rambling, two-story house set among locusts and elms,"[8] she recalled. Her mother's flowers adorned the yard and, with no school available, Cornelia homeschooled her daughters in writing, reading, arithmetic, geography, physiology, and sewing.

"Mother was determined that even if we were just a farmer's daughters, our education should not suffer," Corabelle remembered. "We might marry in a higher walk."

In *Blue Star*, Corabelle said those "exacting" practices of education, her harping against "untidiness," remained with her, "for as I sit blind in my old age, the verses of poetry, the answers to questions I learned there in that upstairs room, pass through my mind and are extremely comforting."[9]

That experience in Missouri did not last long. Cajoled by extended family to raise their daughters in "proper privileges" of a city, they moved to Washington, DC.[10] Homer, who also never emotionally recovered from the loss of his only son, again worked as a photographer, then got a job as doorkeeper at the Capitol, a job he did not like but kept for the family's sake.

The family lived in a four-story house with views of Capitol Hill. *Blue Star* describes an expansive view of the rough-hewn city out the front door. Washington then may have been populated with high-society aspirants like Cornelia Haight Fellows, but the nation's capital looked like it was not much beyond the swampy wilderness it had been built on. A disease-carrying canal flowed through stagnant marshlands south of the White House; brothels outnumbered restaurants; and cattle and other animals grazed freely on the unkempt expanse along the mile-long mall stretching westward from the Capitol to the Potomac River. There were more saloons than salons; the Smithsonian Institution and other eventual pillars of capital culture were in their infancies.

When it was available, Corabelle and Marian went to public school. During play time, they often played on the steps of the Capitol to be near their father as he stood watch. The girls frequently played near or went on walks past the half-built Washington Monument, its construction restarted after a pause over the lack of funds and workers during the war. That was a child's dreamscape of bustle and mystery, with massive stones strewn all about the site, and armies of workers cutting, hoisting, and placing giant pieces of the ascending obelisk. The Fellows sisters also spent hours in the majestic Library of Congress and the Corcoran Art Gallery, took dancing and piano lessons, and sat in the visitors' gallery when Congress was in session. Corabelle read every book she could get her Uncle Thomas to check out from the Library of Congress.

She became a good writer, blessed with the gift of original observation and a sharp eye for meaningful detail. She loved a good story, and she developed a knack of conveying that she was in the moment when she was telling them. Corabelle honed a capacity for self-reflection, of compassion toward those who did not share her background.

Eventually, Corabelle devoted a big part of her life to writing. Writing the details of her trip west was one of the first things she did upon her arrival at the Santee Agency. That made the peculiar arrangement with Isely/Duncan and the publication of *Blue Star* all the more difficult to understand. The book came out after Corabelle died. It was presented as Corabelle's story, "told from the life of Corabelle Fellows," not the more direct "as told to." Was that an indication from the ghostwriter that she had taken license in telling Corabelle's story? Perhaps. Indeed, a few passages in the book contradicted the written memoirs Corabelle put together in that last decade of her life.

In Washington, DC, cousins Rachel and Bess Updegraff—daughters of her uncle, Thomas Updegraff, a congressman from northeastern Iowa—sometimes came to visit. But they were homesick for the openness and newness of Iowa, which fed Cousin Corabelle's sense of adventure. America after the Civil War was being pulled westward. There was always something more mysterious and adventurous about Out There, the land far beyond the constraints and expectations of her mother's social life.

The Fellows family hosted card parties and musical performances. Her mother "talked much to Marian and me about the necessity of social training and saw that we lost no opportunity to learn all that was needful to meet and associate with the 'best' people,"[11] Corabelle recounted.

Soon, they became regular invitees to presidential and congressional receptions. The children were dressed for high society, too. "Always we wore three stiff linen petticoats, and our hair was confined in a net," Corabelle said in *Blue Star*. Life fell into a rhythm, with "father going to work every morning and mother being more and more taken by parties."[12]

Then the wandering Homer sparked another shock. He came home one day from work and announced that he'd rented a farm across the Potomac River in Virginia. Her mother and sister cried. Corabelle ran about the Capitol Hill house rejoicing. She was moving to a place of a thousand fruit trees, of lush patches of strawberries and blackberries, of animals of all sizes and shapes. An aging man she called "Uncle Peter" and his Black wife, Kate—a rare and convention-defying racial intermarriage—had tended the farm for years with the help of a German immigrant farmhand. Towering oak and beech trees stood guard around a sixteen-room farmhouse, which was ringed by a veranda on the first floor and a portico on the second.

It was paradise for a girl then coming into her teenage years, a girl who loved the outdoors, animals, and adventure. Corabelle spent days in woods and dales, distant from judgmental eyes and the buttoned-down dress of a society girl. Even her mother, she remembered, "soon acquired the idea that it was possible to be a lady even in the country."[13] Soon followed parties with friends from Washington, DC, who crossed the Potomac for a country getaway. Homer boarded city dwellers' horses and raised chickens for sale. Marian and Corabelle took weekly trips into Georgetown to study science and take piano and dancing lessons. The sisters made their own clothes, and Corabelle became an expert darner after learning from her mother the intimate art of repairing holes in knitted clothing.

"We eased, almost at once, into cheerful, peaceful living," she recalled.[14]

As they grew older, Marian and Corabelle were sent to school at Georgetown Academy, where their mother stayed with them in a rented room during the week, returning across the river to the farm for weekends. The girls were educated for two years there, spending adventurous summers on the farm in between.

Then came another move, to Maryland Avenue back in DC, where Homer Fellows again set up a photography shop, and seventeen-year-old Corabelle helped in her father's business by retouching photos with pen and India ink.

There, she had her first real romance. It was short and secret and quickly and severely ended by her father. But it was a separation so sudden and permanent that it launched Corabelle on a course that led to Dakota Territory, never to return for long to the East Coast. In her handwritten account decades later, Corabelle equated that first love with her romance of missionary work and explained how one led to the other.

"I was sent to my aunt in Aurora, Illinois, to make an extended visit, and go to the seminary," she wrote in her memoirs. "It was there, while with a helpful friend, that I was converted, and upon my return [to Washington, DC], found the First Presbyterian Church's missionary work among the Santee Sioux Indians."

Her handwritten memoirs and *Blue Star* went into detail about the interrupted romance.

"In Washington, where I was raised from seven years to twenty-one, girls did not come out in society until they were eighteen years old,"

Corabelle said. "We were living on Maryland Avenue in a large, four-story house, and had more rooms than we needed, so my mother kept several roomers and boarders, among whom was a Capt. K, an Englishman, toward who I looked upon as a hero."

He was "a Captain in some Royal Regiment back in England. He was over 6 feet tall and . . . thoroughly English."

Captain K "wore nothing but English-knit clothes made in London" and "perfumes from England." She was smitten, even when he "continuously corrected me in my use of English."

"I admired him," Corabelle remembered, even though "he was twenty years my senior."

Her parents were wary of suitors. "I was never allowed to go alone with my escort because I was only seventeen. So my sister and parents always went along. I was also not permitted to accept presents from gentlemen, at least nothing of much value."

At Christmas, when this mysterious Captain gave Marian and Corabelle lockets with gold charms, their mother told them they could keep the locket but not the charm, which she substituted with a blue ribbon.

"I believe my parents were right," Corabelle wrote more than forty years later in her memoirs, "tho[ugh] it is not the ways of today."

Soon, Corabelle was calling Captain K "my lover" and he—despite the age difference—asked Homer Fellows if he could court his daughter. Her father "politely and very curtly nipped (it) in the bud," Corabelle remembered. "My dear father ordered the haughty Captain from our home, stating he 'considered it an insult to ask for a child twenty years (his) junior.'"

"I, of course, was heartbroken, and wept alone, writing sentimental poetry in my diary book."

Then one day Corabelle received a secret delivery. The captain had sent a note for Corabelle to walk to a "rustic bridge" in a nearby park, and to look for a note from him under a distinctive rock. She was to place her note of return under the same rock, and to destroy any notes she got from him. Its choreographed secrecy resembled that of twentieth-century Cold War spy craft, but this was the espionage of forbidden love.

"I ran to my room and hastily wrote a few fervent words, put it in my dress, took my hat, and telling my mother I was going to see a girl, I ran as swiftly to the park as I could," Corabelle wrote.

The captain's note was under the rock, just as he had said it would be. Corabelle placed hers under the rock, and—filled with jubilation—ran home to read the secret message from her suitor. But on the way home, she ran into "my father dear," who noticed a portion of the envelope sticking from her dress.

"I begged him to destroy it, but he said he would think about it. I felt humiliated but that was not all," Corabelle remembered. "He then told me to go back with him and get the note I had placed there, which I was compelled to do."

They found the note as she had left it, and her father took possession. "But what was hurting me [was] that my father should have my note and unread," Corabelle wrote. "I felt like running away. No doubt my father was red and my eyes full of tears, but my father knew hurt and taking my hand he walked along and in a kind manner told me what he thought of a man who would lure an innocent girl away from her home and have her deceive and tell lies.

"My father talked kindly but sternly," she remembered. "And from that time on I never saw my Captain again."[15]

Chapter 4
Go West, Young Woman

Heartbroken over her father breaking up her first love, Corabelle eventually did what a lot of people of her generation did: She went west. She would never completely and comfortably return to the places of her childhood, and it was the beginning of a permanent separation from her family, especially from her mother and sister.

Very soon after the lost love with "the Captain," Corabelle's parents sent her to live with her aunt in Aurora, Illinois, where she attended seminary. Immediately, she felt "connected" to missions and to teaching, she wrote later in her memoirs. After spending a few months with her aunt and attending the seminary, she returned to Washington, DC, and—still a teenager herself—started her own school.

"From childhood I had always [had] great desires to be a school teacher . . . or missionary," she recounted. "Before I had finished my school career, at seventeen years of age, I had an opportunity to carry out my first ambition, and always fond of children, my friends urged me to open a private school."

She broached the idea with her father, always her sounding board, and Homer Fellows urged her to ask for sponsorship from the leaders of the First Presbyterian Church in Washington, DC. Its pastor, Rev. Byron Sunderland, had been a leading abolitionist and the chaplain of the US Senate early in the Civil War.

First Presbyterian leaders "gave me free use of the old chapel," Corabelle said. She decorated the brick walls with her own art, the windows with her handmade curtains, and she dressed it up with other homemade items aimed at elementary school children.

"On opening day, I had twenty-three pupils, boys and girls. I taught all grades. I taught the entire year except for the month of August, which in Washington, DC, is very hot," she wrote in her memoirs.

Corabelle ran this school for two years. In her spare time, she painted watercolors, often under the tutelage of her father, who painted for much of his adult life. She had dreams of being an artist. But, upon the insistence of her mother that she finish her seminary education, Corabelle took a train west again at around age twenty to live with her aunt in Aurora, and to return to the seminary there. It was there, Corabelle remembered, that she was "born again." She returned to Washington, DC, "with a new urge to be a missionary among the Indians."

First Presbyterian, which would help sponsor her, "thoroughly encouraged me, and I was thoroughly questioned and examined" as to the depth of her faith and commitment. Her attitudes toward the Dakota and Lakota—indeed, the attitudes of white Americans in general—had been largely shaped by the newspapers and books of the day. They often treated news from the territories as sensational and scary. Later, the yellow journalism approaching the turn of the twentieth century would sensationalize events in Dakota Territory, including Corabelle's marriage, even more.

By the 1880s the newspapers, which had grown exponentially in reach and influence during the Civil War, were routinely portraying Dakota, Lakota, and other Native people as enemies bent on bending or ending Manifest Destiny. In the two decades that followed the 1862 uprising in Minnesota, that war and other battles with Indigenous people on the plains had been used by the US government as justification for more federal seizure of lands granted to Dakota and Lakota in a series of treaties.

The Little Big Horn defeat of Custer, while a spectacular military victory for the Native tribes at that battle, which they called Greasy Grass, unleashed a more aggressive federal response that lasted into the next century. Treaties were abrogated; the Black Hills were opened wide to gold-seekers, rogues, outlaws, and other fortune hunters; and the

Homestead Act and other congressional action opened Dakota Territory to settlers and railroads as the region's Native inhabitants were forced from Great Sioux Nation treaty lands into separated and smaller reserves.

The American press largely covered these events under the "go west, young man," credo pushed by the most famous editor of the last half of the nineteenth century, Horace Greeley.

The attitudes portraying Native people as warlike and obstinate dominated the public press and literature even though there were many examples of Dakota and Lakota acting as peacemakers. Elizabeth Winyan was one of them. Her story was known by few, but those who knew her deeply respected and loved her. By the 1880s, she had been teaching and preaching in Riggs's mission schools for several years. She had developed a reputation as a woman of extraordinary moral, intellectual, and physical strength. Her own life could have been seen as a myth were her adventures not verifiably true.

During the 1862 Minnesota Sioux uprising, Winyan, then in her early thirties, had gained notoriety among both Dakota and whites by swimming bread and meat to Stephen Return Riggs's missionary family and a few dozen accompanying white settlers as they hid on an island of the Minnesota River during the violence.

Corabelle was a year old when that happened. A quarter century later, she would live and serve with Winyan. She felt she had been adequately prepared, theologically and physically, for the rigors ahead. "Kindness of the church and other friends nicely equipped me for my long journey north among the semi-civilized tribes of the Sioux Indians," she wrote in her memoirs.

"Semi-civilized" was one of the most benevolent descriptions of the Dakota and Lakota in that late fall of 1884 when Corabelle arrived at Santee. By and large, politicians and newspapers were hell-bent on assimilation, and some pushed extermination for recalcitrant tribes. While some missionaries and white politicians were advocating for a less abrupt conversion and for acknowledging and preserving at least some Native traditions and practices, there was little room devoted to that on the pages of the nation's newspapers.

Weeks before she arrived at the Santee agency the St. Paul, Minnesota, *Daily Globe,* whose pages would four years later describe Corabelle's marriage to Sam Campbell in the vilest of racist, sexist terms, headlined an article, "Indian Civilization." The author argued there was evidence that the government's assimilation-removal-reservation policies could eventually create a self-sustaining culture for the Dakota, Lakota, and other Natives.

"There seems to be some hope of solving the Indian problem without continuing unending appropriations for the 'savages,' or, by wronging them, inciting Indian wars," the author began. The story went on to cite statistics showing more Dakota living in homes rather than tents or teepees, and "more devoting themselves to farming," fewer to hunting.

"Schools for Indian children are better attended, and more of the adult Indians are accepting mechanical construction, and more are becoming self-supporting and less will be required of the government in the future in the shape of annuities," the *Daily Globe* reported. "The true solution of the long vexed Indian question is, to civilize the aborigines and to train them into the ways, habits and customs of civil life, education, and labor. Civilization and Christianity are the true modifiers of Indian character, instead of war and bloodshed, cheating, wrongdoing, and oppressing them."[1]

But there were great inconsistencies in the policy and messaging. A day before Corabelle's arrival at Santee, the newspaper reported that a man in Dakota Territory was "training an Indian quartette, two squaws and two bucks, to great efficiency on roller skates, with a view to a tour of the states."[2]

It was becoming the age of big shows. By then, Buffalo Bill's Wild West extravaganza had opened a three-decade run as a nationally known attraction that toured the country and Europe. It eventually traveled by train, crisscrossing the country, a village on wheels that would pick up and reassemble at each stop. It advertised "wild Indians" and "sharpshooters," and for a time featured both the victor of the Little Big Horn, Sitting Bull, and the deadeye-shooting Annie Oakley.

And, for a brief time, Corabelle and Sam Campbell would be featured attractions.

But even as the Wild West show was touring the country and exposing Native people to white audiences, voices of genocide persisted. A year before Corabelle arrived at Santee to teach, the Black Hills *Daily Times* in Deadwood, Dakota Territory, expressly called for extermination of resisting Indians. In a report on the US Army Brigadier General George Crook's cavalry war with the Apache in the Sierra Madre Mountains of the southwest, the paper called for killing all the Apache. "This is the only solution of the Apache question; all other plans have been tried time and again and have failed," the paper proclaimed.

"All honor to Crook and his command for thus clearing the path for civilization and progress," the *Daily Times* said.[3]

The enigmatic Crook, who had survived a Confederate prisoner of war camp during the Civil War, was no stranger to the Dakota and Lakota. He led columns of US Cavalry against the Sioux in battles at Rosebud and Slim Buttes in Dakota Territory within weeks on either side of Custer's death and defeat at Little Bighorn. But later in his life, as head of the US Army's Department of the Platte in Omaha, Crook also spoke out on behalf of Natives he had fought against. As the Great Sioux Reservation was being fractured, Crook spent the last year of his life trying to convince recalcitrant Sioux in Dakota Territory to accept government offers of land and permanent peace as their last, best chance of surviving the changes thrust upon them.

Speaking to the graduates at West Point not long before Corabelle's arrival at Santee, Crook said that "with all his faults, and he has many, the American Indian is not half so black as he has been painted. He is cruel in war, treacherous at times, and not overly cleanly. But so were our forefathers."

Despite the government's assimilation policies and its record of abrogating treaties, Crook argued that there still was hope for long-term coexistence—as long as it came with good faith from the government and settlers flooding into the land considered home by the Sioux.

"His nature, however, is responsive to a treatment which assures him that it is based upon justice, truth, honesty and common sense; it is not impossible that with a fair and square system of dealing with him the American Indian would make a better citizen than many who neglect the duties and abuse the privileges of that proud title," Crook told the graduates.[4]

The very week Corabelle arrived at Santee, US Secretary of the Interior Henry M. Teller issued his final annual report, and it was heavily focused on what he called "the Indian question." The election of Grover Cleveland as president meant Teller was losing his job under his boss, Republican President Chester A. Arthur.

Teller was a strong opponent of the Dawes Act, which Congress later passed, and which was designed to break up Native holdings and force assimilation through individual land grants. In that final report, Teller lauded the reality that "the past year has been one of peace among the Indians, and that no outbreaks have occurred. All the tribes are at peace with each other and with their white neighbors."

The government in 1884 was running seventy-six day schools and six "industrial or manual labor schools" for Indians all over the country, he reported. Fourteen additional boarding schools and four day schools were being run by religious organizations supported by the government. This arrangement with religious sponsors was necessary, the Interior Secretary said, because the government had not appropriated enough money to educate all Indian children who wanted to go to school. In addition, Teller reported, there had been established twenty-three religious schools supported by donations, such as the Santee school where Corabelle taught. The government was annually spending $167 per capita to educate Native children in boarding schools and was millions behind in funding overall education for them. The government also supported boarding Native children in white homes for the purpose of education. But the main obstacle, Teller reported to Congress, was that it was becoming increasingly harder on ever-shrinking Indian land for even the newly educated Natives to make a living.

"It has been the great object of the department in dealing with the Indian to make himself supporting," Teller wrote. "When an Indian youth has been taught to labor he is self-supporting, if an opportunity is presented to him to secure employment. One great difficulty met with is that when the young of both sexes return to the agency there is no remunerative employment for them. They lack capital to open and cultivate a farm, and if they have acquired a trade, they find no employment of that character."

Teller closed his report on the "Indian question" by maintaining that Congress had vastly underfunded payment of land seized by the government from the Indians. Federal policies inhibited Indians' ability to lease lands they still held, he wrote, so Native populations had become "beggar(s) and dependent on the government" and "brought to the verge of starvation."

"Left to himself, he will continue in this wretched condition until the vices of savage life shall destroy his race," Teller predicted. "His destruction will not be speedy, but it will certainly come unless he can be induced to adopt the civilization of the age, which he has until recently scorned. At no time in the history of our intercourse with the Indians have they shown a greater desire to abandon their savage life than during the last year."[5]

It was against this backdrop that Corabelle arrived at Santee. When she left Washington, DC, her parents were not happy, and she recalled the scene with a mixture of sadness and hopefulness in her handwritten memoirs.

"Very reluctantly my parents took me to the train that would soon put many miles of distance between us, and with many loving words and caution, they bid me goodbye," she wrote. "And my journey kept on. I never saw my mother again, though I made a visit home and saw my father. My heart was filled with lively prospects of my future work and also of much good work to be accomplished."

Isely/Duncan's *Blue Star* only hinted at this estrangement from her mother. Corabelle and Cornelia would write back and forth during her first three years in Nebraska and Dakota Territory, but the split would become forever after her engagement to Sam.

In her memoirs, Corabelle remembered the practical things she took with her from home when she moved west. They included a trunk filled with soft wool blankets and wraps designed to fend off the Dakota cold. They were her most tangible connection between the comfort of her childhood and the challenges of the life she had set course on. Looking back as she wrote, line by line, those memoirs as an old lady, she said she always felt "God gave me the strength and ambition which I even have today even though I am seventy and blind." But, oh, what she had seen.

Chapter 5

A Big, Wide World

"I left my home in Washington, DC, the 20th of November, 1884," Corabelle Fellows wrote weeks after her arrival in Santee, Nebraska. "I left on a beautiful, warm morning, with my heart full of doubts and misgivings as to whether I should reach Santee in safety, or do the good upon arrival there that I had it in my heart to do. To travel alone is never as pleasant, especially when one is leaving home, but I tried not to look behind me—only ahead—picturing in my imagination how I should find things at Santee."[1]

Her imagination could not grasp what she would see and feel and experience over the next four years: first, at Santee in Nebraska, then at a series of postings at government schools and Riggs's missions in Dakota Territory. She was twenty-three years old, more worldly than most women her age at the time, but the country she traversed on the way to her new position and the new home she had chosen were awash in political, economic, and social change. Corabelle wrote in her memoirs that she'd had a choice of missions in Arizona or Nebraska, and that she chose the latter because of the depictions of the plains she had read about in the papers.

Her father had tried to stop her, saying, "Don't you realize, child, what a slight little body you have? Indians are big, burly people. Their country out there in Dakota is rough and uncivilized. Besides it is very cold, and you know you have a cough." She tried to assuage his concerns and headed west.[2]

The frontier was closing, and change had come to all aspects of American life. Male citizens had just elected Grover Cleveland, the first Democratic president since before the Civil War. Labor unrest was widespread; two days after Corabelle left her uncle's home in Chicago on her way to the mission in Santee, thousands marched on Thanksgiving Day for higher wages. Science and engineering were pushing convenience. A St. Louis researcher patented evaporated milk the same month Corabelle arrived in Santee. The fountain pen and self-powered machine gun were invented that year.

Days after her arrival at Santee, the Washington Monument—the place where Corabelle and her sister once played among the unassembled granite boulders—was finally dedicated. At 555 feet, it was declared the tallest man-made structure in the world.

It was still thirty-six years before women could vote, but women were making indelible marks on the frontier. Much of Corabelle's missionary life in *Blue Star* is told in exciting anecdotes, but the book is occasionally telling in its subtle references to the broad changes sweeping the nation and its territories. The book largely ignores the tectonic forces then grinding between federal and territorial governments and the Sioux, conflicts that would lead to Sitting Bull's killing by tribal police and the slaughter at Wounded Knee. In the third year of Corabelle's mission among the Sioux, Alfred Riggs would ignore a federal directive that all teaching at mission schools and government schools be in English, calling it "illegal, unscientific, irreligious."[3]

But English was the mandated classroom language when Corabelle arrived that cold November day in 1884. Along with the soft blankets and sweaters she'd brought from home, she carried to Santee a sense of cultural and civil superiority of her upbringing.

"They are slow, shy and often sullen, but if you use the right authority, by not laying them too often in fault, they are not difficult to control," Corabelle wrote. "I think from observation, they are quite artistic, and I was again surprised to find them musical. Their drawing and music teachers have much to be proud of in these two talents."[4]

Natives were to be controlled, to be taught to adhere to the ways of white civilization. Her first job was teaching sewing to young girls. "And yes! It was a pleasure to see a group of round, smiling faces in a sewing room sitting in little chairs in a circle, waiting for their work of dress, or underwear, or patchwork.

"They were not allowed to speak in Indian," Corabelle wrote in her memoirs, "and should any little one do it, a dozen hands would go up and say, "teacher, Maggie, 'she talks Dakota!'"

Little did Corabelle know then of just how much she would learn of the Dakota language and music, of many Sioux people's knowledge of the natural world, of horsemanship, of friendship and devotion, of the longing for authenticity and the power of place, all of it from people she had come to "control." Soon after her arrival at Santee she began learning Dakota in a class that started out full of teachers but soon dropped to just her and the missionary Alfred Riggs. His father, Stephen, had a few years earlier published a Dakota-English dictionary; the son could not very well give up that pursuit of the spoken language. Corabelle treated it as another learning adventure.

In mid-1885, Corabelle was transferred to the Riggs's Oahe Mission near Fort Sully, a modest horse ride north of what is now the South Dakota state capital, Pierre. Established a decade before, it was headed by Alfred Riggs's younger brother, Thomas Lawrence Riggs, a young man whom Elizabeth Winyan had helped raise after his mother had died. By then, as the historian Bruce David Forbes has noted, the mission was established as a "formal industrial school for Indian children." It included a school, a chapel, homes, and outbuildings, and it was tucked along the Missouri's east banks at a place called Peoria Bottom.

A network of thirteen outstations was established, including one of the most remote being run by Winyan. Some called it the Two Kettles station after the village where it was located. Many of these outposts were on what, four years later, would officially become the Cheyenne River Reservation. Reaching them often required days-long horse-and-wagon journeys and river crossings.

Amelia Stone Quinton, the chair of the Women's National Indian Association, her sponsor, wrote her a letter expressing hope that the posting in such a remote place would give Corabelle an opportunity to hone in on the language of the people who needed help the most. "It will be to you a new experience and test your missionary metal very surely, I think," Quinton wrote.

"You ask, 'what do we do when we get on the field?' My dear sister, do you not see that that wholly depends upon the field itself?" She suggested that Corabelle should seek to learn from the people as well as teach them. "Pray for help, and, take advice," Quinton wrote.[5]

For all their controversial positions and actions, the Riggs believed that Native missionaries were the most effective messengers to the Dakota and Lakota. "Thomas Riggs firmly believed in Native leadership," Forbes wrote, "claiming that 'the Indian was a great deal more effective as a preacher and teacher among his own people than any white man could be.'"[6]

Of all of them, Elizabeth Winyan was unparalleled.

Chapter 6

Mother, Protector

Elizabeth Winyan was born three decades before Corabelle, on the shores of Swan Lake near present-day Mankato, Minnesota. The name she was most known by, Winyan, meant "mother-protector" in Dakota. At about age ten, inspired by schooling she received from the missionaries Stephen and Mary Riggs, and Thomas and Margaret Williamson, she took the English name, Elizabeth.

Winyan was the granddaughter of the peacemaking Sisseton Dakota Chief Ishtakhaba, known in English as Sleepy Eyes for his drooping eyelids. Winyan's father was described in some accounts as Sleepy Eyes's top soldier. Both of her parents died when she was young. One ancestry account identifies them as "Mrs. and Wambdi Sapa Black Eagle."[1]

In 1824, in one of the early meetings between territorial Indigenous leaders and government officials, Winyan's grandfather, Sleepy Eyes, led a delegation of Dakota and Ojibway to Washington, DC, to meet with President James Monroe. Monroe, in the last full year of his presidency, had decided that policies of assimilation of eastern Indians were not working, and that Washington should begin negotiating with individual tribes inside the twenty-four states to move Indigenous people to territories west of the Mississippi River. Monroe wanted it to be a "voluntary" process, declaring that "to remove them from (their lands) by force, even with a view to their own security and happiness, would be revolting to history and utterly unjustified."[2]

But that policy would soon die on Andrew Jackson's Trail of Tears and its forced Cherokee relocation and a relentless parade of other broken treaties, military battles, and forced relocations that followed.

Sleepy Eyes, who was relocated along with his granddaughter, Winyan, later became one of the most recognized Sioux leaders to sign the 1851 Traverse des Sioux Treaty. He did so reluctantly. In that treaty, Sisseton and Wahpeton bands sold 21 million acres, stretching from northwestern Iowa through Minnesota to present-day South Dakota, for roughly $1.7 million. Sleepy Eyes and his followers were confined to a narrow reservation about twenty miles wide along the Minnesota River, a gentle 332-mile tributary of the Mississippi.[3]

The governor of Minnesota Territory, Alexander Ramsey, and US Indian Commissioner Luke Lea justified the treaty by declaring to Congress that "it is needed as an additional outlet to the overwhelming tide of migration, which is both increasing and irresistible in its westward progress."

The two federal agents foresaw it as a giant step toward forced assimilation of the Sioux and other Natives living in the land of lakes and coteau prairies. They believed that forcing a civilization based on community to adapt to one based on individual rights was the only way forward. Private property, a foreign concept to Dakota and Lakota, would be their basis of survival.

"It was our constant aim to do what we could to break up the community system among the Indians, and cause them to recognize the individuality of property," Ramsey and Lea told Congress. "If timely measures are taken for the proper location and management of these tribes, they may, at no distant period, become an intelligent and Christian people."[4]

All told, Winyan's grandfather signed four treaties with the US government. He died around 1860 while hunting near what is now Sisseton, South Dakota. Among his many acts, Sleepy Eyes is credited for helping plot the current site of Mankato, Minnesota, at the confluence of the Minnesota and Blue Earth Rivers.

Sleepy Eyes had instilled in his descendants a love for their home around Swan Lake and the Minnesota River, a longing that never left his granddaughter, Winyan. It was a bountiful natural table of unspoiled beauty, with clusters of wild rice and ample populations of ducks, geese, swans, turtles, muskrats, and fish. Sleepy Eyes loved it so much that in the negotiations over the 1851 Traverse des Sioux Treaty with the government, he asked that it include a provision granting him the "privilege" of living and dying there, and it was granted by Commissioner Lea.

The Dakota Chief had resisted signing this treaty, telling government commissioners he was dubious they would honor it, and that he knew it would further preserve a system in which his people would be subject to a downward system of dependency upon white traders. "I am a poor man and have difficulty in maintaining myself," he declared, "but these traders wear very good coats." He was persuaded to sign the treaty by younger men, but he asked for a copy "so that we may look at it and see whether you have changed it." He was correct in his suspicions. Eventually, his granddaughter would be forced west to live on a reservation in Dakota Territory.

"Promises made even by officers of the government in such circumstances are of very little account, when the stipulation of the Treaty and the fears of the interests of the white race require the red man's removal,"[5] Stephen Riggs recounted. By 1857, after the killing of settlers in what became known as the Spirit Lake Massacre shook the burgeoning white population near Sleepy Eyes's village, "a group of home guards marched one day to Sleepy Eyes' camp on Swan Lake . . . and demanded that he remove at once to the Reservation," the historian Thomas Hughes wrote. "Being a man of peace, the old Chief left the beloved home of his father and settled at Sleepy Eye Lake, near where the city of Sleepy Eye now stands," about thirty miles away.[6]

As a young woman, Winyan became widely known for her physical strength and powerful moral center. She considered herself a conciliator between her Dakota and Ramsey's "overwhelming tide of migration" that was pushing her people ever westward. Throughout her life, Winyan survived multiple close calls on her life, and she more than once helped save others from unhappy fates, including Corabelle Fellows.

"She was one of the grandest women I ever knew," the noted missionary, writer, translator, and Indian rights proponent Mary Collins said.[7]

A Winyan cousin, Julia LaFramboise, the daughter of the trader Joseph LaFramboise and another granddaughter of Sleepy Eyes, also became a Christian missionary. But she died young; Winyan lived into her late fifties.[8]

During her childhood, Winyan and her younger brother would often be awakened at dawn by their grandfather. Sleepy Eyes would take them to the banks of the Minnesota River near present-day Mankato and give them pieces of paper and other presents to toss into the river as an offering to a greater spirit. He "would pray devoutly to the Great Mystery with uplifted arms and eyes," Hughes wrote.

One of Winyan's earliest memories was being tied to a board that was then securely affixed up in a tree for safekeeping while her mother worked in a nearby cornfield. One day, when a very young Elizabeth and her family had gathered with a group of Dakota men and women to make maple syrup, they were attacked by hostiles from an unidentified tribe. Shouting and gunshots rang through the air. Elizabeth's father was killed. Her mother, realizing she could not escape carrying both children, grabbed her brother and hastily emptied a pot of boiling water and hid the tiny Elizabeth beneath the overturned pot. There, the girl stayed for two days and one night, before being rescued by her mother during the second night.

"Even in her old age," the historian Hughes recounted, "Winyan never forgot that terrible experience and how, when her mother lifted the kettle, the moonlight shown on the bloody faces of the outstretched dead, her father among them."[9]

As a young woman, Elizabeth gave birth to a son, Edwin Phelps, who would also become a missionary in Dakota Territory. Some accounts said Elizabeth had been married more than once, including to an abusive Native man who had accidentally drowned. Elizabeth was known as one of the early converts of frontier missionaries Stephen Riggs and Thomas Smith Williamson; the latter was also a medical doctor. She lived at Riggs's missions or served them across the Upper Midwest for the rest of her life. Although she never became fluent in English, she understood it and could speak phrases, and she often translated. Winyan learned to sew and to read the Bible, which Riggs had translated into Dakota, Elizabeth's native language.

Once, when she was a young woman visiting her grandfather Sleepy Eyes, Winyan hid a few pages of the Bible in her dress. Somehow Sleepy Eyes found out, and she was summoned before him.

"I was trembling," she said of the man who had taught her to offer thanks to a great spirit by tossing tiny tributes into the Minnesota River. "I did not know what he would do." But Sleepy Eyes gave his blessing, and he called others to listen to her read. And from there, she began teaching the Bible to other Native women. Winyan blossomed into a regular teacher and childcare provider at the Riggs's missions in the Upper Midwest. As she got older, she was given some of the toughest, hardest tasks, sometimes living solitarily through Dakota winters, opening her home for fellowship and food to Dakota struggling against the elements and the change brought by white neighbors.[10]

Her physical strength helped save others. During the deadly Sioux uprising of 1862, friendly Dakota had warned the Riggses to leave their mission, and they and a small band of missionaries took refuge on a small island in the Minnesota River to hide from bands of Dakota who were attacking and killing whites and sacking their homes and businesses. Winyan, whom the Riggses sometimes called Zoe, swam the bread and meat to the island. Eight days later, in a journey beset by frequent bad weather and close calls with bands of hostile Sioux, the Riggs party of about forty, its ranks swollen by other displaced white settlers who had fled their homes, made it to Shakopee, more than one hundred miles from their mission, where they waited out the hostilities.[11]

In a letter to a Cincinnati newspaper after that 1862 uprising, Stephen Riggs's daughter, Martha, described in harrowing detail the family's flight to safety. Martha's account included how the Native Winyan had put her own life in danger, and she cited Winyan and others who had tried to end the violence to plead with readers to not blame all Dakota for the violence.

"It was not my intention, when I began this article, to enter at all into the causes of this outbreak," Martha wrote. "But what I have written will excite your indignation against all Dakotas, and I cannot bear that it should be so. It must be remembered that the [Dakota] church members, as a whole, have had no hand in it. One, John Otherday, guided a party of sixty-two across the prairies. Two others, Lorenzo Lawrence and Simon Anawangmane, have recently brought into Fort Ridgely three captive women and eleven children; and we doubt not that others will 'let their light shine'—at the peril of their own lives, remember."

Martha closed with a plea against escalating demands for the extermination of all Dakota.

"Our own people have given them intoxicating drinks, taught them to swear, violated the rights of womanhood among them, robbed them of their dues, and then insulted them! What more would be necessary for one nation to rise against another? What more, I ask. And yet there are many who curse this people and cry, 'Exterminate the fiends.' Dare we, as a nation, thus bring a curse upon ourselves and on future generations."[12]

Winyan taught Dakota to anyone who would listen. She taught it to Margaret Louisa Irvine Riggs, the second wife of missionary Thomas Riggs, with whom Winyan served in stations along the Missouri and Cheyenne Rivers as the march of white settlers approached.

By the time Corabelle arrived in Dakota Territory, Winyan was known as one of the first Native missionaries, a giver and provider with an independent spirit and open heart, equally devoted to preserving what she could of her culture yet attuned to the reality that far more powerful forces were bearing down. Forced to change, to abandon her beloved homeland in Minnesota, Winyan was determined to co-exist by preserving as much of her Dakota identity as she could, to seek commonality through what her grandfather had taught her: service, humility, attention to the poor and suffering, and a reverence for nature and its splendor. Acts, not words, would define her. It was also what her Christian Bible had taught her.

"Winyan was a woman of strong character, fine mind, and a natural leader," the historian Hughes wrote. "Her great desire was that her people should hear the Gospel, so as the years went by, her work widened, and she was sent to various fields. She held meetings, explained the Bible, visited the sick, buried the dead, and occasionally addressed conferences of white people. Even the Indian men held her in the highest esteem."[13]

Mary Collins, an Iowan by birth and long-time white missionary in Dakota Territory with Thomas Riggs and his first wife, Nina Foster Riggs, became one of Winyan's closest confidants.

"She is a faithful friend, true to her character as a Dakota," Collins said. "She enjoys camp life with us, and evenings, as we sit by the campfire, she will tell stories of her early life, or fables, or legends of the stars. She is quite an astronomer. She reads the sky like an open book."[14]

Like Corabelle Fellows, Collins also wrote late in life of the challenges she had faced, of the great unknowns she had encountered, and of the people with whom she worked. Missionaries, like the Natives they encountered, were being asked to step beyond the past. In 1875, enroute with the Riggs family to her first mission post along the Missouri River, Collins literally hugged a telegraph pole near Fort Thompson as a touchstone to the life she was leaving behind. It "seemed like a hand reaching back home," Collins remembered.

Collins met Winyan for the first time on that journey. The Riggs party reached the mission they called Oahe, which means foundation, or a place to stand, in English. It was at a place called Peoria Bottom and close to Fort Sully, a US Army outpost on the eastern flank of the Missouri, just north of the eventual South Dakota Capital in Pierre. Like many others' first encounters with Winyan, Collins's was memorable. Winyan had traveled from the Sioux agency at Sisseton, in the very northeast corner of the territory, with her son and his family.

"On the way, a baby girl was born," Collins recalled. "For a long time this family had been praying for a child and now the prayer was heard." The little girl—Winyan's granddaughter—was named Hannah.

"The trip had been rather hard on the new baby and her food did not agree with her," Collins wrote. "So the first work I did for the Indians was to fill a bottle with milk and kneel down before the mother and feed little Hannah."

After Nina Foster Riggs died suddenly in 1878, Elizabeth Winyan and Mary Collins became the primary caregivers for Theodore, the Thomas and Nina's four-year-old son. "Elizabeth was a great comfort," Collins said.

Elizabeth Winyan
COURTESY OF LORA MEINZER

Once, walking together while serving at Oahe, Collins and Winyan entered a small patch of woods along the river and came across a tragic scene. "The faint voice of a crying woman said, 'mini wachin, mini wachin,'" Collins wrote. "I said, 'Elizabeth, someone is crying for water. We must find her.' Going further into the timber we saw what we recognized as a tent for a dying person. I went in and found an old woman. I said, 'grandmother, I will give you water,' and a quart cup of water was left there for her but she could not lift it.

"Her daughter came to the tent and explained that she was dying. And she said, 'I have four little children and my husband made me put her out lest the evil spirit leaving her might enter into me after her death and cause my death.' Poor woman, leaving her mother but such the mother's heart trying to protect her offspring."

Collins and Winyan gave the woman bread and water, and Winyan stayed with her until she died. "The daughter never forgot it and she and her family became followers of the meek and lowly savior who went about healing the sick," Collins wrote.

It was an illustrative moment. Winyan was caught between tradition and faith, between fear and action. She ignored the Native warnings of evil spirits from the dying woman's son-in-law. She saw another in need, and she acted. Did it matter if she was acting in communal mercy in the Dakota tradition, or as a converted Christian following Christ's teachings about comforting the suffering?

On one mission trip, Collins found herself on the prairie in a tent next to where Winyan and her granddaughter were sleeping. "Elizabeth snored so loudly that no one could sleep," Collins recalled. "Little Pilgrim awoke and said, 'grandmother, sleep softly. Sleep softly.' Their expressions are very beautiful when correctly translated, but many interpreters do not interpret correctly. How can they, when they are illiterate and know very little English and what they know has been picked up mostly by people from those who depend upon slang largely to express themselves."

One day, Winyan sat down next to Collins and opened her heart to a gnawing reality that the freedom of her childhood was gone forever.

"I have just seen something that well represents our present condition as a race," Winyan told Collins. "A man named Longfeather, dressed in Indian dress paint and feathers, was teaching some boys the Indian dance and song. There were three boys: One with long hair and painted face and Indian dress, one with long hair and shirt and leggings and a white boy's shoes and stockings on, the third dressed well in entire white men's clothes. One represents the past, the second the present, and the third the future. I know it has to be, but to me the one dressed all in the Indian child's clothing looked the best, but I'm only an Indian."[15]

Chapter 7

A Mysterious Captor Comes Calling

By October of 1885, Corabelle was settling in at Winyan's missionary outpost at the Oahenoupa village on the Cheyenne River. The two women would live and teach together there until the following summer. Grasslands rolled below a fulsome sky, often roiled into more vigorous motions by the wind. Winter temperatures that plunged to thirty or forty degrees below zero pushed humans constantly to the edge of survival, to one failed fire away from freezing to death.

Corabelle's journey to the camp had been rough and long. Thomas Riggs led in a party that included his young son, Theodore; another missionary, Mr. Collins, and his four children. There is no indication this Mr. Collins was related to the missionary Mary Collins.

"We had the Missouri River to cross," Corabelle wrote in the *Word Carrier*, then wryly added: "And one always had a hard time on that river."[1]

Searching for a good place to cross, hired men harnessed a horse named Jack to tow a flat-bottomed boat a quarter mile along treacherous shores in search of a crossing point. "Finally, we all jumped in the boat: men, women, children, horses, provisions, and all," Corabelle wrote. "They rowed us over, but the current was very swift, and it was a hard pull."[2]

Once across, a hard pull on land still lay ahead. They continued on their seventy-five-mile journey, stopping after twelve miles on the first day. Corabelle described it this way: "We found a nice little spring of water and drove our wagon over a hill to keep off the wind. After the horses were watered and enjoying their oats, we made a camp fire. I rather enjoyed, for the first time in my life, eating out on the prairie. We had a very good supper, coffee, boiled eggs, bread, doughnuts and cookies. Mr. Collins made his bed under the wagon, and we made our bed on top of the six barrels of lime."

They slept under a buffalo robe on a feather bed draped over those barrels, "and were as cozy as possible, for the wagon had a cover to keep off the dew and wind," Corabelle told the *Word Carrier* readers. She nearly fell out of bed that night when the wagon jerked as the horses, tethered to the wagon for the night, strained against their constraints to reach for more grass. The moon that night "shone brightly," but the only other living creature they saw was a coyote, "a small, yellowish fellow, who was not one bit afraid of us." As they moved day by day toward Winyan's outstation along the Cheyenne River, they saw plentiful populations of jackrabbits, wild ducks, and prairie chickens.

After about a week on the trail, they arrived at Winyan's log home one evening after crossing the Cheyenne River, a smaller stream than the Missouri but no less daunting because its banks were of heavy clay earth commonly called "gumbo." When wet, that clay turns into a heavy, pasty quagmire that can quickly clog the feet of horse and human, and render stuck and useless the wheels of a wagon. In her memoirs, Corabelle described the mud in the Cheyenne River bottom as a thick "quicksand."

Winyan's granddaughter, Hannah Phelps, the child born when Mary Collins first met Winyan, was staying with her when the Riggs party arrived. On her first day at Winyan's, Corabelle was thrust right into the work. She was left alone to preside over the mission; Winyan and Hannah left with the rest of the party to return Mr. Collins to Oahe, leaving Corabelle to teach school that day. After an uneventful day of classes, a young man visited that night. He came in unannounced, as was the custom, and asked after Winyan.

"I told him I could not speak much Dakota, and had come to learn," Corabelle said, in a notable change from her attitude just a year earlier. "Whereupon he immediately began to teach me; went to the shelf where the school books were and had me read several pages. Then write on the blackboard and say the Lord's Prayer. He was a very pleasant . . . young man and after asking my Dakota name and telling me his, left."

Alfred Riggs had warned Fellows she would be among the "rougher Indians" in her station with Winyan. Corabelle herself wrote that she was "surrounded by painted faces, and never a white person in sight for many, many miles."[3]

Isolated almost to the point of intimidation on the vastness of the country, Corabelle nonetheless quickly began to feel at home in Winyan's house on a hill overlooking the Cheyenne River. It was here that she began calling Winyan Ina (mother). This place was akin to a community center, a gathering place for widely dispersed people living in log homes or tepees scattered about the prairie for miles around.

"Elizabeth's home was neat, a long log house well chinked with straw and plaster," Corabelle wrote in her memoirs. "A place in the center of the room for the stovepipe, and so there in the center stood the large cook stove brought by the government. Always warm and cozy and giving space everywhere for people to get near and warm. A few chairs and benches all around the wall, for Elizabeth held meetings every Sunday. In one corner was a homemade bed and plenty of wool blankets at the foot. In the other corner was a good-sized homemade table where we kept our books and papers. On the other side of the room in each corner were two large, covered boxes, with clothing in one and dishes and food stuffs in the other. All around on the walls were hung herbs and dried corn."

Winyan "was preacher and example to all the semi-civilized Indians and they respected her way, and I was sent there to learn to speak the Indian language and do missionary work in every way I could." Winyan, she wrote, "was to protect and help me."

But in *Blue Star*, Winyan is falsely portrayed as a hapless subordinate. Isely/Duncan simply refers to her as "Elizabeth" a "fat old Indian squaw" who "proved to have many chins and merry eyes." Although Corabelle described Winyan as a "widow" in her memoirs, Duncan's book also inaccurately described Winyan as an "old maid," intimating that she was childless, even though by then her son, Edwin Phelps, had become a missionary and teacher of renown. *Blue Star* also described Winyan as Corabelle's assistant, when in reality it was a relationship of equals, with Winyan having the motherly final say on many occasions.

To further the inaccuracies, Elizabeth was described in Duncan's book as just educated enough to "learn something of a white man's house and its keeping." Nowhere in *Blue Star* were there mentions of Winyan's long service with the Riggs's missions, including the fact that she had helped raise several children of missionaries.

Historian Bruce David Forbes noted the slight in his introduction to a later volume of *Blue Star*. "Winyan was the missionary in charge of the station and was the teacher in its one-room school," he wrote. "Fellows was her assistant."[4]

In that initial *Word Carrier* article from her new station on the Cheyenne River, Corabelle described Winyan as "an excellent Indian woman, the missionary for the station," adding that "there are few in these regions who do not know her, as she was among the first Christian Indians, and has lived with and known the Riggs family for a good many years.

"She is strong and active, and always cheerful and full of fun," Corabelle continued. "She teaches school here, and as I am right in the room, I study and recite Dakota, also help her teach arithmetic. Her little room is always neat and fixed up quite nicely for a school."

By then, Corabelle—despite political pressure to declare Native languages forbidden in schools—was well into learning to teach in Dakota and English.

"There is a blackboard upon the wall, a Dakota chart, and the Lord's prayer in Dakota," she wrote. "They read in Dakota first, from their reading books, then write on the blackboard, then read from the Bible, sing, and close by repeating the Lord's Prayer."

As she was writing the *Word Carrier* article, a young Native man sat in the classroom as Winyan taught younger children. The man was perusing a Dakota language dictionary Corabelle owned.

"He is very handsome," she told readers." "His hair is long and black, and has a little lock finely braided, beginning at his scalp, and tied with a string of beads at the end. He has long leggings and moccasins, and although he cannot understand much that I say to him, and has not spoken a word himself, he seems contented, and does not offer to go away."[5]

Writing in a later volume of the *Word Carrier*, Corabelle described Winyan as "about sixty years old, and her work among this, her own people, is wonderful. She has no husband, and is quite independent of everyone. Carries wood and water and thinks nothing of chopping all her own wood. Sometimes I go with her to the river, which is about one-half mile from here. It is a pleasant walk, and she seems to enjoy it as well as I, although she carries a little keg of water on her back."

By now, well into her second year of teaching Natives, Corabelle had developed relationships with many women, including a young mother, whom she described as "quite pretty if she was clean.

"Her eyes are large and black and her features are good," Corabelle wrote in the article, which was headlined, "Among the Wild Indians." "She has a dear little baby, who is always in a good humor, notwithstanding the dirt and streaks of paint upon his face."

Corabelle had nicknamed him "Charlie," and she would care for him while his mother took school and religious lessons in Dakota from Winyan.[6]

In her handwritten memoirs, Corabelle described her time with Winyan as a rebirth of motherly love. She would soon discover just how permanently distant she had become from her own mother, but in that rough winter of 1885 and 1886, she and Winyan forged a bond through trying physical conditions by honing in on a shared humanity, and by leaning on humor.

"In this log home, with Elizabeth Winyan (woman) Ina (or mother), I learned many profitable things," Corabelle wrote. "The Indian homes are quiet and orderly, a place for everything, and everything in its place. The bow and arrow over the door to grab if an enemy appeared, the beds and blankets on one side and the clothing. The food and dry corn, berries, meats in sacks upon the wall, and cooking utensils in a box, sometimes made of skins. The floor in winter was covered with buffalo skins.

"Mother was the Native missionary. Every Sunday she called together the people around and preached to them the gospel stories she had heard at the Riggs missions, telling them of Wakan Tanka, the great Spirit, who watched them that they did not steal or kill.

"The large room was always filled with men and women and dogs. . . . My duties in the camp [were] both mission and educational. We would visit the sick, sometimes walk miles, the sick lying upon the ground within the tent, the tent full of smoke in the center of the room, or the smoke from their pipes. We were always welcome. They would say, 'shake hands, my friend Blue Star, and mother, my heart is glad to see you."

They subsisted on the dried food hanging on the wall, and meat, flour, and coffee hauled from government commissaries miles away.

"The Indian men would bring mother wood, but the long, cold winters consumed a great deal of wood, so often mother and I would tie on our blankets and start out. She carried a large hatchet to cut small branches and I helped out, placing them in her blanket around her waist." They carried these small branches in blanket pouches that they eventually tied around their heads. Elizabeth could carry twenty gallons of water from the Cheyenne River a half mile distant, one straddled across her shoulders, one in her hand.

"We would go down to the Cheyenne River, which was filled with quicksand, and dangerous for man or beast," Corabelle remembered. "Mother would submerge the keg in the cold, clear water, until it was filled, then put in the cork and one was ready to strap on her shoulders. But sometimes while in one place too long, we would feel ourselves slowly sinking, then we moved away quickly for a new place. I carried a keg also."

Their school lasted from morning until after dark, children in class during the daylight hours, adults at night. They taught geography, reading, writing, and arithmetic. "Their inspiration inspired me, and I could notice how they were improving," Corabelle remembered. Routinely, a combination of the same ten or twelve young men would come late in the evenings, often after Winyan had gone to bed, and with Corabelle leading they would sing songs like "Shall We Gather at The River" in Dakota. Outside the cabin, windchills could surpass fifty degrees below zero, but inside, a fire burned. The adult class had started with four young men named Dog Bear, Grey Bear, Grey Hound, and Good Bear. The men, who were soon joined by others, agreed to not paint their faces before school.

"Their voices were clear and strong, and they were pleased to sing in their own language," Corabelle's handwritten account recounts. "In those days my voice was fairly good and the boys readily learned the tunes. Mother would sometimes wake up and join us but usually she would sleep and snore, for she worked hard every day preparing the fuel and meals and attending to mission work in the camp."

Corabelle kept her bed clothes and straw mattress in a willow-poled tepee outside the log hut, for there was no room for it during classes.

"The missionaries and Indians told me to never go out of the house at night—it was not safe," Corabelle remembered. One night, nine of her regular young men showed up, walking in with a greeting and handshake. Corabelle noticed a tenth face, an unfamiliar young man wearing a white blanket. He refused to sit throughout the lessons, preferring to stand near the stove.

"I turned to the boys at the table and asked, 'who is your friend? Does he wish to join the class?' The regular students merely shrugged, answering in Dakota, 'perhaps.'

"I was a little vexed at the attitude he took," Corabelle remembered, "and ignored him until after the study hour."

After the students and mysterious stranger left, Corabelle tried to awaken the snoring Winyan to help her to retrieve her straw mattress and bed clothes stored in the willow-poled tepee nearby. But Elizabeth was in a deep sleep, "so I stood at the door watching the tall Sioux boys drift down the slope giving an Indian call as they went."

With Winyan still sleeping, Corabelle went out alone to retrieve the bedding. It was a big mistake. At the corner of the house, "a blanket was thrown over my head, and I felt myself being carried down the hill. I was too surprised to call or shout. But upon garnering my sense, also knowing the predicament I was in was unusual, I kicked and screamed, but of no avail. . . . My captor held me firmly."

She was carried through deep snow toward the river, "further and further away from home and my Indian mother." Her captor was the young man with the white blanket.

Corabelle was saved by an open door. She had left the front door of Winyan's log cabin ajar, thinking she would be out retrieving the bedding only a few seconds. The frigid blast from outside awakened Winyan, who heard the muffled screams and struggle down the slope toward the river. Winyan ran toward the struggle.

Corabelle's handwritten account goes on to describe Winyan, speaking in Dakota, "calling in a loud and angry voice: 'What bad thing is this? Now, you stop!'" Scolded by this angry woman, Corabelle's captor dropped her in the snow and fled with his white blanket.

"The snow was deep. I had on no hat or wraps. My silent Indian strode on without a word. . . . Mother, upon reaching me, found me crouched in the snow, crying. No hood or cloak, a cold shivering girl. She scolded and shook me and pulled me upon my feet." With Corabelle wrapped in a blanket Winyan had grabbed on her way out of the cabin, they made their way back to its warmth and safety. "I was very much a frightened girl," Corabelle recalled in her memoirs. "I took my seat by the stove to warm, while mother began preparing some herbs in two separate cups and placing them upon the stove in water. I was curious and asked, 'mother, what are you going to do and she said, 'to keep you from being stolen.'"

Elizabeth helped Corabelle strip to the waist, and she began bathing the young woman in the mixture. "I was rather uneasy over this procedure and wanted to know if it would darken my skin or poison me. 'No, no, no, Blue Star, I would not hurt you, but no one will want to steal you again.'" Corabelle took it as "she was putting a charm on me."

Whether a charm or an herbal remedy to stave off the effects of the cold, the act of treatment further bonded the women. *Blue Star* features this story, and one can deduce that Corabelle and Isely/Duncan spent a lot of time talking about it, for it is also prominent in Corabelle's handwritten memoirs. But *Blue Star* does not mention the "charm," instead describing the herbal potion as a "nauseating potion" of "slimy stuff, a thick greenish brown soup."[7]

The white blanket should have been a clue as to the aborted kidnapping, for as Winyan explained, it was a signal that the young man had come to carry Corabelle into marriage. It was the culmination of a traditional courting ritual. Had Elizabeth been awake during their lessons, she would have immediately noticed the white-blanket intentions and driven him out. Corabelle had ignored the warnings to not go out in the night alone and had nearly been carried off into matrimony.

"So if a young girl ventures out of her house or tent, she is likely to be stolen, carried off to his tent and is his wife," she wrote in her memoirs. "Next day, he has to pay for his wife with a horse or any money that the parents should ask (for). As to what my future would have been had not mother, my protector, frightened off my captor, for he had a dread of being put in the guard house?" She does not answer this question which appeared in her memoirs, but not in the book, and her gratitude to Winyan for saving her was palpable.

Although not named in Corabelle's handwritten memoirs, in *Blue Star*, Isely/Duncan identified the prospective suitor as a young man named Matela, whom, Isely/Duncan wrote, already had several wives. According to the book, the shaken young woman finally regained her composure, and she and her Indian mother stayed awake late into the night, alternating between laughter and tears. Then came a moment that bonded them forever.

"Impulsively, I threw my arms about Ina's neck and kissed her. She stood back, arms akimbo, and eyed me with a strange new emotion twisting her old face. Then Ina bent and kissed me. . . . Weak and unstrung, I lay snugly between the blankets Ina tucked about me, and cried and cried."[8]

Chapter 8

Cut Meat Creek and Rowdy Cowboys

Corabelle left her post on the Cheyenne River with Winyan in mid-1886. After a vacation with extended family in Iowa, and a short speaking tour in which she tried, but failed, to raise enough money to start her own Dakota Territory school, she returned to Dakota Territory in December of 1886 to take charge of a government day school at Cut Meat Creek, on what would later become the Rosebud Indian Reservation. Rosebud, like Cheyenne River, was as rustic as it was beautiful, home to the Sicangu (burnt thigh) Lakota.

Her handwritten memoirs described an adventurous vacation in Iowa. Corabelle spent it with her congressman uncle, Thomas Updegraff, who, along with his wife, Florence, owned a "lovely home" on a bluff overlooking the Mississippi River in the town of McGregor. Their daughters joined Corabelle in frequent hikes along the river and its rocky outcroppings. Midway through that vacation, an uncle from Florida sent them a live baby alligator through the US mail. "Which created a great deal of fun and excitement," Corabelle deadpanned in her memoirs.

Then, she added: "But afterward, we found he was less savage than the wild Indians I had to encounter, and we let him roam about the library at will, much to Florence's disgust, and the poor little ugly looking creature at last got away."

It was one of the few places in her memoirs that Corabelle referred so crudely to the Native population of Dakota and Lakota with whom she had spent the previous two years. In other aspects of her life in Dakota

Territory, Corabelle showed by her actions and words that she was shedding those preconceptions.

After the time off in McGregor, Corabelle boarded a train for Valentine, Nebraska, where she would have to take a stagecoach across the border into Dakota Territory to the Indian agency in Rosebud. It was late in 1886, and she was immediately reminded of the "severity of a Dakota winter." She thought she was well prepared but was grateful for the "extra coats and blankets and hot stones and bricks" provided to warm the stage on the way to Rosebud. By then, Corabelle was a veteran of the remote challenges on the frontier, accustomed to overcoming obstacles that would have sent many fleeing back to where they came from. But, as she explained extensively in her memoirs and briefly in *Blue Star*, the welcome she received in Valentine surprised even her.

Valentine itself was raw and new, established three years earlier as a spawn of houses and businesses along the Sioux City and Pacific Railroad that traversed Nebraska's grasslands and Sandhill country. That region's expansive geography would later be popularized by the novelist Willa Cather, who lived as a young girl in Red Cloud, Nebraska, when Corabelle arrived in 1886.

Snow piling along the tracks delayed the arrival of Corabelle's train into Valentine, but when it did arrive the whole town seemed to turn out for her on a bitterly cold evening. "It seemed as like the Indian population and cowboys knew there was to arrive a young woman teacher from the east that evening to teach among the Indians, and the Indians and cowboys had hung around the town the whole afternoon in order to meet me (and as I heard later, to give me a big scare of initiation. They deemed me a tenderfoot as they dubbed a new person from the east)," Corabelle recalled.

"I had made up my mind before leaving home that I would not allow myself to be frightened by anything the Indians might do. But I had not counted on cowboys' stunts. So [I] was really taken aback by what did happen, though I tried not to show any concern over the incident, though I really believe I must have turned pale."

The crowd that gathered near the train station, Corabelle wrote, was led by "a tall cowboy with a large cowboy hat, highly animated, and with a large red silk kerchief about his neck, buckskin shirt, also beautifully ornamented, white fur cowskin leggings, and loudly clicking spurs on his boots.

"And as he shook hands with me with his right hand, he fired a revolver off over my head, which was the signal for many others to do the same. Then he backed down the steps and was gone, amid a noise of whoops and shouts."

Given that wild welcome, it would be logical to believe anything to follow on the trip to Rosebud would be anti-climactic. But Dakota Territory always offered its surprises. The next day's stagecoach journey to Rosebud was over "thirty-four miles of snow-covered, rocky, muddy roads with their slippery, winding, and steep hills and almost impassable, snow-piled roads," Corabelle wrote in her memoirs.

The memory of writing about it fifty years later caused her to marvel at the conveniences that had made life easier in the twentieth century but wonder if those conveniences had made people less caring, less willing to strive to serve others.

"I look upon most wonderful and conveniently equipped hotels and also beautiful highways so convenient and comfortable, but as time advances and material ways and means improve, no one is anxious to venture out in the selfish world to help save a soul," she wrote.

At Cut Meat Creek, Corabelle performed missionary aid work during the day and taught adult school at night. A colleague, a woman she called "Miss Minnie" from Keokuk, Iowa, taught children in day school. The school had an organ, and Corabelle played and led singing from a Dakota hymn book. She would put on a pot of coffee and make fry bread to attract students for the night sessions.

Corabelle befriended a camp leader, Yellow Hat, and she often visited his home, a sturdy log hut with one end caged off for pigeons. Weeks into Corabelle's assignment at Cut Meat, Yellow Hat came by one day to ask for translations of words in English. She also gave him some government-issued teaching materials.

"I thought nothing of it, but in a week or so, I noticed the children dropping out of school, and that week I did not have a half dozen children in school," Corabelle wrote in her memoirs. She sent for the camp policeman, Red Eyes, who determined that Yellow Hat had started his own school. A confrontation ensued; if the children came back the following Monday, by the time she raised the US flag, Corabelle told Yellow Hat, she would not tell "Uncle Sam." He could keep the chalkboard and other school materials she had given him. That following Monday, the children came back.

At Cut Meat, Corabelle witnessed a celebration central to the communal culture of the Sioux, but she described it differently in her handwritten memoirs than the way Isely/Duncan depicted it in *Blue Star.* In the book, it was described as an "annual occasion when the Teton Sioux entertained their neighbors, the Crows." Elaborate food, costuming, and jewelry preparations took place for a month leading into the big gathering. "English society makes extensive preparations for its functions, but this function could have been paralleled only by a British coronation," *Blue Star* described it. "There was not the littlest acorn jangling with its fellows from its leathern thong that did not get a magnificent polishing."

When the dancing began, it soon turned into a "near frenzy" that was "frightening to behold." The book's account ends with Corabelle "trembling violently," entering a "vortex" of "yelling, whirling, naked men" on the dance floor. She was declared a "brave heart" and given a pony, but retired, afraid.[1]

If this indeed did happen, if indeed Corabelle was frightened and trembling, that sentiment must have come in the interviews Isely/Duncan said she had with Corabelle, or she simply embellished them. In her own words in her memoirs in the 1930s, Corabelle had a gentler memory of the event.

She described it as happening in August of 1887. In her handwritten account, Corabelle went into detail about the planning. Beef cattle were slaughtered and cooked, women baked bread, huge containers of coffee were brewed. Women sewed fancy shirts adorned with beads and porcupine quills. People were painted with "fine designs" on arms and legs, and ponies, which were to be given away, were gathered in pens. She was fascinated watching a "good-sized village unfold before our very eyes, wood being chopped, children playing at home before their own doors, and all nicely settled before night."

A dance arena in a large log structure was prepared, "beaten hard" by pounding feet, then soaked with boiling water, and again "beaten hard and smooth, then swept clean and dry ready for dancing." Large blankets were placed around the smooth, dry dance arena for dancers to rest and spectators to watch.

"We watched the wagons coming over the hills and in less than half an hour the whole long slope was alive with hundreds of tipi tents and smoke coming out of them," she remembered. "They are quick experts in setting. The horses are hobbled, staked and eating grass, and later are all driven to the river to drink."

Colored lamps were hung on poles around the dance arena, and ornately painted drums were strategically placed. Corabelle remembered details of that and other dances for the rest of her life. "I have seen women beat the drums hour after hour for the squaws to dance, standing in line and in their peculiar swaying, up and down, and bending the knees," she recalled in her memoirs. "They also have beaten the drums for men to dance. The men dance in many forms singly and in groups, and wear very little clothing, a breech cloth."

She and three other teachers were invited and attended. Men, elaborately painted and many smoking pipes, squatted together at one end of the dance floor. Women congregated at the other end. A teacher companion refused the first offer to join the dance, but Corabelle jumped in. Instead of being terrified, as *Blue Star* had her, in her handwritten memoirs she described her "heart beating fast with excitement."

"Round and round they danced, menacingly, with quick, up-lifting lurches toward me, then retreating, then again circling with thumbs on my arms and sometimes twirling me around and rubbing paint on my face. Finally, to cap the whole performance a blanket was thrown around me and my cheeks dabbed with red paint."

She was awarded an eagle feather, moccasins, and a blanket, and the "head Teton" man gave a speech "about how glad their hearts were for the friends gathered there." She and her fellow teachers finally left the dance "amid whoops and shouts." Excited? For sure. Terrified? Not really.

Corabelle left that Cut Meat post after another failed marital attempt from a Native suitor. He had arrived with a ring and intercepted her one night as she—again flaunting custom—went briefly outside for firewood. After quick thinking of sending him off for more firewood, Corabelle locked herself in her cabin. The scorned suitor spent hours outside the house, knocking on windows and calling, "Come here, Blue Star!" He eventually left. The next day, a terrified Miss Minnie packed and fled home to Keokuk, and Corabelle's employers felt "it was too risky for me to stay alone." Corabelle then spent the next several weeks at the home of the Indian agent before receiving her next teaching offer.[2]

That late summer and fall of 1887, Corabelle taught briefly at a boarding school at Fort Bennett, Dakota Territory, a military outpost on the west side of the Missouri near the Cheyenne River Agency. There, she met and began a courtship with Sam Campbell. Eventually, she landed at Swift Bird's Camp on the Missouri River, about fifty miles east of present-day Eagle Butte, where she was employed until May of 1888, two months after her marriage to Sam, and the end of her mission work. Along the way, much more risk, challenge, and adventure beckoned.

Chapter 9

Women Work

"When I left my home in Washington, DC, I had fully made up my mind to do all I knew best to do for the Sioux women," Corabelle recalled in her memoirs. "I had often heard of the brave acts that brave men had performed, but very little of the women. They are brave, too, and hard workers, and they are not in bondage as many supposed, but proud of the duties imposed on them, because there are no other outlets for their activities."

Her handwritten recollections—some, but not all of which are included in *Blue Star*—are filled with what she learned from Sioux women. She described them as "socially inclined, in many instances willing to adopt some of our ways and customs, but knowing their ways were already adapted to their environment." As a result, she wrote, many of the women she befriended "often refused to accept a change, especially in food and dress customs."

She taught sewing, but found she also learned much about this skill from the Native women. They "liked the full skirt gathering on the waist, but disliked the long sleeves, so I compromised" by teaching dressmaking with shorter sleeves, "making it more convenient to nurse their babies." Corabelle took note of how Native women focused first on making a garment that would last before adorning it with creative designs and colors. She went into detail in her memoirs about the natural materials and tools that Dakota and Lakota women used to make lasting garments.

Hairstyles, she wrote in her memoirs, were sometimes a point of conflict. "It was always parted and pleated in two braids. The Santee Sioux women tied and looped their hair over their shoulders, while the Teton Sioux let their pleats hang straight in front."

Schoolboys left a long lock of hair on a shaved head, and she developed a begrudging admiration for boys' refusal to change. "The only difficulty I encountered was their refusal to have the scalp lock cut off. It was a mark of distinction and something to fight for."

Corabelle was enthralled by the food-gathering and preparation, and she developed an appreciation for the nutritional benefits of plants gleaned from the wild prairie. But at other times, she was dismissive of the use of Native plants in medicine, and she had little good to say about other practices, like sweat lodges, that could have health-related benefits. But 1880s medicine was still decades from the invention of penicillin, and American medicine was only then coming around to how sanitary conditions and germ-fighting was integral to treating many wounds and diseases.

Nutritionally, she observed practices that had been handed down for generations. She described Native food preparation as culinary art. "The Sioux women cut up all the meat and hung it on scaffolds to dry," she wrote in her memoirs. "They also prepared what to them was a very choice dish called wasna. I have watched them prepare it and confess it is very palatable. They take a long slab of dried beef, slightly cook, and then pound fluffy and fine, take marrow from the bones, melt and mix, take wild cherries and pound them very fine, pits and all, mix all together sweeten with sugar, press into cakes and slightly bake. Then dry and place in sacks for future use. When needed, it is soaked and thickened with flour and cooked into sauce."

Gleaning excursions on the prairie were also social events. She described delighted little girls running across the prairie and along the river bottoms in search of wild sustenance, mothers following behind. In her handwritten memoirs, she recalled: "I have been with the Sioux women often to find the wild vegetables to eat. They gather the little wild beans that the field mice store away for their own use. They are found in small mounds all over the prairie. The women and children have quite a scramble to obtain them first. Then there are wild sweet potatoes and turnips, which grow scatteringly over the prairie, and have to be dug with a sharp, pointed sticks or crow bars. There are quite a variety of berries" which were picked and eaten fresh, the surplus dried for future use.

Dining was a traditional ritual. Inside tepees, a mother's place was usually at the right of the opening, and girls would sit to her right on the same side. Facing the tepee's opening, fathers sat in a "seat of honor and to watch an enemy," while boys generally sat to his right.

"The women put up the tent and that is done quickly and skillfully," Corabelle recalled. Three poles were hoisted into a triangle and tethered together, and the covering—canvas or buffalo hides or something else—was anchored with "picket pins," stakes pounded into the ground to hold the shelter in place "against wind and storm."

She sat with Sioux women as they mourned deaths, watched as bodies were placed on scaffolds in isolated locations. Fifty years later, the memories were so vivid she alternately described them in the present tense. "They mourn a long while, cut their hair and sometimes their bodies, and expose themselves to extreme cold. They mourn on the hills or some desolate place. The wailing is saddening to listen to, and they would place on the scaffold a dish of rice or other food for the spirit to get. The body was tightly wrapped and tied to the scaffold, away from wild creatures. And at the end of a year, the family would have a big feast in memory of them."

She handwashed clothes in streams with Dakota women using "issue soap"—a reference to what was likely government-provided soap. Wash day was an important day. "Their clothes were clean and they, not having conveniences, were content and happy."

It was here, in these handwritten reminisces, that the elderly Corabelle acknowledged that a civilization could be defined in ways she would not have imagined as a young woman arriving in Dakota Territory. The friendships, the intimate moments—they provided the best memories. The Christianity that she had come to teach was not that different from the beliefs of the Dakota and Lakota people.

"Civilization and convenience are wonderful but are not necessary toward making us happy or contented," she wrote in her memoirs. "The

Bible tells us to 'be content with such as we have, for it is written, I will never leave you nor forsake you.' The Sioux are faithful in their belief in the Great Spirit, Wakan Tanka."

Chapter 10

A Good Dog Night

During the summer of 1887, before her last appointment at the Swift Bird day school, instead of returning to Washington, DC, or traveling to Iowa to visit her uncles and cousins, Corabelle, decided to go on a mission circuit with the Good Dog family. She had secretly become engaged to Sam Campbell, and perhaps that helped keep her in Dakota Territory. Whatever the reason, it was a memorable summer.

Corabelle had come to know the Good Dogs as helpers and givers. She had become attached to her new home in the wide-open spaces, and it was people like the Good Dogs who had helped make it her home. Tough living conditions had become a way of life rather than an obstacle to it, and she took pride in being able to answer almost every invitation to venture out.

Corabelle had previously described Mr. Good Dog as a good-hearted servant in her "Among the Wild Indians" article in the *Word Carrier*. In that earlier encounter, he had asked about her home. She had pulled out a map of the United States to show Good Dog, and he "was quite astonished that I would come so far away from my home and parents to be among his people."[1] Whether or not she fully acknowledged it at that moment, her home was in Dakota Territory.

The story of her journey with the Good Dogs is told in *Blue Star*, but not in as much detail, or with as much nostalgia, as it appears in her handwritten memoirs. There, Corabelle wrote at length about their days-long journey from one small Native settlement to the next.

She, Good Dog, his wife, and their two little girls (Isely/Duncan identified them as two little boys) traveled in a horse-drawn lumber wagon, packed with a large tepee and "all necessary things to camp and for a week or more" at a time.

"I took my own necessities and bedding to sleep in their tent," she wrote. "I was given the place of honor opposite the tent door, and the arrangement for three beds were properly made, with the fire irons in the center as customary. We went different places preaching and talking, and I believe Mr. Good Dog was a very good Christian man and I hope much good work was done."

She soon discovered in one settlement, where "much was going on," that some Sioux people "do not mind the least sitting up all night."

Late one evening, long after she and Good Dog's wife, whom she did not name, and her small girls had gone to bed, Corabelle heard distant, rhythmic drumming. It was soothing, "an incentive for sleep." It was very dark in the tepee, with the light-giving fire having been snuffed out at bedtime. She drifted off to sleep to the distant drums. Good Dog, however, had stayed outside to tend a fire. The drumming got louder and closer, and so did men's voices. Soon, she was wide awake.

Corabelle peered out of the tepee to see "Mr. Good Dog and several of his Indian friends in their Native skin, feathers and paint, roasting meat on wooden spits before the fire and coals, and jabbering in Dakota to their heart's content, utterly oblivious of the fact that four women folk had retired. Good Dog called out, 'Blue Star arise—meat, meat, plenty of meat. Get up and eat.'"

To celebrate Good Dog's visit, someone in the tiny settlement had slaughtered a steer. A midnight feast was on, the word had gotten out, people were gathering around the fire. Clearly, it was a highlight of her life on the high plains, for Corabelle recalled details a half century later.

Duncan/Isely's book described her as frightened in that moment, a sentiment that did not appear in Corabelle's handwritten accounts. Indeed, in her own writing she remembered being happy to be invited out, if a little irritated at having her sleep interrupted. She described herself as thrilled to join the party, honored to participate in a special feast.

"Quite contrary to our customs," she wrote in her memoirs, "I wrapped my blanket around me and sat up to eat. The meat was quite good, though [it] had no salt. They roasted it partially through on one side then turned it around, and by holding it near a wood fire it is made perfectly tender and done.

"Then Mrs. Good Dog found some fried Indian bread in a flour sack and with the big coffee pot set over the fire and drinking out of tin cups we had a fine feast." They talked and ate long into the night.

In both her handwritten memoirs and in Isely/Duncan's portrayal in *Blue Star*, Corabelle had an epiphany around that campfire. Sitting among Native people, engaged to a man of Native blood, she glanced into what she thought would be her future, and how different it was from her mother's life and for Cornelia's aspirations for her daughter. She weighed the conveniences of her formative life with the relationships she had made on the frontier.

"Before me rushed the pictures of my mother's dining room, of shortcakes and loin roasts, linen, flowers and finger bowls," Corabelle said in *Blue Star*. "I felt keenly my lack of baths, my half-combed hair, and my wrinkled clothing. With something like consternation, I realized how I was enjoying myself, being one with the Indians, that I was doing their way, not they, mine."

As the men "talked loudly and with abandon," and "the women jabbered as usual," she sipped a "hot and savory" tea that she had to admit was "not unpleasant." Then, "I sat solemnly considering my future among these people. I was affianced to an educated man, who, however, had Indian blood. I wondered if a generation or two of education could change completely the age-old tradition of man and wife, of cleanliness, of interest in affairs outside the village."

She continued: "What, after all, was the difference between these people and, say, my mother? They were anxious to learn all that my race knew which theirs did not. My mother was sure that they had nothing of the intellect or heart which she would wish to know. Yet their friendship was the most vital thing I had yet experienced. There was no quarreling, no carping, no greed, no grasping. They toadied to their chief not as much as my mother toadied to her social leaders." [2]

Her handwritten memoirs contained an important observation that did not appear in the book. Corabelle also remembered the night with the Good Dogs as a lesson in trust and friendship. The Sioux, Corabelle wrote, are "very hospitable toward friends of whom they are not afraid, but afraid is not possibly the word I should have used in connection with the Sioux, for they are a very brave people and tribe."

Then, she added: "The manners in which the government and soldiers have regarded and treated them has caused them to become suspicious of the whites."

Soon, it was not soldiers or government, but press and family, that would create suspicion, condemnation, and separation in her own life. It would be anything but hospitable. Corabelle seemed to sense it that Good Dog night. As the party was ending and rosy hues of dawn swathed the eastern skyline, Corabelle suddenly felt "an eerie sense of impending disaster."

Chapter 11

Wild Horses and Raging Blizzards

Corabelle's last posting in Dakota Territory was at the Cheyenne River Agency's Number 4 day school, roughly seventy-five miles northwest of her previous brief teaching appointment at Fort Bennett, astride the Missouri River in a little community called Swift Bird. The position had opened up, she wrote in her memoirs, because the teacher hired there had decided to go prove a homestead claim with her brother.

It was the fall of 1887, two years before statehood for South and North Dakota. The trickles of white settlers into the glacial lakes and river valleys east of the Missouri River had turned into torrents. Immigrants from Germany, England, Holland, Sweden, Norway, Russia, Finland, Ireland, and other European countries were homesteading, carving out the grasslands east of the river into square-mile grids of corn, wheat, oats, and alfalfa, sometimes four families to a section. The proverbial melting pot was spilling over west of the Missouri River onto lands that had for centuries been roamed by the Sioux and preceding Native tribes.

Swift Bird was a new settlement that was more camp than town, one of many little collectives along the Missouri's sheltered bottomlands or on the bluffs overlooking it. In these clusters and hovels, missions and government schools were being built. After leaving her mission appointment with Winyan, Corabelle had expressed an interest to stay in Dakota Territory, but some schools were not ready. The government agent at the Cheyenne River Agency, Charles McChesney, had written her in early 1886 about lumber being hauled onto the reservation and carpenters building schools and homes for prospective teachers. "I cannot build to advantage before April on account of the cold weather," McChesney wrote.

If she came, the agent wrote, Corabelle would be in an "Indian camp with no white person near. This would be unpleasant, but as far as safety is concerned, you could be as safe as in Washington (DC). An Indian Policeman is stationed at the camp, and he will be instructed by me to afford you every protection and assistance in his power."[1]

Corabelle's new home was part of a growing network of schools run by either the government or church missions, or both. "The mission schools were scattered all along the river, Swift Bird, Chargers Camp, White Horse, and others," Corabelle wrote in her memoirs. "There were little churches, one in every camp. At the agency was also a large Roman Catholic Church."

At Swift Bird, Corabelle lived with a dog and two horses. She reveled in her independence, in meeting the rugged physical and mental challenges of a solitary posting. She made frequent seven-mile trips by horse and wagon to Forest City, a supply outpost on the opposite side of the Missouri River. She learned the best spots to ford the river which, in winter, was partially dry and partially frozen. "I could drive my pony over without wading much for the river was full of sand bars," she recalled. Traveling on winter ice was often smoother and easier than taking the rutted dirt roads, and she visited friends up and down the river by taking the frozen route.

"The camp school was named after the old chief, Swift Bird, an excellent old man, having a large family," Corabelle remembered. "The houses in this camp were nearer together than the other camp schools and [their occupants] seemed a little more social than the other schools. My policeman had quite a family, and five of his children were in school. And as a policeman, his name was very appropriate, 'Mr. Runs the Enemy.'"

Besides the two horses, Corabelle drove a team of oxen early every morning to the river to get water. In the winter, she sometimes needed to chop through ice first. She drove the oxen back to the school, and after bedding them in the barn, would "go and get ready for school, first by putting up my flag on the pole which flew over the school house, and served for a bell," she wrote in her memoirs. "The children could see it quite a long way away, and would soon begin to come to school. I had them bring in the wood and sweep the snow."

She had about twenty-five pupils that school year of 1887 to 1888. Even for Dakota Territory, it was a harsh winter. A storm on January 12, 1888, forever known as the "Children's Blizzard," killed roughly two hundred people, many of them children of new settlers walking home from school in southeastern Dakota Territory. In her memoirs, she does not write about any people dying during that blizzard in the Swift Bird camp.

Corabelle continued her pivot into accepting Native customs and habits, and she was increasingly understanding their origins and the usefulness of them. More and more, she considered herself as much a friend and companion as teacher and missionary. Her writing is brightened with stories about individuals who made lasting impressions upon her, and on whom she had depended to survive. Most importantly, at Swift Bird Corabelle began carrying on a long-distance courtship with Sam Campbell.

She slept and lived in two rooms above a large schoolhouse, a space accessible only by an outside staircase that was treacherous in ice and snow. A log house adjacent to the school contained her kitchen. Homes on the frontier occasionally separated the kitchen from sleeping accommodations so a fire in one wouldn't burn the other. A small barn sheltered her horses. Sioux men supplied her with beef, venison, and bear meat, the carcasses of which often hung frozen from rafters in the winter. The government supplied her with fifteen cords of firewood for that winter, but keeping fires in three locations—school, living space, and kitchen—quickly exhausted that store, and she continuously sought new wood supplies in a country where trees grew sparsely. To make up for that deficiency, Natives and settlers—some in sod huts—heated their homes with dried cattle or bison dung, or dried grass twisted into tight clumps.

Corabelle taught Dakota girls jelly making and bread baking over a stove in the log kitchen. The children "were always interested and tried to exceed one another making rolls and light bread, and coffee for their lunches," Corabelle wrote. Jars upon jars of preserved jellies soon lined the kitchen shelves. That spring Corabelle planted a garden where she raised beans, corn, and assorted other vegetables. She eventually turned it over to Native women.

She was making $55 a month and had access to government commodities such as sugar and coffee at cost, although some of it had to be hauled in from more than fifty miles away. Shortly after her arrival at Swift Bird, Corabelle bought, for $25, a pony she named Bess from a kind, patient elder named Harry Dog Bear. Bess had not been broken, but Harry Dog Bear was there to help. Corabelle's handwritten memoirs of the spirited event covered several pages.

Harry brought Bess "around by the schoolhouse, and I held the rope while Harry put on the bridle. Then I dropped the long rope while he jumped on her back. She sprang up and down a few times then ran around the schoolhouse, but the bridle bit soon made her stop. Then he brought her back to the steps and put on my new red velvet saddle my Uncle Tom Updegraff gave me when I visited.

"Bess did not like that any better, so Harry led her around, and once more brought her to the steps. And I sprang into the saddle. That was the finishing touch. She sprang forward stiff legged and threw me against the schoolhouse. I jumped up, not much hurt, or at all discouraged, knowing with one more trial I would conquer the pony. Harry took off my saddle and put his on. I carefully got on so she would not notice the weight, took the bridle in my hand, still leaving the long rope around her neck. And by that time, she was tired and finding we did not intend to murder her she trotted a dozen times around the school yard, a quiet and conquered pony.

"I thought I would probably break my neck before she was broke," Corabelle reminisced, but "from that time I began riding . . . as the Indian women did."

After she wrote her parents about that experience, her mother responded with a letter chiding her to "be careful of that pony—you will break your neck." Cornelia, worried about what the wind and cold would do to a woman's skin, also pleaded with her daughter: "Do be careful of your complexion."[2]

Despite her mother's worries, Corabelle and Bess were thereafter inseparable, and she eventually bought a second horse and named it

Prince. Harry Dog Bear built her a bobsled. Corabelle hitched Prince and Bess and used the sleigh many times that winter to visit friends, especially fellow missionaries Rebecca and William Holmes forty miles upriver. The Holmes's school at the time was along the Moreau River, another tributary of the Missouri.

In the fall and the following spring at Swift Bird, Corabelle frequently foraged with Dakota mothers on the Native prairie and along the river bottom for wild plums, sweet potatoes, turnips, and berries. "The women gathered and hung [them] up on the wall of their homes," she wrote. What Corabelle in the 1930s called "squaw corn"—which produced an ear whose kernels were red, yellow, orange, and other brilliant colors—would also be hung on walls to dry, providing both sustenance and decoration. She became more immersed in the social lives of the Native families. She was re-assessing notions of ownership, of sharing, of self-reliance, of defiance against the elements, in virtually every aspect of her life.

"The Indians have always cared for one another in quite a socialite [sic] manner, never turning away kin folks," she remembered. "When their food supplies gave out [they] would go to another relative and eat and stay with them. They have been able for many years to get all the meat they needed and robes and hides from the animals, and their thread from the sinews off strips of the strong muscle of the buffalo or cattle. The thread is not long but is very stout and the hides do not wear off the sinew thread."

That last line was telling. The things that mattered were the things that lasted. That was true in the tools and materials she had been introduced to, and it was true in the friendships she remembered almost fifty years later. It may have also explained why Corabelle surrounded herself with her own family in the last decade of her life in Wichita.

Corabelle became increasingly enthralled with Dakota women's patient seamstress work, describing in detail clothing decorated with dyed porcupine quills and made of buckskin hides. Individuality and community melded in ways she was not accustomed to. There were hierarchies, for sure, but status was based on good deeds. Corabelle reconnected with her own interest in painting and art by recognizing the creativity of clothing, tool-making, and other expressions of the Dakota and Lakota. "Every nation and tribe [had their own] artistic designs," she recalled. "And art is shown everywhere, even music, among heathen or wild people."

She had transformed from being an advocate for total assimilation into heartfelt appreciation for unique cultural practices of the Sioux. But as her use of "heathen" in her description showed, Corabelle never entirely shed the pretenses of white cultural superiority she had carried with her to Santee as a young woman. Now, in her late-in-life memoirs, was she being sarcastic and mocking labels, or simply being harsh? Judging her memoirs, as a whole, the former seems most likely.

Corabelle praised Native women for their work ethic, their knowledge of how the earth could naturally sustain them and their loved ones, and above all else, their devotion to their children. But she also commented frequently on the lack of cleanliness among the Sioux, looked askance at eating dogs, and was dubious about Native medicine and its practitioners. In truth, when she was in Dakota Territory scarcely two decades after the butchery of the Civil War, American medicine was not exactly advanced science. Just three years before Corabelle arrived at Santee, President James Garfield had been assassinated and died after suffering terribly for eighty days from a wound that was probed in unsanitary conditions and misdiagnosed, a wound that medical professionals later said could have easily healed had doctors cleaned the wound and removed the bullet, rather than continuously probing and pushing it deeper into the suffering president's body.[3]

In *Blue Star*, Corabelle said Native women had often come to her with sick children, upsetting traditional medicine men. But her treatment course was often not much different from the medicine men's in its dependence on natural remedies. The medicine men, she wrote, would employ salves or powders or other variations of snakeroot, a cousin of the sunflower; oxalis, an edible clover-like groundcover; mandrake, the root of a nightshade plant; wild flag plant, a wild iris; kinnikinnick, a low-growing shrub; wild sage; and wild onions. They would be dried and crushed and often given as teas to lower fevers or turned into salves to treat wounds. "My treatment was usually a dose of castor oil with warm or cold sponge baths," Corabelle said. The latter course—frequent sponge baths for the ill—was not that different, she acknowledged, from what Dakota women did to treat children with measles.[4]

In their defense, missionaries like Corabelle should be looked at through the prisms of their age. They entered unsettled and unfamiliar territory, lived among people being pushed onto places they had not chosen to settle, surrounded by US military soldiers that could be called in at any time, and written about by a press that often treated them as saviors and the Natives they lived with as lesser humans.

When she had first stepped off the train at Springfield in 1884, the echoes of Custer's defeat at the place the Natives called Greasy Grass were still highly resonant in Sioux culture, even though the heroes like Sitting Bull were living ostensibly pacified lives on reservations. The defeated Custer had been canonized as the hero of Little Big Horn, celebrated in books, theater, and in the traveling Wild West shows. And the slaughter at Wounded Knee, which took place scarcely two years after Corabelle left her work at Swift Bird, was testament to what could happen when a spark landed in the tinderbox.

Decades later, she recognized that assimilation and Christianity may have been her ambition, but in that she had not totally succeeded. She seemed fine with that.

"I often look back at my dear camp people and wonder after forty-five and fifty-five years if they can remember their ambitious little teacher, who was so anxious for their welfare, and wanted them to put away their wild Indian ways and be happy, true Christians," Corabelle wrote in her memoirs. But, she discovered, "they do believe in the Great Spirit, 'Wakan Tanka,' and are inclined to be serious and to live quiet lives."

Corabelle came to believe that Native beliefs and rituals the government banned, even those she once considered barbaric, were not for her to judge. Although some Native customs could be "cruel," Corabelle wrote in her memoirs, she had decided that God "takes no delight in the loss of a single soul, and hears every earnest petition we send, which they think to torture their bodies and starve themselves is pleasing to God."

She wrote of how she had often clashed with Sioux mothers in how they dressed their children, or more accurately, sometimes did not dress them at all. But "we generally settled matters in a kindly manner, giving and taking," recognizing that clothing was an "acquired custom," and that "my opinion is to be more modest" and "to cover our bodies." Others had different opinions, she acknowledged, and that was part of her education in the "delightful and happy experiences" she had had in Nebraska and Dakota Territory.

Corabelle said Dakota and Lakota friends had "hearts of flowers" and many she met had an unusual ability to "read your heart and know the touch of your hand, [to determine] if you are friend or foe." She pitied soldiers, some of them boys themselves, over the predicament they'd been placed—themselves strangers in a strange land.

"Soldiers with faint and fearful hearts that shot down good, honest-hearted Indians because of their fierce looks or feathers, have often created that destruct[ion] for the white face, 'Ite Ska,' as we are called," she wrote in her memoirs.

"I like the Sioux Indian. There is much that is noble, natural and true," Corabelle wrote, and "they look at you in the eye and shake hands if you are true." But if they decide otherwise, she warned, "you can seldom win them back."

At Swift Bird, some traditions often clashed with classroom practices. Corabelle wrote in her memoirs that Sioux parents coddled their children too much, and that that could interfere with classroom discipline. But she was continuously impressed with the curiosity and intimacy that Indian children exhibited once she was proven as "Blue Star," as friend.

Corporal punishment was widely accepted in education at the time, and revelations and investigations in later decades would reveal how punishment in Native boarding schools could turn brutal, even deadly. In one instance, Corabelle described using it herself.

Remembering decades later, Corabelle wrote about how the man hired to provide her water at the Swift Bird camp, High Bear, temporarily stopped bringing it because she had disciplined his boy. She said that in her four years teaching in Nebraska and Dakota Territory, she engaged "but twice" in "light" corporal punishment. One involved the son of High Bear, a boy named Two Horns.

Two Horns had gotten crossways with his teacher by insisting on being the first to speak in a lesson. When she insisted just as firmly that he wait his turn, the boy pouted, and he would not speak when that turn came. In *Blue Star,* Corabelle is quoted saying she used a tree branch and "switched his legs soundly" and that the boy "made no sound, offered no resistance, and sat back in his seat, a statue still, without expression of any kind."[5]

That's when the water was cut off. In her handwritten memoirs, Corabelle said she threatened to put High Bear in the guard house if he "did not do as I wished." In *Blue Star*, Corabelle tells High Bear that "the way of the Great Father is not your way." Faced with that threat and lecture, High Bear began hauling water again. If, indeed, she said it, it was an unvarnished reminder that she was an agent of change that High Bear could not stop.

At Swift Bird, Corabelle was cook as well as teacher for her students, some of whom walked eight miles round trip to school and back each day. She cooked the meat that Native men brought her, and she served it with government-issued hardtack, the brick-hard crackers that had sustained Civil War armies. Coffee was a staple even for children, and to go with it she and her students made biscuits from government flour, lard, and baking powder, on which homemade jelly was spread. Each week, two girls were tasked with making the dough in the morning and cooking it in time for afternoon breaks. Eventually, Corabelle opened a night school for young men. Her assistant there was Walter Swift Bird, son of the camp leader.

On Saturday evenings Corabelle boiled a large pot of meat and played the organ for anyone who gathered at the schoolhouse. Children played games and drew pictures on paper and the blackboard. Families came together.

The vast buffalo herds that once roamed the unfenced country, herds that had sustained the Native people, were nearly extinct. Once estimated to number between thirty and sixty million, their population had dwindled to around one thousand during Corabelle's time in Dakota

Territory.[6] Millions had been slaughtered for their hides, tongues, or simply for rich men's sport. In their place came beef cattle, who ate whatever they could find to survive. One bitterly cold winter night, that new reality forced Corabelle into drastic action to save the hay for the small herd she had been granted as a supply of meat.

It was well below zero outside, snow was drifting in high banks around her house and barn, and a hard wind was shooting tiny daggers of ice and snow crystals onto faces or any exposed skin. Soon, she heard bellowing cattle near her two tons of hay for which she had paid $14. The hay was surrounded by a shaky corral fence that the hungry herd would almost certainly break down. They could wipe out the remaining winter food source virtually overnight.

Corabelle by then had adopted a dog named Mazepha, a name she said she derived and adapted from Lord Byron's poem, "Mozeppa."

"She was as fearless as her mistress," Corabelle wrote in her memoirs, "and I had seen her tackle a big rattlesnake and shake it to pieces."

Mazepha slept in a bed beneath Corabelle's. On this cold night the dog stirred and woke her. About twenty-five head of cattle soon appeared in the swirling snow outside her window, "sniffing and bellowing."

"My dog was truly mad now, and from our window we watched the herd going round and round the big Swift Bird corral," where camp residents had stored about fifty tons of hay, she wrote. That fence was too sturdy for the cattle to break down, so when the hungry cattle turned toward her haystack, Corabelle went to work.

"So Mazepha and I shouted at them and drove them away, but before we went back and shut the door, they would come back. I finally made up my mind I would wrap up, take my blankets and dog and stay all night in that stack.

"Mazepha was willing to go with me," Corabelle recalled. "I fixed [dampered] my fire, armed myself with blankets, and the dog and I crawled into the haystack away from the wind." Throughout the sub-zero night, the dog barked any time the cattle came close. Corabelle and her dog saved the haystack by burrowing into it.

She wrote her father of the experience, and sent him a package of "curiosities," including tanned animal hides, perhaps of cows or deer. Homer wrote back with concern and some friendly agricultural advice.

"We imagined blizzards and cyclones and every possible catastrophe when your letter failed to come on the usual day," her father wrote. "But such lengths you went to over that hay! Your fence should be strong enough to make such doings unnecessary."

He wrote that the skins she had sent "have a familiar look and remind me of boyhood."[7]

Blue Star devotes only a few pages to Corabelle's school year at Swift Bird. But some of the biggest scares and greatest adventures of her life occurred there, and her handwritten memoirs devote lengthy passages to it.

Almost every Friday after school, she would ride or drive a wagon to Forest City to get groceries. On the way, she would stop to rest and warm at a school run by a native family named Smith. For extra layers in the winter, she would cut holes for head and arms in a gunny sack—a burlap bag that might have contained potatoes or grain—and wear it over her winter clothes for extra warmth. So much for high-tea fashion. Survival and adaptability reigned. Once a month a Dakota woman at Swift Bird named Nancy Dupre drove what Corabelle called a "lively" mule team and "spring wagon" the seventy-five miles to Fort Bennett to pick up government commodities and other supplies for the school and community. Nancy knew little English, except for "meat, flour, soap, sugar, bread, etc.," Corabelle recalled in her memoirs, and they often conversed in Dakota. Once, she invited Corabelle to come along, and the teacher readily accepted.

They drove "miles and miles over gumbo roads," camping overnight and sleeping in a smoky tepee. As they continued the next day, things got very interesting, very quickly. After a few miles the wheels of the wagon stopped turning altogether from the gumbo stuck to them.

Dakota gumbo is like nothing else. It is one of the great nuisance wonders of the natural world. When wet, it coagulates into a heavy, gristly mix that sticks to anything it touches. It takes sturdy tools and strong muscles to clear moving parts.

"I was sitting in the back of the wagon on blankets," Corabelle recalled in her memoirs. "We had first stopped to scrape off the wheels with the little wooden paddles they keep handy, for the black gumbo loads the wheels, making travel hard for the team."

Once the wheels were scraped and cleaned enough to travel again, Corabelle climbed back into the wagon and was about to settle in when "Nancy whipped up the team. And off we started again but found to our dismay the team was running away, and since the wagon was open at the back, I rolled out. Nancy could not stop them, so I was left behind. I felt like the girl in the song, 'The Girl I Left Behind.'"

The memoirs continued: "I never thought of bumps, but scrambled to my feet, not wishing to be left a prey to wandering Indians or savage wolves, and started on a run after my guide. I could see Nancy and the team a long distance ahead. Over that barren country one can see a long way. Nancy had succeeded in stopping her runaways for the wagon was getting heavy with gumbo. . . . At last puffing and tired, I reached her. She sat upon the wagon seat laughing loudly, her dimpled cheeks showing no concern over me as to my safety, only saying 'I never saw a white woman run so fast in my life!' We drove onto the agency without further excitement."

She didn't know it then, but almost fifty years later, Corabelle and Nancy Dupre would remember that episode with smiles.

On one journey, Corabelle made the largely uneventful trip to Forest City, although she did notice there were none of the usual walkers and riders along the seven-mile dirt road. On the way back, she planned to stop and drop off supplies the Smiths had requested. After a pleasant visit and early supper, "we noticed a blizzard coming on."

It is unclear in Corabelle's memoirs if this was the "Children's Blizzard" that killed so many schoolchildren. That happened on a Thursday; Corabelle normally took her supply trips to Forest City on Fridays when school let out. Either way, once she noticed the storm gathering while visiting the Smiths, she knew it was time to head for home or risk being stranded for days away from her school.

"So I hurried, and finding a little Indian boy on his pony, I hired him to go back with me," her handwritten memoirs record. "It was getting quite dark, and I would be facing the blizzard most of the way, and I was afraid I might lose my way."

They rode into the intensifying storm, along the way crossing paths with a bobcat. They heard coyotes yipping and a screech owl making its distinctive, high-pitched call. Breaking off from the river bottom and heading into open country toward her home, Corabelle decided to let the boy lead, "for he knew the country.

"We traveled and traveled. I put my head down and the bridle over the pommel of the saddle and let my pony go. After a while, I called the boy and asked him if he knew he was right and he replied he was not sure," she recalled in her memoirs. "Then I began to think we were lost. Well, we surely were, so I went ahead of him. . . . We traveled along lost in the blizzard. At last, the little cold Indian boy discovered our camp schoolhouse. And we reached there so cold we were hardly able to put the ponies in the little barn and give them hay."

In her schoolhouse-home, her dog greeted them with a "mournful bark." She made the boy supper and Corabelle brought in extra blankets for him to sleep in the schoolhouse, which gradually warmed with fresh wood on the fire. The next morning, the storm passed, Corabelle awoke early to cook her visitor breakfast. But by then her young friend who had helped her through the storm had headed for home.

She wrote home to assure her parents that she had survived the great storm. "Glad you came through safe," Homer Fellows wrote back. "Do be careful about going far at this season of the year."

Her father's letter went on to describe the life she had left behind. They had seen First Lady Frances Cleveland at church. Homer went on about her mother's social activities. Some of it—a care package for a sick friend—was not that different from Corabelle's work. Other parts—formal appointments to go on sightseeing tours, name-dropping famous folks—came from a world away.

"Yesterday your momma made some salad and custard and other little fixings for Mrs. Ellis who is sick," Homer wrote. "Tomorrow that Mr. Ebbstrom of the picture-card firm proposes to bring a carriage around and take your momma sight-seeing. Your momma went to Mrs.

Cleveland's reception last week—got terribly squeezed—was introduced to Mrs. Cleveland and the cabinet ladies, all very pleasant, etc."

In letters home, she apparently had only vaguely described Sam, not telling her family that he was part Dakota. Her father wrote back with an ominous premonition. "You write about a partnership," Homer wrote. "There is always more or less danger in partnership—especially for you."

Homer mentioned that Corabelle had been praised from the pulpit in Sunderland's Presbyterian Church. "One little girl—a member of this church—deserves special praise, for unmarried, alone and unprotected she has gone among untutored savages to the inclement climate of Dakota," the preacher said. "She is a veritable female Caesar."[8] The "little girl" who had broken horses, survived blizzards, forded rivers, fought off unwanted suitors, foraged for Native plants? One can imagine the bold young woman smiling at that slight.

Chapter 12

A Quiet Courtship Becomes a National Sensation

In the spring of 1888, Corabelle's solitary teaching life at Swift Bird ended. She was about to become famous, but it was not the kind of notoriety she, or anyone, would have wanted. A peaceful, patient romance was about to turn into a sensational national scandal that, just like Nancy Dupre's mules, soon ran out of control.

In *Blue Star*, Corabelle said she had met Sam Campbell, "a handsome young man," whose "clothing and mien were that of an English gentleman," on her way to the post office while she was teaching at Fort Bennett. She described Sam as "the son of a trader and a Sioux woman" whose mother had died when he was young. Sam, she said, "had been reared by the Episcopal clergyman of the little church at Fort Bennett and had taken his foster father's name. We rode and talked together, and fell in love."[1] The reference to taking the foster surname is almost certainly wrong, or incredibly coincidental, for subsequent family-tree research has identified Sam's father as the trader and interpreter Antoine Joseph Campbell.[2]

Sam was one of the Native children educated in government schools who returned as an adult to his adopted home at Fort Bennett sometime in the mid-1880s. He was quiet, tall for that time, and often described as handsome. He was born in Marshall, Minnesota, in 1867, the son of Antoine Joseph Campbell, a mixed-blood trader, scout, and interpreter;

Samuel C. Campbell
WICHITA STATE UNIVERSITY LIBRARIES SPECIAL COLLECTION AND UNIVERSITY ARCHIVES

and Hanyetusawin, a Santee Sioux woman. His birth is recorded in a Santee Episcopal Mission baptismal register.[3]

Sam Campbell was a child of dual—and dueling—history. His Santee ancestors had roamed the glacial lakes and plains of the Upper Midwest, had been pushed into what is now Minnesota in the 1600s by Ojibwe and Algonquin tribes around the Great Lakes. Including Samuel's brief but passionate and, ultimately, tragic love affair with Corabelle Fellows, the Campbell family exemplified as much as any the history of exploration and exploitation on the Dakota and Minnesota frontiers of the nineteenth century.

Samuel's grandfather, Antoine Scott Campbell, was thought to be of Scottish and Dakota blood, although some said he was part French.

Known through his life as Scott, he had joined Lewis and Clark as a teenager during the historic expedition's latter-stage return to St. Louis, then journeyed back to Fort Snelling at the confluence of the Mississippi and Missouri Rivers after Meriwether Lewis's death in 1809.

As an adult Scott Campbell worked, like his son, as a trader and interpreter. Samuel's grandfather knew four languages and he worked with Indian agents and military officers putting the Dakota language on paper. And he had a connection to the missionary Riggs family that would later employ Corabelle Fellows.

According to a family history, "missionary Samuel W. Pond credits Scott for his part in the manuscript that Ogden passed on to Samuel and [Pond's] brother Gideon Pond, which was helpful in their work in developing a Dakota dictionary that was finished and published through the efforts of fellow missionary, Stephen Riggs."

Scott Campbell was also the interpreter for the Treaty of Prairie du Chien, the US government's attempt in 1825 to forge peace between long-warring tribes of Sioux, Chippewa, Winnebago, and others who lived in what is now the Upper Midwest. A son, Baptiste Scott Campbell—Sam Campbell's uncle—was one of thirty-eight men hanged after the 1862 Sioux uprising in Minnesota. Baptiste said he had participated in the uprising only under duress.[4]

Scott Campbell was described as "very mild, quiet and gentlemanly, always ready to smoke or chat with white men or Indians" but with a "fiery temper which sometimes broke through."[5] His grandson, Samuel Campbell, would also be described as mild and quiet but never of fiery temper by the yellow press of the late nineteenth century.

The men in the Campbell line were described as attractive: tall and muscular, black-haired, with dark eyes and pleasant facial features. The Campbells had a gift of language. By the mid-nineteenth century, Sam's father, Antoine Joseph, took over Scott's role as interpreter between the US Army and Native leaders.

Antoine Joseph served in that role during the 1851 treaties of Traverse des Sioux and Mendota. In 1857 he acted as an interpreter and guide during the expedition to capture and punish the instigators of the Spirit Lake Massacre, an attack by a small group of Santee on white settlers in northwest Iowa that resulted in roughly three dozen dead settlers, and four abducted women. Antoine also traveled as a member of a Dakota delegation to Washington in 1858, just weeks after Minnesota was granted statehood in which Little Crow and other Dakota leaders were forced to relinquish all lands north and east of the Minnesota River.

During the 1862 Sioux uprising, Antoine Joseph Campbell was a driver for Little Crow and a go-between with Col. Henry Sibley, commander of the army's expedition trying to put down the rebellion. Antoine Campbell convinced Little Crow to turn over forty-six white captives to Sibley, and the next year Antoine scouted for Sibley as Sibley continued to hunt down those thought to have perpetrated the uprising.[6]

Little was recorded of Sam Campbell's childhood. His mother died when he was a small boy, and, according to Corabelle's memoirs, he lived with the Native Episcopal missionary George Pay Pay at Fort Bennett, Dakota Territory, for much of his childhood. In a later marriage, Sam would name a son George Pay Pay Campbell.

Corabelle wrote in her memoirs that Sam had been educated at the Carlisle Industrial Indian School, the preeminent Indian boarding school in Pennsylvania, and at another, the Lincoln Institute in Philadelphia. There is no known record of him attending either, although he could have been enrolled under a different name.

Like his father and grandfather, Sam was described by one newspaper reporter as a "rather good looking fellow" with high but not overly prominent cheekbones and straight black hair. His "fine features" were slightly pocked with smallpox scars on his face, after he had apparently survived the disease that killed many Native children. He was also described as "sullen," but that description was often applied to Natives who were quiet and reserved. He was said to be "bright" and a good writer.[7]

Newspapers routinely described Sam as taller than he was, with one saying he was six-foot, eight inches, a giant in those days.[8] In reality, he was just under six feet tall. It's one of the many times newspapers were not reliable in their descriptions of Sam, but his exaggerated height was a mild transgression in an age when racist caricatures of Native people were prevalent in the press. The published vitriol directed at people, like Sam, of mixed white and Native backgrounds was often the worst. They were sometimes portrayed as refugees from both white and Native civilization and were treated badly by both whites and full-blooded Natives. One reporter called Sam a "stranger in a strange land under exceedingly strange circumstances."[9]

That line, more than any, would describe Sam Campbell's short life. He would have multiple relationships and father children with three women. He tried farming, he became embroiled in the sticky politics of Native land grants, and he suffered some of the worst slights and racist scribblings ever written about a man in the American press.

By the spring of 1888, Corabelle was quoted in *Blue Star* as saying that Sam "had been adding to his herd of cattle, and now he was telling me that he thought himself wealthy enough to marry. I promised to marry him, but I was afraid to tell my people."[10]

In Corabelle's handwritten memoirs, she offers a slightly different version of how they met:

> *I met my husband Samuel Campbell while I was teaching at the government school. I used to walk the mile to the Post Office for my mail, and I would many times stop at Rev. George Pay Pay's home to visit them awhile. Rev. Pay Pay was an uncle of Sam's who had raised him, and when Sam returned from his eastern school, he always stayed with his uncle. Therefore, I often met Sam and he would walk back to the school with me and we became very good friends, and were by our own consent engaged to be married some time after my school term.*

They settled into a courtship built around her weekends off from teaching school. Sam would ride on horseback from Fort Bennett to Swift Bird on Fridays and he would stay with friends he knew in Swift Bird's camp. They cooked supper together Friday nights, after Corabelle returned from her Forest City journeys, and on Saturdays Sam "helped me prepare for Sunday and a trip to the next camp, where we went to church. And on Sunday evenings, he took his departure for home seventy-five miles away.

"Those were pleasant and romantic days for me, and we decided to get married on my birthday (March 4, 1888), and I appointed Walter Swift Bird to finish my school term."

The couple initially told neither family nor friends of their engagement. But in her memoirs, Corabelle wrote that she did send $50 home to her mother to ask her to "buy enough . . . sateen [a satin weave] to make me a dress." As testament to her willingness to flout custom, she requested that the dress be black and trimmed with black beads. Corabelle also instructed her mother to buy a hat "of the style then of black lace and a bit of salmon pink ribbon to trim it." She also asked for a pair of black gloves.

"They made the dress and sent it to me, with a letter asking why I wished [for] such a very nice outfit there among the Indians," she recalled. "I wrote them of our engagement, and Sam wrote my father a nice letter also, but it did not prevent the storm of indignant rebukes I received from my home folks. And after the paper had printed the news of our very romantic engagement, we were then beleaguered by newspaper reporters from everywhere, because they made a sensational affair out of it."

"Sensational" barely describes the reaction. The news about the engagement and her family's opposition to it had leaked out the last week of February 1888, cascading in newspapers across the country in racist stereotypes and outright falsehoods. Egregious errors of fact and description became commonplace. Escalating the furor and confusion, one reporter, having failed to find Sam, had a photo made of an elderly Sioux man he called "Chaska." That illustration was falsely depicted in newspapers across the country as Sam, and a claim was made that Corabelle was marrying an older "chief."[11] It was pure fantasy—Sam was not "Chaska"—and he was in his early twenties, younger than the twenty-seven-year-old Corabelle, not an old "chief." But by then, the press was making the marriage a Rorschach Test of interracial relationships. Facts were left by the wayside, the couple's love for one another became secondary to the sensation of disapproved love in the press. The letters from her family and the articles in the newspapers turned into a blizzard of condemnation and ridicule.

Both in *Blue Star* and in her handwritten memoirs, Corabelle professed to be shocked at the vehement objections of her family. In the book she is described as reading one letter from home "with hand trembling almost past using."

"Their daughter marrying an Indian was sufficient disgrace, but this cheap nation-wide publicity," Corabelle said. "With a torrent of words they attempted to forestall the proposed wedding. They sent almost daily telegrams to the agent, the minister of the little white church, and to myself. Not knowing what the newspapers were saying, and feeling that these superlatives were to be expected from Mother, I wrote back that I was very much in love, and went ahead with my plans."[12]

On March 2, roughly two weeks before Corabelle and Sam were to be married, the St. Paul *Daily Globe,* whose pages were routinely filled with gross distortions and blatantly racist depictions of the Sioux, headlined a front-page article, "A Red Man's Bride." The subhead said: "Chaska, the Cheyenne Brave, and Miss Fellows will Wed on March 16."[13]

The article was reprinted in newspapers around the country. It purported to include an interview with Corabelle done on February 26 at Swift Bird camp. From the very beginning it was infested with inaccuracies, referring to Sam as "Tom Cummings," and describing him as an uneducated "full-blooded Indian." It referred to the bride-to-be as "Belle." The newspaper's story was also wrong on Corabelle's time in Dakota Territory, saying she'd only been there six months, when it was her fourth year there or in Nebraska. It spoke of a "prominent captain" who had wooed Corabelle at Forts Bennett and Sully, a supposed romance that appeared nowhere in Corabelle's reminisces or in *Blue Star*. It could have been a reference to the British captain back in Washington, DC, who had secretly tried to court her when she was seventeen, but that would have meant the information came from Corabelle's family and was twisted into a Dakota Territory context. If it did come from her mother or father, that is stark evidence of how far her family was going to try to stop the wedding.

The *Daily Globe* article went on to recreate a conversation that the unnamed reporter (newspapers then generally did not put bylines on stories) claimed he had had with Corabelle. It started with the bride-to-be purportedly asking the reporter a question.

"So you have come from Fort Bennett?" she laughingly asked. "And I suppose they have told you about my coming marriage?"

> *"Coming marriage?"*
>
> *"Why, yes. March 16, I will be married to Chaska, [which means Child-First-Born], or Tom Cummings. The date has been fixed, and today Chaska went to see Agent McChesney [Charles McChesney was the government agent at Cheyenne River] and ask him if he would allow the marriage to take place on the reservation, accompanied by all the Indian ceremonies. I hope he will succeed."*
>
> *"But is this not a foolish fancy, Miss Fellows?"*
>
> *"Not a bit of it. I love Chaska and Chaska loves me. He means to be a good, true, and honest husband. I have always avowed that whom I love, I would marry him, and I love Chaska, and I will marry him just as sure as I live."*
>
> *"But Miss Cora, he cannot support you."*
>
> *"I care not for that. I shall strive to educate him, and I fell [sic] that I can."*

The author then claims that, as he was leaving the tiny Swift Bird camp, Corabelle called after him to ask if he would come to the wedding.

The *Daily Globe* article further described Corabelle as "the daughter of Homer Fellows, who fills an important position in the pension department at Washington. The family ranks well in Washington society, and the coming marriage will no doubt be a surprise. Chaska is a full-blooded Sioux, and has no education."[14]

That same story in the St. Paul paper included a purported interview out of Washington, DC, also supposedly conducted on February 26, with Corabelle's mother, who had just received Corabelle's letter telling of her upcoming marriage to Sam.

"The parents of Cora Fellows refuse to believe she is going to wed an Indian," the article began. "They do, however, suspect that she has made arrangements to marry a white man who is a stranger to them. At their home on Capitol Hill this morning, a letter was received from Cora and it was read to the friends who came in to inquire about the newspaper dispatch which announced her coming match with the Indian Chaska."

The article went on to say that friends of the family agreed that Corabelle would never marry a Native man. It described her as filled with the “missionary spirit,” who was “petite in face and figure, and a good-looking young woman, with plenty of energy and self-reliance.”

The article depicted Corabelle’s mother in utter despair and disbelief over the thought that her daughter would marry a Native man. The paper said that the family was unanimous in their opposition if, indeed, Corabelle was marrying a man of Native blood. Cornelia Fellows thought it was a ruse.

“We can’t believe this monstrous story,” the newspaper quoted Cornelia, describing Corabelle’s father and sister nodding in assent.

> *“Today, we have been looking over her letters and we have concluded that probably she does intend on getting married, but to a respectable white man. She used to write about the kindness the head farmer, a Mr. Wright, showed her, and once she said something about a ring which had been given her. We at once wrote begging her not to think about marrying and settling out there. She has a good home here with plenty of friends and a school to teach if she likes. We couldn’t bear the idea of living in Dakota, but she has seemed to be happy and contented ever since she went there. Her health was never good in Washington, and she has to be so taken with Dakota that nothing would induce her to come back here to live.”*

“She has written us all about her Indian pupils and mentioned a great many of the Indians by name, but we never heard of Chaska,” the *Daily Globe* continued, ostensibly quoting Cornelia Fellows. “It is a cruel story started by someone out there. The girl would never marry an Indian.”[15]

But Cornelia was wrong. In her handwritten memoirs, Corabelle wrote at length of her firm intention to go ahead with the marriage despite her family’s very public opposition, and despite the tempest in the press.

“When my father in Washington, DC, found I was going to marry an Indian and as the papers put it, an Indian Chief, as the papers had pictured Mr. Campbell, my parents were furious about it and sent telegrams to the agent and to the minister of the church I was to be married in. [But] it was of no avail, for we were both of age, so nothing could be done to prevent our marriage."

Whether either of the newspaper interviews accurately depicted conversations with mother and daughter on the same day is impossible to verify. But one thing is certain: Newspapers all over the country had turned the impending marriage of this white missionary and a mixed-race man into a national scandal. The furor was fed by almost daily reports for weeks, many of them continuing to get even the basic facts wrong. The *Daily Globe* story had gotten so much wrong it was laughable. The wedding originally was set for March 4, not March 16. Her fiancé was Sam Campbell, not "Tom Cummings." And the illustration of "Chaska" that was showing up in many newspapers all over the country was a complete fake.

In Corabelle's handwritten memoirs more than four decades later, the pain of recounting what should have been a happy, hopeful time, was still evident.

"Much was printed and passed over in the newspapers, so for a time we were getting advertised from my Washington [DC] home to California, for my family was well-known in Washington circles, and in excellent standing," she recalled. People back home, she wrote, "were more or less quite prejudiced against the Indians, and my parents were not pleased with the big notoriety I had received.

"Though today," she wrote, almost pleadingly in the 1930s, "they might well be proud of the three grandchildren" that eventually came from her marriage to Sam.

Blue Star did not dwell on the family's strident objections, and Isely/Duncan tried to stamp a happy face at the end of the book, ultimately portraying Corabelle reconciling with her father, but not with her mother or sister. Even that left an inaccurate impression that Homer had finally come around. Corabelle's memoirs never indicated a relationship with him beyond one meeting after her marriage that was described in *Blue Star.* And there is ample evidence that, when the story of the marriage was exploding in the sensationalist press, Homer tried to deny or temper reports that his daughter was marrying a man with Native ancestry, although some of the accounts proved to be pure fantasy.

The Pierre *Journal* in Dakota Territory reported in early March that Homer Fellows had arrived in the Twin Cities and was heading to Swift Bird "determined to prevent the marriage of his daughter, Cora, to Chaska, the Sioux Indian." It said Homer intended to "take his recreant daughter in hand."[16] There is no evidence beyond this claim that Homer Fellows ever traveled west attempting to do this. Then, after the marriage, Homer Fellows reportedly tried to play down Sam's Native lineage. Less than two weeks after Sam and Corabelle were married, a Kansas newspaper printed a dispatch out of Washington, DC, claiming that Corabelle had written her father a letter saying Sam had only a "slight trace of Indian blood in his veins," and that "Miss Fellows asserts from this frail foundation has sprung the sensational reports that have been published."[17]

Other egregiously incorrect stories about the relationship were printed. More than a week after the actual nuptials had taken place, the Bismarck *Tribune* claimed the wedding had not happened, and that the couple was waiting for a member of the family to arrive. Corabelle's "big brother will be present and it is hinted will lead the war dance," the paper claimed.[18] Corabelle's only brother had died as a toddler, and the very idea of celebrating her marriage with a "war dance" would have been too offensive for either Sam or Corabelle to even consider.

Three days later, the Washington, DC, *Evening Star* reported on an interview it said it had with Homer Fellows, who disclosed he had received letters from both Corabelle and Sam. Homer claimed Corabelle had wanted to get married that summer in her parents' house, but that Sam had nixed that idea and had wanted to get married as soon as possible. In her memoirs, Corabelle was clear in declaring that she had chosen the original date of the wedding to be on her birthday, and that only delays from mail and bad roads had pushed it back twelve days to March 16.

The *Star* also said that the letter Sam had written his prospective father-in-law had been a "great surprise" and that Sam had "told the story of his love and promised to make his daughter's future life a happy one."

"Mr. Campbell has a slight trace of Indian blood in his veins, but is intelligent, and when Miss Fellows met him last August at Fort Bennett he was in the employ of the Indian bureau," the paper went on. But the paper said the Indian bureau also had no record of Sam ever working for the federal government.

Homer Fellows blamed all the furor on an unnamed reporter in Pierre, Dakota Territory, who, despite never meeting his daughter, had sensationalized and falsified facts about the marriage from the beginning. "He said that his family had felt deeply the publicity which had been forced upon them and the unjust statements that had been made relative to his daughter," the *Star* reported. "He hoped that now the newspapers would let them alone."[19]

That was futile hope. Although she didn't know it at the time, the divide in Corabelle's family was permanent, and the newspapers kept up their obsession with Sam and Corabelle for years.

It is no surprise Corabelle never sought reconciliation with her family after the letters they wrote her. Judging by them, it is also doubtful they ever would have given their blessing to a marriage that included a man with even a "slight trace" of Native blood.

One letter came from Corabelle's "Auntie May." It was written from her home in Washington, DC's Takoma Park neighborhood on February 26, 1888, a Sunday, the day the local papers printed news of Corabelle's impending wedding, the same day both Corabelle and Cornelia ostensibly were interviewed by reporters 1,500 miles apart.

Aunt May wrote Corabelle that she had stopped by the Fellows's house on Capitol Hill for breakfast and had been shown the morning paper. The letter oozed a toxic brew of remonstration and self-pity. Aunt May got right to it, laying on the guilt with a thick layer of religion.

"I have just come from Washington and from church," she wrote. "I left a sad, sad house of your mother's. You will perhaps before this reaches you receive some of the Washington papers, with the terrible report about yourself. Of course, we know there is no truth in it. It is too dreadful and an insult to you to believe for a moment, but that such a thing should be published has nearly killed your mother and made the whole family too wretched to describe."

Aunt May kept piling on the guilt. "Your mother fell over dead, as it were, at the breakfast table. I did not know what was the matter until they showed me the papers. I was shocked, of course, but treated it as a lie, and tried to have her feel the same, but the very thought seemed to crush her so that I feared paralysis, as her tongue was thick, so she could not talk for some time."

According to Aunt May, Cornelia declared: "I would rather die than to live and suffer such disgrace." Aunt May went on to describe her own shame of having been approached by a neighbor, a man she identified as a "German professor," who was outraged that not only was a "white teacher" going to marry an Indian, "but a convict, too."

"I said, 'Professor, that is my niece, and there is no truth to it,'" Aunt May wrote Corabelle.

She harangued and questioned over six pages of tight cursive. Aunt May said she knew something was up when Corabelle had asked for the dress but had not said precisely why. Aunt May was too self-absorbed to realize her blatant judgment and blind condemnation was proof of why Corabelle had been so secretive about her wedding in the first place.

"Now Cora, what has started such a fearful story?" Aunt May asked. Another family member, she claimed, "has thought you were to be married or you would not want such a dress there, and because you did not explain, feared you might have chosen someone beneath you. But she said she [Corabelle] has a right to marry anyone if he is a white man and respectable.

"My dear child," Aunt May wrote to her soon to be twenty-seven-year-old niece, "I cannot think or believe that you will do anything to bring so much trouble on your family. You surely would not isolate yourself from your family by linking yourself with Indian blood in his veins; think what an inheritance to children. I think if such a thing were true your mother would die or be insane. You know how she is. And how even the shadow of disgrace would affect her."

Aunt May had underlined with sharp strokes "Indian blood" and "shadow." She was adamant in her guilt-laying and self-pity.

"I have written only of the effect upon your family, but my dear, I think of you and would not have you do what you will repent of and what will surely bring yourself misery. If you wish to marry a respectable white man, I do not care how poor he may be, I have nothing to say, it is all right. But for your own sake, [and she heavily underlined, 'own sake'] and for the sake of your poor father, mother, and sister, consider what you do or do not do an irreparable wrong to yourself and to them."

Aunt May closed with a plea. "This life is short, at best and let us live so that our Father can say, 'well done, good and faithful servant.'"

She signed the letter, "With much love, Auntie May."[20]

Three weeks later, Corabelle responded with a letter and a telegram from Fort Sully, confirming that she and Sam had indeed been married on March 16. Her sister, Marian, wrote back on March 24. Like her aunt's letter, Marian's was filled with condemnation and disbelief, and she scolded Corabelle for not writing sooner. The family, Marian said, had given her the benefit of the doubt because of slow mail service and "bad roads" in Dakota Territory.

"For one solid month we have been kept in suspense," Marian complained. "It was exactly that length of time between the first publication that came out in the papers and your letter received last night. Of course, we did all we could to stop them, but as they did not originate here or anywhere but in the very place where you live and where the events referenced were supposed to have happened, we had very little hold, and your continued silence made it worse."

She complained of "newspaper reporters who have literally run us to death and made our lives miserable." She said their father had "refuted at once" the papers' reports, but as they kept piling up, story after story, he had given up trying to dispel them. When Corabelle's telegram announcing the wedding arrived it confirmed the family's worst fears, Marian told her sister. She was ashamed, she said, to appear in public.

"I do not think anything more unpleasant has happened to me in my whole life than I have been through for the last few weeks," Miriam complained. "To go out among people and have to hear their comments and insinuations and not be able to contradict them has just been terrible."

Their mother, she said, fearing those reactions, had not left the house in a month. But at this point in the letter, at least, Miriam displayed some recognition of Corabelle's love for Sam. The sister at least held the door open to Sam to someday be welcomed in the family, although it may have been an empty gesture, given the letter's greater context.

"I am not at all sorry but very glad you are married, and hope that when the time comes that we become acquainted that I may be pleased with your husband and my brother. Of course, I can think of a thousand different ways wherein I might have been better pleased that you could live nearer home, could be better off and that your husband did not even have that little tinge of Indian blood in his veins."

Marian referred to the engagement letter that Sam had written to Homer Fellows, calling it a "very straightforward and manly letter" that "shows on the face of the kind, honest heart which the writer must possess." Then she asked for a picture of Sam, "for we are very curious." By then the false image of Chaska—that dishonest photo of an old man used to depict Sam—had been plastered on the pages of newspapers all over the country.

Despite Marian's begrudging promise to try to someday accept Sam, in a bold plea signaling the family's continued denunciation and disbelief, Marian asked Corabelle to send their mother the marriage certificate to "please her," promising that "she will take the best care of it." There is no evidence Corabelle did this and it is highly unlikely she would have. At this point, her mother's intentions would have been highly suspect based on what Cornelia had been quoted saying in the newspaper interview about her distress over the marriage. In her memoirs almost fifty years later, Corabelle said she never saw her mother again; it may have been episodes like this that created the permanent divide.

Closing out her letter to her sister, Marian pleaded for Corabelle to "move out of that part of the country" to try to stem the sensationalist press reports that played so heavily into the Wild West and the crude and racist depictions of the people Native to it. Marian wanted her sister to move closer to home where, she hoped, the furor could more quickly subside. But this modern technology! The mass media, the yellow press's thirst for sensational conflict, was destroying privacy and exploiting family disputes. There was no place they could go to escape it. "The railroad and telegraph has [sic] annihilated distance in this country," Marian wrote, "and effectively prevents anyone from hiding their light under a bushel." [21]

Chapter 13

A Prairie-Gumbo-Splattered Wedding Day

As weddings go, the union of Sam Campbell and Corabelle Fellows was unconventional, even for that time and place. But it spoke to the spirit of independence the young woman from Washington, DC, had cultivated in Dakota Territory. Corabelle even baked her own wedding cake. She shaped it like a pyramid.

But she had to wait to make it. Weather, muddy roads, slow mail, and rivers running over their banks from melting snow all conspired to move the wedding back twelve days after the couple's intended date of March 4, Corabelle's twenty-seventh birthday. And even at that, a scheduled 11 a.m. wedding for the new date on March 16 had to be pushed back into the afternoon after a gumbo-hampered wagon ride.

The wedding took place in an Episcopal Church twelve miles up the Missouri River from the Swift Bird camp. It was presided over by an Episcopal clergy named the Rev. J.W. Hanford, "who heard my story, met my fiance and approved my decision to go on with the wedding," Corabelle recalled in her memoirs. The wedding dress made by her mother had arrived just in time. The Missouri River was so jammed with ice that Corabelle could not get across to the post office in Forest City to retrieve it—hence the postponement from the original date. Eventually, she paid an "Indian man" $5 to brave the ice jams and retrieve the dress, hat, and gloves Cornelia had sent. Sam looked fine in a "new tailor-made suit," and her "satin bonnet and gown were stylish indeed."[1]

Corabelle had bonded with fellow missionary Hanford, the father of five "little children, like stairsteps," that "were the pride of everyone around." In *Blue Star*, the reverend's name is spelled "Hansford," but records of the Episcopal Church in Dakota Territory record it minus the "s."[2] Numerous press reports at the time falsely identified Reverend Hanford as Sam Campbell's uncle.

Hanford and his wife, Corabelle recalled in her handwritten memoirs, were "thoroughly English" and "missionarys [sic] in the true sense [who] helped all they were able and did their own work."

Less than five months later, while cutting hay, Reverend Hanford's team of horses was spooked and broke into a run. He fell onto the sharp blades of the hay mower and was cut so severely he bled to death. He had acquired a spritz of fame just for conducting Sam and Corabelle's wedding. Newspapers all over the country noted his death and the fact he had presided over the wedding of Corabelle and Sam.[3]

Corabelle's handwritten memories of her wedding day are a jumble of words; this passage is one where she had accidentally written over a previous page; understandable given her blindness at the time she wrote her memoirs. Her wedding had been quite a day and even those many years later, the memories excited her. A careful reading of those entangled lines and combining them with Isely/Duncan's account in *Blue Star*, fills in many details.

March 16, 1888, began with an early-morning sendoff in Swift Bird camp. Dressed in their wedding finery, Sam and Corabelle set off by wagon to Reverend Hanford's church. "Ice still jammed and creaked in the river; snow lay heavily on the earth, but the sky was brilliant with a warming sun, and there was a crowd out to cheer us as we drove away," Corabelle remembered.

Melting snow was turning the dirt roads into sticky trails of gumbo. "As the snow melted the mud grew worse and worse. The winding road developed one mudhole after another. We slipped and slid up and down the interminable hills with greater and greater difficulty, until finally the wheels refused to turn."[4]

Faced with no other choice, wearing his finest wedding clothes, Sam "climbed down to dislodge the mud from the wheels." He spent "a long weary time tugging at the sunken wheels. Finally we got out of it and

Corabelle in her wedding dress
COURTESY OF CARRIE LINDSEY

drove on, but our spirits were sadly dashed. It was after 3 in the afternoon when the little white church spire came in sight."

The 11 a.m. "English breakfast" wedding that Corabelle had dreamed of had passed its hour, and many guests had long gone by the time Sam and Corabelle arrived mid-afternoon. About a dozen hard-core attendees had hung around for a ceremony that took place at 3:30 p.m.

Surprisingly, Corabelle's pyramidal wedding cake had safely been tucked into the wagon and survived the trip. Upon arrival, the couple learned that Mrs. Hanford had also baked a cake for the couple, so the newlyweds celebrated with two.

"After a mud session in the woodshed and another session with the wash basin, we went into the cold little church and were married. Happy, in spite of the misadventures of the day, I cut my pyramidal bride's cake, which was frosted in elaborate colored designs, and enjoyed the tea which was to have been a breakfast."[5]

The newly married couple went on a three-day honeymoon at the home of William and Rebecca Holmes. Amid the furor, this couple could provide comfort. "Rebecca Holmes, like myself, was a schoolteacher who had married a man with Indian blood," Corabelle wrote in her memoirs.

Although the Holmes's lived roughly forty miles from Swift Bird, early in their marriage, Corabelle and Sam considered them their best friends, and strove to meet as much as they could. "We often exchanged visits," Corabelle wrote. They were "very cultured in those days, and distance was nothing to us, for a trip of forty or fifty miles was not considered much even though we went in a lumber wagon."

According to her memoirs and *Blue Star*, Corabelle and Sam then returned to Swift Bird on the Tuesday after their wedding, where they were warmly welcomed. Her pupils showered them with gifts of "arrowheads, moccasins, food, and blankets."

"I was now nearer them since I had married a man of Indian blood," Corabelle remembered. "Now I was 'Sister Blue Star.' In grave curiosity the children looked Mr. Campbell over and named him Mr. Blue Star!"[6]

Chapter 14

Dime Museums and Buffalo Bill's Wild West Show

Just weeks after their marriage, Corabelle and Sam accepted an invitation to go on a speaking tour promoted by a "Mr. Dewitt," owner of a "stereopticon bureau" in Washington, DC.[1] Corabelle had resigned her teaching position and, on June 14, while on tour in Ohio, Corabelle signed a power of attorney to resolve all outstanding legal matters, including anything she owed to the government commissary back on the Cheyenne River.[2]

With their marriage plastered all over American newspapers, the newlyweds had been inundated with offers to cash in on their fame. At first, seeking only to settle down and start a farm at a village not far from Swift Bird called Chargers Camp, they resisted. It had been named for a Lakota leader who rescued nine white women and children captured in the 1862 Sioux uprising in Minnesota and was situated between the Missouri and Moreau Rivers.

For a while the camp served as the Cheyenne River Agency. Its history is marked with some of the most significant events of the nineteenth and twentieth centuries on the upper Plains. Lewis and Clark camped nearby in 1804. In the late 1950s, as the Oahe Dam began causing flooding in the lowlands along the river, the site was abandoned, although a historic marker still overlooks the original site today.[3]

In her memoirs, Corabelle said she and Sam had been "beguiled by people from the east to go east" as soon as the sensational news of their marriage went national. Despite misgivings from her family reported in the press and the unforgiving letters from her aunt and sister, they had decided to take advantage of the offers. They "made a contract finally with a gentleman I used to know in Washington," she wrote in her memoirs. She and Sam "were to go and give short talks and tell them of my work in Dakota and Nebraska."

Corabelle said that "with the handsome salary we earned" she and Sam were able to "buy complete equipment and furnishings for the farm we had purchased."[4]

The stereopticon, commonly called a "magic lantern," was another of that age's high-tech innovations. It used a light to project photographic negatives, and it was wildly popular before motion pictures began taking over popular culture after the turn of the century. In the 1880s a stereopticon show was a popular form of entertainment as well as education, and elaborate showings were often Easterners' first and primary depictions of the vanishing western frontier. Attendees could see places they probably could never go themselves and meet people who had lived actual adventures there.

"We made quite an extensive tour with him, speaking on Indians and explaining his pictures," Corabelle is quoted as saying of "Mr. Dewitt." "Later, we made a second tour, the two covering most of the large cities of eastern and northern United States."[5]

Using a common term for taking photographs, Corabelle noted in her memoirs that an unnamed person—perhaps the mysterious "Mr. DeWitt" referenced in *Blue Star*—"had made some burns of the children and Indian homes" to show to audiences.

"Sam and I [went] lecturing about my work while he also had pictures to show and the canvas of beautiful scenes to please the people." The promoter, Corabelle wrote, had daughters who played the violin and coronet during their presentations. "So we were a little company and made considerable money."

They toured as far east as Cincinnati, and "then I made a contract with another company," where they began "traveling in many cities in the east, always being introduced as 'Mr. and Mrs. Chaska.'" The name, she wrote in her handwritten memoirs, "means the first-born son" and "that was the Indian name my husband was called."

The vague reference to "another company" is certainly a dressed-up memory. The record shows something quite different from Sam and Corabelle's participation in a high-brow "stereopticon" tour, which was the only tour mentioned in *Blue Star*.

By that spring of 1888, Sam and Corabelle were being advertised as participants in a "dime museum" show by the Chicago-based Kohl & Middleton Co. Sometimes called "freak shows," they often portrayed people in the extreme: the world's tallest, or heaviest, or strongest. Later, according to Corabelle's memoirs, she and Sam would also be paid to appear for a short time as novelties in Buffalo Bill's Wild West show that was touring the country and abroad. They had been blindsided by their fame; they decided to capitalize on it.

"We were much sought after and feted everywhere we went and enjoyed our trip and the good salary as well as being popular for a season," Corabelle wrote. But it wasn't all good. It "was our first venture into the big world, and there are some things I regret. I am not sorry I saw so much of beauty in the large cities of the east. We made a second trip a year later, and took our little son [Claude], a fine little fellow with dark eyes and hair, perfect in size and form and at four months old, weighing twenty pounds."

The second tour in 1889 took them to many eastern cities and included what her memoirs described as a side trip, perhaps a delayed honeymoon, to the lighthouse at Old Point Comfort at Fortress Monroe, Virginia. Later was when they joined up with Buffalo Bill's Wild West tour, introduced as the famous Corabelle and her husband Sam.

The privilege of assuming a place of honor in the biggest show in the country, to be seen on something close to their own terms, must have seemed like a luxury after the dime museums. But the newspapers were still sensationalizing their marriage, and they had new fodder for ridicule and exploitation. They were early victims of the infamous yellow press of the late nineteenth century—a sensationalist journalism in which speculation and hype supplanted fact and reality. It was brutal.

Like the participants in reality shows of the twenty-first century, Sam and Corabelle had become caricature commodities in an exclamation-point age. Propelled by a press that had grown exponentially during the Civil War and exploiting an American public whose literacy rate had grown just as fast, mass media was growing in size and influence in America, the advertising and promotional professions exploding. Promoters pushed everything from land rushes for homesteaders to castor oil for what ailed them. The St. Paul *Daily Globe* launched the exploitative assault.

"She Loves a Savage" blared a Kohl & Middleton advertisement of their "wedding tour" tour in early May of 1888.

"Read and Be Convinced!" wrote a promoter named E.R. Richards.

"Chaska and His Lovely Bride" would be on display for all to see, the advertisement said. It included a drawing of Corabelle in a white wedding gown and a bare-chested Sam in leggings and a feather in his hair.

"High-born, beautiful and accomplished CORA BELLE FELLOWS, who was wooed and won by a Red-Skin!" the advertisement blared.

St. Paul *Daily Globe*
COURTESY OF NEWSPAPERS.COM

"It costs thousands to satisfy the public demand," the advertisement went on. "FIVE agents were sent for them. They forded rivers, traveled miles on horseback, and AT LAST SUCCEEDED."[6] A news story in the same edition called the young couple "full fledged freaks."[7]

Along with appearances by Sam and Corabelle, Kohl & Middleton was getting evermore freakish in its acts. A man wrestled a bear; shows featured a woman purportedly nine feet tall, another weighing 732 pounds. "Goliath," the "strongest man alive," exhibited feats of strength. Kohl & Middleton was first to feature Harry Houdini and his family, escape artists the museum advertised as the "Greatest Illusionists" alive. Attendees were invited to bring their own handcuffs to challenge the "Wizard of Shackles." Another featured act, "Lady Swimmers" performed "Fancy Swimming and Diving." That they were dressed in bathing suits in a Victorian age, where women went into public fully corseted and covered, was undoubtedly a part of the Lady Swimmers' appeal.[8]

Like Buffalo Bill's extravaganza, dime museums had also become a staple of mass-appeal theatrics in the late nineteenth century—a grandiose urban counterpart to the Wild West shows. They were aimed at new immigrant populations dreaming of the prosperity and elusive promises of their new country. Frequently confined to the harsh and often mundane limitations of tenement life in America's teeming cities, these new immigrants sought the dime museums for a shared thrill.

Dime museums were "as popular an institution in the United States as the movies are today," author Andrea Stulman Dennett observed more than a century later. In the late nineteenth century, she wrote, they were "a byproduct of the enormous expansion of the American urban landscape."[9]

Hype, sensationalism, racism, lies—it all added up to monetized exploitation. Adventure and mystery abounded. And, if promoter E.R. Richards, who brought Sam and Corabelle to the stage, was to be believed, the heroes of the story were the PR agents who brought this spectacular story of forbidden marriage to the masses. Why, these intrepid PR agents had risked their comfort, maybe even their lives, to bring this fantastic story to the paying public! They had forded rivers! They had ridden horses for miles! They had SUCCEEDED!

A rival newspaper reported that thirty-five thousand people saw Sam and Corabelle in their first week on tour with Kohl & Middleton in St. Paul, and that the audience included "some of the most prominent people in the city." The show also featured "Zinman, the giant skeleton; Alice, the largest of women; Zoe Zeleke, the beautiful bird charmer; and other things of interest, besides good stage performances."[10]

A month before its sensational ads, the *Daily Globe* had been scooped on the $5,000 contract Sam and Corabelle had signed with Kohl & Middleton. Iowa's Sioux City *Journal* reported that a telegram had been sent to "Mrs. Chaska, nee Fellows" that offered the new couple "$5,000 to appear in a ten weeks' engagement as freaks."

The messenger who delivered the telegram, the paper reported then, "states that Mrs. Chaska and her husband received the offer in a friendly manner and wrote the museum for a few days in which to consider the matter."[11]

In 1884, a $5,000 payout for ten weeks of work would have been beyond the dreams of anyone but the wealthy. In 2023 dollars, it would be about $150,000, almost a million-dollar annual salary. It would have been a huge temptation for a young couple trying to establish a farm in that unbroken prairie between the Moreau and Missouri Rivers. Eventually, they agreed to the tours, and over the next two summers Sam and Corabelle were turned into "curiosities"—a word regularly used to describe them in the press—before tens of thousands of people.

At ten cents a head, fifty thousand people—five thousand a week, more than seven hundred a day—would have had to come to see them for the promoters to break even. The payout was big for the participants, but the risk was big, too. Who knew what biases could trigger violence in big crowds like that? Would the tour seal for good the estrangement between Corabelle and her disapproving family?

The idea of fame as commodity and an avenue toward wealth was getting a lasting foothold in American culture in the late nineteenth century. It was a brawny, expansive age, and the hype helped both create and fill voids. By the time Sam and Corabelle went on tour, Sitting Bull and other Lakota and Dakota leaders had participated in Buffalo Bill's Wild West show. Newspapers reported William Cody's visits to Dakota

Territory reservations to find new performers. He offered decent pay and a chance to see the world, and he had plenty of takers.

"Buffalo Bill has recently been at Pine Ridge for the purpose of securing 100 Indians to accompany his 'Wild West' to Paris the coming spring," the Black Hills *Weekly Journal* reported in March of 1889, just as Sam and Corabelle were preparing to go on their second Kohl & Middleton tour. "He had no trouble in securing the bower of the flock, and consequently South Dakota will be represented at the World's exhibition the coming summer by 100 of her original Natives." (Technically, it would not become a state until November of that year although Cleveland had signed the bill granting statehood to the two Dakotas in February).

The paper reported that the Oglala Lakota leader Red Shirt, "the gentleman who had created such a furore [sic] among the crowned heads on the other side of the big waters last season, will not accompany the gang."[12]

On Buffalo Bill's European tour the year before, Britain's Queen Victoria had "commanded personal meetings with Annie Oakley and Lillian Smith, and with Red Shirt, who was advertised as 'chief' of the show Indians, too," the historian Louis S. Warren wrote. "She burbled over two Lakota babies. Her mere presence was the highest honor a show could receive in Britain. Her enthusiasm for Cody's entertainment played a huge part in its success that season, and in all years to come."[13]

Cody's extravaganza got a similar reaction at the 1889 Paris Exposition Universelle, where the Eiffel Tower—just opened in March that year—was celebrated. There, Cody and some of his Native performers met with the French president and the shah of Persia.[14]

There is no mention in Corabelle's memoirs of her and Sam touring overseas with Buffalo Bill, but in her handwritten account she did briefly describe appearing at his show in the United States. Their fame had certainly preceded them. Cody apparently received word they were coming, and he offered a contract and built a prominent seat of honor from which to promote the now-famous white woman who had married the now-famous Native man.

"We were expected, and there was a special balcony built for us where we could see the whole show to advantage, also to be seen, for which privilege we received quite a nice little sum in a nice purse," Corabelle wrote in her memoirs.

Corabelle made no observations about what she or Sam thought of the show. It was quite a spectacle. Three trains moved what was essentially a village of eight hundred performers and workers (and a small herd of buffalo) from city to city. Cody was sometimes an ally of beleaguered Sioux, but as a scout and soldier, Cody proclaimed that in his more solitary life on the Plains he had "stood between savagery and civilization most all of my early days." To show how he protected "civilization," one act in the show had Cody taking scalps in revenge of Custer.[15]

Yet there was at least an attempt at preserving some elements of Native culture and to incorporate the end of the frontier firmly into the American narrative. While Cody was a "harbinger of American expansion," Warren wrote, Cody's "efforts in this direction were in some ways analogous to those of American historians, notably Frederick Jackson Turner, who sought to expand the nation's historical consciousness beyond the eastern seaboard, and to incorporate at least a limited range of non-English immigrants in national histories and myths."

The show, Warren continued, "became a touchstone for Americans seeking to understand their own rapidly urbanizing, racially conflicted, industrial communities and country, and for Europeans contemplating a host of concerns, including industrialism, colonialism, race progress and race decay."[16]

Depicting intermarriage between a white woman and Native man—Sam and Corabelle—would have fit into several aspects of this entertainment script: "Civilization" taming the wild, risky love between people of different races, adventurers on a vanishing frontier. Yet by spotlighting love, even a quasi-forbidden kind, Sam and Corabelle's marriage was also a link to tradition. Marriage was a familiar and comforting norm, even if divorce was a common result. Was their marriage ultimately to be seen as a lesson in the power of love over prejudice? Were promoters showcasing a future of wider acceptance of interracial relationships? Or were they put on display as mere curiosities, as what the newspapers were describing as gold-digging flaunters of racial hierarchies and cultural norms?

In 1893, five years after Sam and Corabelle married, the historian Frederick Jackson Turner declared the end of the American frontier, "the closing of a great historical movement." White civilization, he said, had succeeded in "winning a wilderness."[17]

Cody's production lasted until it went bankrupt in 1913. A new war was looming, and America's twentieth century gaze would be pulled in other directions, to world wars in Europe, Africa, the Middle East, and Asia. But the mythology of the American frontier and its famous actors continued well into the twenty-first century.

Either way, Corabelle's story in *Blue Star* ended before this sensational chapter in their lives began. Neither Isely/Duncan in *Blue Star* nor Corabelle in her memoirs mentioned the sordid treatment they received for two years. She wrote nothing of the dime museums, the "She Loves A Savage" advertisements, the demeaning and dishonestly inaccurate depictions of their marriage. Perhaps it was all encapsulated in the "regrets" she had expressed in one line in her memoirs.

While on tour that first summer, Sam and Corabelle had sent word ahead to her family that they would be in Washington, DC, and that they would be staying at the newly renovated St. James Hotel at Sixth Street and Pennsylvania Avenue. It was a status declaration for the newlyweds. In that summer of 1888, the St. James was a fancy, new hotel that was advertising it was soon to get electric lights. It featured such high-society offerings as carpets imported from Brussels, black walnut furniture, toilets on every floor, and a "ladies waiting room."[18]

Despite the bitter, racist, scolding letters from her aunt and sister, Corabelle still wanted her family to meet her new husband. Perhaps he could win them over with his quiet dignity; perhaps they could see how in love they were. But Homer Fellows sent back a note saying that, while he was available, her mother and sister had gone to Atlantic City and would not see her.

"I knew what he meant," Corabelle said in *Blue Star*, cryptically acknowledging the opposition from her mother and sister.[19] In her memoirs, Corabelle was more blunt, referring to the letters she had received from her family, and she said it was not a surprise Cornelia and Marian chose to avoid her and Sam.

The book *Blue Star* depicted Sam and her father cordially meeting in the lobby of the St. James. At the end, Isely/Duncan wrote, Homer Fellows turned and wrapped Corabelle in a bear hug, planting a "smother of kisses on my face." That's the way *Blue Star* ended, in smothering kisses.[20] Perhaps Corabelle simply wanted to remember her father that way. It was better than dwelling on what happened next.

Chapter 15

Lies and Distortions That Never End

It is a challenge to describe how shamefully and dishonestly the American press depicted the marriage between a white woman and her husband of Dakota and white ancestry. The yellow press assault—and it *was* an early example of that sensationalist era of journalism at the close of the nineteenth century—lasted from their marriage in 1888 well into the next decade. Fiction masqueraded as fact. Racist, libelous terms were commonplace. Sam and Corabelle had merely fallen in love. They were treated like freaks and actors on the age's biggest stages, and the paying public played along. Some even accused Corabelle of a most cynical ulterior motive.

"It now turns out that Miss Cora Fellows married the Indian, Chaska, simply to advertise herself," the Atlanta *Constitution* speculated. "She wants to write a novel and is under the impression that her marriage will create so much talk that people will be crazy to read her book. Perhaps her story deals with border life, and she is trying to get the proper local color. 'Painted Red' would be a good title for her novel."[1]

There is no evidence in anything Corabelle had written or left behind that she had gone to Dakota Territory for anything other than to teach and serve in mission. In both *Blue Star* and in the handwritten memoirs handed down through generations of descendants, Corabelle focused most of her adult memories on her time teaching and doing mission work, and she described a marriage based on love and respect. She may have had other Dakota Territory suitors, but Sam was the only man she mentioned at any length. In her memoirs, she did say that while living with Winyan, "I had quite a few callers when I came to live with my Indian mother. Some were earnest, some were not." She fell in love with only one man.

But it was no use trying to explain; the public's picture of their marriage had completely escaped their grasp. They were trapped no matter what they did. If they stayed at home on a quiet farm along the river, her family still opposed the marriage and the newspapers wrote about them, anyway. Yet one main reason Corabelle said they went on tour—to finance their new farm and farm equipment—only added to the exploitation and denouncement in the public press and fed the narrative that they were in it just for the money.

The day after the "She Loves a Savage" advertisement in the St. Paul *Daily Globe,* the paper published a story purporting to be an interview with Corabelle and Sam. It was less than two months after the wedding. The headline on the article read: "Six feet of Indian and a White Woman Not at All Pretty." The subhead announced: "His Siouxness and She Who Was Known as Miss Fellows Are in St. Paul."[2]

The lead paragraph began: "Attired in a buckskin shirt, with historical fringe about the shoulders and the breast embroidered in several brilliant colors; a pair of civilized trousers, new moccasins purchased at any store on Seventh Street, and a cowboy hat decorated with bear's paws, Chaska, the noble red man who went gunning for the heart of Cora Belle Fellows and hit the mark, arrived in St. Paul yesterday, and took up quarters in Parlor 'D' at the Ryan."

"The people of civilized St. Paul now have an opportunity to gaze upon the faces of the Indian and white maiden whose romantic marriage at Swift Bird's Camp, in Dakota, caused such a decided sensation at the national capitol, whence Mrs. Chaska emanated, and throughout America."

The unnamed author assured readers that despite concerns "the whole thing is a most ingeniously gotten-up 'fake,'" there nonetheless "seems to be no doubt but that the story of the marriage is true, and that these persons at the Ryan are as represented, for every necessary proof is submitted."[3]

Again, the setting sent an important, subliminal message. "Civilized" local citizens would recognize how this novelty attraction was being treated like celebrity. The Ryan Hotel, then just three years old, was considered a "Victorian masterpiece." It had been built by a millionaire who made his fortune mining gold and silver in Utah. Its opulent features, which included "towers, pinnacles, pedimented dormers, bays, bracketed balconies" and other Gothic features, made it "the kind of eye-catching building that merrily eluded the perils of understatement."[4]

As such, the seven-story bastion (which was demolished in 2014) also perfectly depicted the new wealth that was assembling among the grain merchants and shipping magnates of Minneapolis and St. Paul. They had capitalized on the boom of white settlement in the emerging grain belt west of the Twin Cities by shipping wheat and other grain down the Mississippi River and out to the world. By 1888 the Twin Cities had surpassed St. Louis as the nation's leading shipping point for grain, and the Pillsburys and other big names in the trade had built mansions of their own on St. Paul's Summit Avenue, still one of the world's longest avenues of Victorian homes.[5] So the *Daily Globe*'s readers would have known that this celebrity couple was being put up in the most regal accommodations St. Paul could offer. This was high class, even if the paper was crude and demeaning in its depiction of its two famous occupants, and the inference again was that this mixed-race couple out of nowhere was willing to be exploited for the money.

The *Daily Globe* reporter described the first impressions of Sam as "brawny, copper-colored husband, who towers to the height of six feet three, is well proportioned and a handsome fellow, so far as build is concerned. His face showed no marked signs of intelligence, and when he grasped the reporter's hand, with merely an 'ugh,' he lowered his black eyes and kept them directed at the carpet throughout the interview." In reality, Sam was just under six feet tall, and it is hard to fathom him responding to a question with "ugh," given he'd been taught in English in eastern boarding schools.

Corabelle "is about five feet one, fairly well formed, and has a wide face, with sunken cheeks though in perfect health," the reporter wrote. "She is quite plain, but has a pretty mouth, nice teeth, and a merry pair of eyes. A rather small, nicely shaped foot peeped out from her black satin beaded dress."

The author did not say that the foot he had described had also helped keep Corabelle atop horses being broken or immersed in ankle-deep gumbo while freeing stuck wagons on Dakota trails. Or that it was a foot that had traversed prairie meadows in search of Native plants with friends who had accepted her as she was. That foot had carried heavy water vessels with Winyan up the banks of the Cheyenne River. The *Daily Globe* article included another purportedly verbatim account of an interview with the couple. It went as follows:

> *"Well, Mrs. Campbell," the reporter said as he took a seat beside her, "I presume you are aware of the object of my call?"*
>
> *"The same old story, I suppose," she answered with a laugh, looking across the room toward her "hub," who sat on the sofa picking a piece of paper to pieces, and looking at his moccasins.*
>
> *"Are you an unbeliever?" she asked.*
>
> *"Well, I can hardly tell this early in the game. Reel your yarn and I shall spout afterward."*

According to the author, Corabelle introduced Sam as "Chaska, my husband." If so, and it's a big if, it meant she had conceded to a made-up celebrity name for Sam. In her handwritten memoirs, he was always "Sam" or even "Mr. Campbell," although she did occasionally acknowledge that promoters and newspapers called him Chaska.

The *Daily Globe* reported how Corabelle glanced "lovingly" at Sam and said that Corabelle's "eyes wandered affectionately in the direction of his Siouxness." Racist spewing continued. The reporter confessed that they were so afraid to ask Sam a question they had "visions of a split skull and absence of scalp" as a result. Sam did not respond to questions, the *Daily Globe*'s story said, adding that the reporter "might as well telephoned the spirit of Sitting Bull's brother, for all the answer he got."

The article quoted Corabelle as saying that "a dozen times verbally and a hundred times by letter" she had been warned to not marry Sam. One plea purportedly came from a Minneapolis real estate agent.

According to the newspaper, Corabelle showed the reporter another letter from a "Miss Boner, of Langdon, Minnesota." It had been written to Homer Fellows, warning him of terrible things being done to his daughter. Her father had forwarded it to Corabelle, according to the *Daily Globe.*

"Your daughter has undoubtedly been drugged," the supposed "Miss Boner" wrote. "The Indians dig up certain roots and by them can make anybody love them they want to. I want you to get your daughter away from the Indians, as he will make her life 'hell on earth.'"

The reporter asked if Sam had any "noble ancestors." Corabelle was quoted replying: "I never inquired. He was a popular fellow at the camp, and I never thought of his folks. They are all the same as here, although Chaska has some relatives who distinguished themselves on various occasions." This may have been a reference to the scouts and interpreters in Sam's lineage.

The newspaper again messed up even basic facts about the marriage ceremony. It said that Sam and Corabelle had traveled on horseback from Swift Bird to their wedding at Reverend Hanford's church, when in her memoirs Corabelle recounted the intimate details of traveling in a wagon that they had to pull out of the gumbo after it became stuck.

According to the newspaper, Corabelle dispelled the lie that Sam—nee "Chaska"—was a Sioux chief. That claim, she said, had been made up by another reporter she had never met, echoing her father's claim that the initial report of their engagement had been written by a man from Pierre, seventy miles from Swift Bird.

Corabelle allegedly told the *Daily Globe* that since the wedding she and Sam had also received other reproachful letters from Washington, DC, but that her family had begun looking at the marriage "philosophically." There was no further evidence that ever happened, and three days later the newspaper itself printed an article that directly disputed that claim. Corabelle had six weeks earlier received the blistering letters from her aunt and sister. It seems highly suspicious that in the interim, based on the questions she had received in previous correspondence and her own reluctance to disclose Sam's identity to her family, that Corabelle would describe her family as accepting the marriage "philosophically" while on a nationwide tour her family opposed.

Corabelle supposedly showed the reporter another letter in opposition to the marriage. It was from Laura Sunderland, the daughter of the Presbyterian minister in Washington, DC, who had been Corabelle's mentor and early missionary sponsor. "She is a very dear friend of mine," Corabelle allegedly said of Laura Sunderland. The letter, the paper reported, was full of "the very warmest friendship and affection." But Laura Sunderland's opposition, and all others, had not stopped Corabelle from going ahead with the marriage.

Any sense of disapproval from a "dear friend" and the daughter of a prominent abolitionist pastor like Rev. Byron Sunderland would have been hard to take. For decades, Reverend Sunderland had been a well-known abolitionist who continued to decry racial animus and violence. In 1866, the year after the Civil War ended, amidst the severe tensions of Reconstruction, Reverend Sunderland had been the only pastor of a white church in Washington, DC, who allowed the civil rights icon Frederick Douglass to speak to his congregation.[6]

Corabelle also said that the Indian agent overseeing the Swift Bird camp had initially opposed their marriage, but that the agent, Charles McChesney, "was finally won over."

By contrast her Sioux friends, Corabelle told the reporter, were "delighted" with the marriage. "The old and young men called me sister," she said, according to the paper, "and so did the maidens and the squaws. They were afraid they were not attentive enough."

The spirited young bride told the reporter she had also received a letter from a white man living in Dakota Territory. She used it to make a point about love and interracial marriage that the *Daily Globe* and other newspapers were routinely vilifying through her and Sam.

"By the way," Corabelle is quoted as saying in the article, "I received a letter from a young man in Dakota, asking me if I knew of a pretty Indian girl who wanted to marry a young fellow of twenty-three. I could have answered him favorably, for I know a great many pretty Indian girls."[7]

As racist and judgmental as that *Daily Globe* article was, the Chicago *Tribune* outdid it a little over two weeks later when Sam and Corabelle arrived for an appearance at Kohl & Middleton's Chicago dime museum in that city. In an article headlined, "Whoopla there, Chaska," the author descended to depths that are cringe-inducing well over a century later. The article's subhead read: "Arrival of Big-Buck-With-A-Pot-Of-Gold and His Squaw."[8]

"Chaska's heart was happy and his pace was light," the article began. "A buck's pace is always light. That is because his squaw carries the baggage."

The article maintained, without any evidence, that Sam was perpetually drunk, although it did charitably concede that the red eyes it reported Sam having could have come from sitting around too many campfires. The *Tribune* reported that Sam had arrived in the city with "the family shooting irons [slang for guns], scalping utensils, and dog checks. His squaw lugged a hunk of dried beef and two smoked earthen pots of corn-meal, while a brace of frying pans dangled from her belt.

"Protruding from the bosom of her dress was a contract guaranteeing her $5,000 for a 10-week tour of the leading cities. Her demeanor was marked with enthusiasm. Chaska had told her to follow him, and she would wear diamonds. She was therefore hustling to keep up with his prairie stride."

The *Tribune* claimed that both Sam and Corabelle had painted their faces—his with "blood-root," hers in white paint—and that Sam yelled a "war whoop" as they ascended the stairs to the Kohl & Middleton stage. The newspaper said it interviewed people in the audience.

One was a "Mrs. Parker" the *Tribune* reported, "a pale little woman who wore blue glasses and had a baby in each arm." She was reported to exclaim: "I don't see what she wanted to marry him for."

"Nor do I," a "Mrs. Dorsey"—a woman with four children in tow—was said to reply. An old man standing close enough to see "the creases in Mrs. Chaska's face" was reported to have blurted out: "The white man always took advantage of the Indian."

The *Tribune* article said that the "museum orator" introduced Corabelle by pleading, "Should we not commend her?

"She went among these children of the woods as a messenger of civilization and Christianity. She found a man there whom she loved, and she has given him her heart. Would there be more marriages for love! Would there be more Corabelle Fellowses! There may be one before me now, or there may be in this audience of young men some one who will go among the daughters of Chaska's race—"

At this point, the quote is cut off, and the *Tribune* reported that the "boys" in the audience "drowned the remainder of the speech in laughter." As the newspaper described it, this prod toward more interracial relationships between Native people and whites was received as laughably ludicrous. The article then raised doubts about Sam's heritage, quoting "Mrs. Parker" observing that "from the way he pulled up his breeches, I'll bet he ain't an Indian. Why, he did it just like a white man."

Incredibly, the *Tribune* article then goes on to quote Corabelle as claiming that Sam "is not an Indian, though they say he is," and as proof said he had not enrolled as a member of the Santee. This was a direct attack on his mixed-blood status. The article went on to quote Corabelle ostensibly trying to fight back.

"He is a young farmer, hard working, intelligent, honest, of good habits, and a pure man. He loves me and I love him. When this engagement [tour] ends we will return to our farm and resume the work we left. We will be quite well-to-do for people on the plains, because $5,000 is a big sum there."

Corabelle was further quoted saying that after Homer Fellows learned of their Kohl & Middleton tour plans, her father had threatened to sue the dime museum because he was sure that imposters were being used to depict his daughter and her new husband. But, Corabelle said, she had assured Homer he was wrong, and that Homer then dropped the threats to sue. What followed next is pure heartbreak.

"He disowned me," Corabelle said, according to the article. "I do not think I could stand it to go to Washington unless at the end of my journey. I do not suppose my family would come to see me. I have many relatives here in Chicago, and they are well-to-do. I do not care to mention their names. I saw in the crowd before us this morning one of my cousins. I suppose the family had sent him to see if we were really here."[9]

The temporary reconciliation between father and daughter described at the end of *Blue Star* likely came later that summer, when Corabelle and Sam were reported to have visited the government Indian Affairs office in Washington, DC. So, both her observation that she had been disowned, and the closing scene in *Blue Star* could be true.

Despite its racist and demeaning renderings, whether it realized it or not, the *Tribune* article did contain two revealing takes.

The first was that Corabelle's intentions described in the article directly clashed with the freak-show appeal of the dime museums.

"She wants to civilize him, and her ambition to have a husband who can shine in society has already interfered with his value as a dime museum investment," the paper reported. "When he came from the plains, he had the long, straight hair of his race. The showman liked this quality and insisted that it be retained. But Mrs. Chaska stole a march on the showman. Her husband had his hair cut. By the time he reaches New York it is thought he will be wearing a silk hat and a swallow-tail coat. Those who want to see the original and aboriginal Chaska should hurry."

The truth was, Corabelle knew that Sam had been educated in eastern boarding schools. It is why she told white audiences he had qualities ostensibly valued, if not universally practiced, in white civilization: hard-working, honest, a "true man" focused on loving and protecting his family. A glance at the headlines over nonrelated news stories in any of the newspapers that were routinely exploiting their marriage—headlines of crime, divorce, political scandal—would have shattered the lofty claims about white civilization in 1888. But the attributes Corabelle used to describe her husband were seen as elements of a "civilized" society. Even though, as Corabelle had learned, they also were attributes highly valued among Lakota and Dakota.

In the *Tribune*'s view, however, "civilizing" was a negative in the context of Sam and Corabelle. If she "civilized" her husband, Corabelle would threaten the very appeal the museum and the newspapers were counting on in the first place, that of an exotic "savage" from "wildwood" marrying the proper white maiden from Washington, DC. It was all business, after all. The couple's appeal to a mass audience depended upon mass ignorance fed by the mass media that had condemned the marriage. The *Tribune*'s editors apparently missed the obvious contradiction between the article's initial racist descriptions of a drunk Sam carrying guns and scalping tools versus it later describing him cutting his hair to defy stereotypes and quoting Corabelle about his honest, hard-working character.

The second telling point in the article, intended or not, came in the dime museum promoter's suggestion that any man in the crowd could end up falling in love with a Native woman. He did not say the same of white women and Native men. In 1888, the latter union was considered more taboo.

On the frontier, white men marrying Native women was a more acceptable arrangement. Was the *Tribune* adding to this bias by reporting that people laughed at the possibility, or did the mere suggestion of more interracial marriages subtly hold out Sam and Corabelle as trailblazers for more marriages between Natives and whites? In 1888, these were tricky questions.

The dime museum circuit may have been what Corabelle was referring to when she wrote in her late-in-life memoirs that she had a few regrets. To readers of the St. Paul *Daily Globe* and other newspapers across the country she and Sam had become bona fide dime museum "freaks."

Her family's opposition and her subsequent decision to go on tour fueled newspaper reports for days, indeed for several years. On May 10, 1888, three days after publishing its purported interview with Corabelle and Sam at the fancy hotel, the St. Paul paper headlined an article entitled, "Don't Like Cora's Actions," and subheaded it: "Relatives of Mrs. Chaska in Chicago Want Her to Quit the Dime Museum."

The *Daily Globe* referred to a letter Corabelle had received from her sister, Marian. The paper described it as a "scathing letter, the pith of which was if Mrs. Chaska were to debase the family name by appearing in a dime museum, they would leave the country." Since that threat did not appear in the letter in which Marian asked to see the marriage certificate, it's an indication there were multiple letters from her sister protesting the marriage.

The *Daily Globe* also reported that Corabelle had told her father it was no use suing Kohl & Middleton, for she and Sam indeed were the two people appearing in the show, not imposters.

"When the intelligence reached Washington that Chaska and his wife had arrived in St. Paul and were at the museum, Homer Fellows, Mrs. Chaska's father, wired to Kohl, Middleton & Co., saying that a fraud had been practiced and warning them that they would be prosecuted if they continued to advertise Corabelle Fellows as Mrs. Chaska," the *Daily Globe* story said. "This telegram was shown Mrs. Chaska at the museum today, and she immediately telegraphed her father, informing him that it was his daughter that was on exhibition, and telling him that it would be useless to interfere, as she proposed to take care of her husbands [sic] and her own affairs."

The article went on to say that Kohl & Middleton also had received a telegram from a man named Dewitt C. Haight, an employee of the Post Office in Chicago, and purportedly Corabelle's maternal uncle, "asking if something could not be done to have Chaska and his wife leave the museum."[10]

That story rings true. Cornelia's maiden name was Haight, and Dewitt Haight's death records list his vocation as postal clerk.[11]

The *Daily Globe* also reported that a "James Palmetteer" of Chicago, a "wealthy lumberman" and purportedly Corabelle's cousin, had written Kohl & Middleton asking "if the Indian and his wife would be released if the full amount were paid to the museum managers." Was this Palmetteer the mysterious cousin she described showing up at one of their Chicago appearances to verify her identity? The intrigue was promotional gold: What better way to hype a show than by providing proof that Corabelle's family so disapproved of her marriage that they threatened to sue, or to leave the country in shame, or to write the promoter a check to get her and Sam out of their contract?

The newspaper reported that Corabelle's "father, mother and sister had sent letter after letter to dissuade her from the match. So harsh were they in tenor that Miss Fellows finally refused to answer them."

Corabelle was again quoted alleging that her parents were so distraught after hearing she and Sam had married and had gone on the circuit that they would leave the country, and that she had defied their warnings "not to fall in love with an Indian."

The article said that "when she married Chaska, her mother wrote telling her that she would not disown her, but that their correspondence must cease. Then, when it became known that efforts were being made to induce her to go on exhibition, her mother wrote that if she took this last step her daughter (Marian) and herself would be obliged to leave the country. They could not remain in Washington with such a social disgrace hanging over them."

The story went on to quote Corabelle: "I understand father has decided to accept an offer to go to South America. I know just what I am doing. I knew my parents would not support me now. Influences have been brought to bear, so that I will probably lose my school. My husband has no money, but I love him, and I saw this chance to make enough money to buy a farm and make us independent, so I grasped this opportunity."[12]

There is no evidence her family followed through on the threat to leave the country in shame. Homer and Cornelia Fellows lived out their lives in Washington, DC.

Chapter 16

A Child, Vilified and Objectified

Claude Campbell, the first of three children born to Sam and Corabelle, entered the maelstrom of national attention in December of 1888, nine months and one week after the marriage of his parents. Two successive children, Wilber and Flora, followed over the next three years as the family tried to settle down on their farm near Chargers Camp. Of course, this simple birth near Christmas made news. The newspapers' birth announcements frequently came with the usual derision, often aiming it at the mixed race of the newborn.

Claude was born at Fort Bennett with the aid of a midwife. In her memoirs, Corabelle described several people helping her during the labor and in postnatal care, including an "uncle's wife," an "uncle's mother we called grandmother," and a "half-breed girl," all possible references to Sam's relatives. "They were all kind and good to us," Corabelle recalled.

The press wasn't. "Half Injun!" the *Daily Huronite* proclaimed in announcing the birth a day after Christmas 1888.[1]

The *Daily Globe* in St. Paul headlined a Christmas Day—a day to celebrate another birth—with: "One Little Injin," reporting that "Mrs. Chaska, nee Corabelle Fellows, the society belle from Washington who created a sensation by marrying the Indian chief Chaska, of Cheyenne agency, is now a mother." The story was widely reprinted in other newspapers.[2]

Blue Star does not go into depth about the five children Corabelle would eventually bear, three with Sam and two with a later spouse. Her handwritten memoirs make only general references to her children and grandchildren. The book that had ended in a father's embrace said nothing of the brutal attacks on the marriage and of the couple's first son.

The press's attacks on the parents continued. Claims that the young couple had "lived beyond their means," adding that even the farming implements bought from the dime museum dollars "are useless, as Chaska has no talents for farming, and prefers to take it easy as long as he possibly can."[3]

The terms "half-Injun" or "half-breed" were commonplace slurs. People of mixed race were frequently portrayed as being lower on the social ladder than an Indigenous person. Some newspapers expressed sympathy that Corabelle would be raising children of mixed blood. When Sam and Corabelle split a few years later, the Minneapolis *Tribune* reported that Corabelle had "duty to half-breeds that need her protection." The newspaper put mixed-race children in their own category of condemnation.

"The question of Indian civilization involves not the horrors of mixed procreation," the paper reported. "An Indian has to be dead to be decent, which fact has been known a long time—is not recent—and history shows, from the best observations, that half-breeds are worse than their tribal relations."[4]

Despite being subjected to such vulgarities, Sam and Corabelle took young Claude with them on their second dime museum tour for Kohl & Middleton in 1889. The baby became a featured attraction. Just by being born, Claude had expanded the exploitation from interracial marriage to the couple's racially mixed baby.

Advertisements of the couple's first tour, while Corabelle was pregnant, had focused solely on the marriage of "Chaska" and Corabelle as "the sensation of the day." One ad depicted Sam in Native dress, his arms reaching toward the heavens, as an angelic, winged Corabelle, gently descended toward Sam's arms. "Chaska receiving his spotless angel bride," the ad in the Chicago *Tribune* proclaimed. They were on display twelve hours a day. People with a dime could see them from 10 a.m. to 10 p.m., in a "fashionable social event."[5]

In Minneapolis, the Sam-Corabelle marriage also was illustrated with similarly overblown contrasts between two cultures. Sam had been portrayed as shirtless, in Native dress, another blatant misrepresentation of a man who had been raised by an Episcopalian minister and educated in eastern boarding schools. He was just one curiosity of many. A St. Paul *Daily Globe* advertisement that May of 1888 also promised appearances by "Alice, the 750 pounds of African womanhood," a "bird charmer," and "hosts of other novelties."[6]

But the following year, the child, Claude, was the novelty. "Indian Chaska" and his "White Wife" were advertised in St. Paul as appearing "with their papoose baby!" Young Claude would be competing for attention with "the devil fish" and "Morrell the Whittler." Kohl & Middleton advertised young Claude in a limerick about Sam and Corabelle that portrayed Sam as lazy and Corabelle as a victim condemned to a lifetime of parenting a half-breed child.

"Is marriage a failure, or what?," the advertisement began.

"Just come and see what poor Corabelle got.

"With her babe on her bustle

"Sweet Cora must hustle

"For Chaska says work he will not."[7]

Sam and Corabelle and the new baby became closer-to-home attractions. In June of 1889, they were celebrity invites to a "fireman's tournament" in Yankton, South Dakota, which would feature a fire-fighting competition between volunteer departments from "Huron, Parker, Sioux Falls, Scotland, Aberdeen, Kimball, Pierre, DeSmet, Miller, Madison and other towns." A brand-new arena had been constructed for the competition between which departments could aim their hoses most accurately.

"Mrs. Chaska, nee Cora Belle (sic) Fellows, with her husband and papoose, will be one of the features of the tournament," a Huron newspaper reported. They will bring Claude, the paper said, "to please the firemen."[8]

The pressure on the marriage mounted. By the next year, when a second son joined the family, reports began appearing that Sam and Corabelle's relationship was splintering in the aftermath of the dime-museum tours, Buffalo Bill's Wild West show, and the relentlessly negative press. The story lines portrayed Sam as either the villain or a mute accessory to the socialite bride who may have been in it all for the money. By the early 1890s, widespread press reports said that Sam had left Cora and

St. Paul *Daily Globe*
COURTESY OF NEWSPAPERS.COM

had begun a relationship with a Dakota woman from Santee. Corabelle was the victim, some decided, especially so because she was the mother of mixed-race children.

"A moral this tale bears to girls who through folly or strange love of romance imagine it jolly to cast their sad lot with the sons of the wild-wood, and seek a divorce from the friends of their childhood," one newspaper reported. "The romance is short, as in this case related, for Cora now knows she was sadly mis-mated, and has with the rest, the unhappy reflection of duty to half-breeds that need her attention.

"I weep for poor Cora and her two papooses," the story continued. "I feel indignation that Chaska should leave her and skip with another and basely deceive her, and think the law should receive a few patches to shut off these semi-barbarian matches."[9]

Chapter 17

Pulled into Politics

The year Sam and Corabelle married was an unsettled, contentious, suspicious, and exploitative time in America, and their fame dragged them into the maelstrom.

Although the 1876 defeat of Custer was a demarcation line that accelerated the closing of the frontier, the rest of the nineteenth century was filled with roiling undercurrents of challenges yet to come, from women's suffrage to struggles for racial equality, even the Temperance Movement.

The year 1888 had blown in with that monstrous blizzard that killed so many schoolchildren in Dakota Territory. Then just days before Corabelle and Sam's wedding, a March blizzard had slammed the eastern seaboard from Maine to Virginia, killing more than four hundred people and causing widespread property damage. Lynchings frequently grabbed headlines. The beleaguered Democratic President Grover Cleveland, unpopular for taking stands against Civil War pensions and embroiled in debate over immigration policy, lost his bid for a second term.

A potent white nationalism aimed at specific groups had infused American politics. Both political party platforms called for banning Chinese workers, and the Republicans' platform criticized the Democrats for balking on admitting South Dakota as a state. The previous year's passage of the controversial Dawes Act only increased the pressure to open Indian territory to whites and for statehood. The Republicans in their platform also prominently reaffirmed the Homestead Act "for American citizens and settlers—not aliens, which the Republican Party established in 1862 against the persistent opposition of the Democrats in Congress, and which has brought our great Western domain into such magnificent development."

There was no mention, either, in the Republican platform of how more than 204,000 Indigenous people scattered over 135 million acres of land on 171 reservations across the United States and its territories when Cleveland took office fit into that "magnificent development."[1]

After Cleveland signed the Dawes Act on February 8, 1887, immense pressure was being brought on Native people to get them to enroll with the Office of Indian Affairs, later renamed the Bureau of Indian Affairs. When enrolled, those deemed qualified received an allotment of land, usually 80 or 160 acres, and only those who did were eventually eligible for American citizenship. Surplus land would then be sold to benefit the tribes, but those sales often came at very low prices.[2]

Except for the abrogation of treaties, the Dawes Act did more to fracture and marginalize American Indians, especially the Great Sioux Nation, than any other government policy. Columbia University historian Henry F. Graff later called it "a disastrous policy that robbed Native Americans of much of their land and did little to improve their way of life." Over the following decades, millions of acres of land allotted to individual Indians in the Great Plains would be lost through fraud or because the allotments were not large enough to support a farm in a semi-arid region more suited for expansive ranch pasturelands than narrow farm cornrows.[3] Average annual rainfall on the Cheyenne River Reservation is roughly five inches less than the more lush river valleys of the eastern Dakotas. Over the four decades that followed the signing, two-thirds of the 135 million acres held by tribes nationally would be acquired—either legally or by fraud—by white landowners.[4]

Some newspapers around the country began accusing Corabelle of marrying Sam as a ruse to push recalcitrant Sioux leaders to sign up for land allotments granted under the Dawes Act.

The St. Paul *Daily Globe* reported that while "Chaska" was "drawing rations" at the agency, Corabelle snuck off with "one of her old lovers" and let slip her intentions to this mysterious man. She supposedly told him that "her mission at Cheyenne agency was to use her influence with the Indians toward securing signatures for the commission."[5]

The year Corabelle and Sam were married, a commission, led by Richard Henry Pratt, the founder of the Carlisle Indian School and notably the first man known to have used the word *racism* in 1902 to express his disgust at segregation,[6] met with some Dakota Territory Sioux tribes to try to sell the deal, but not with residents of the Cheyenne River, Pine Ridge, and Rosebud agencies, believing it to be futile because of staunch opposition there.[7]

A second commission in 1889 eventually pressured enough men to sign in order for the federal government to begin the breakup of the Great Sioux Reservation. The government agents sent to seal the act, which included the familiar face of Army Gen. George Crook, heard first-hand the depth of the opposition when they met with tribal members at the Cheyenne River Agency in July of 1889.

The Lakota leader White Swan, who had been part of the Native delegation that met with the Pratt Commission the previous year in an October trip to Washington, DC, testified that he had unsuccessfully tried for twenty-one years to be a farmer on the semi-arid prairie. "Sometimes for one year or two years or three years in succession we raise nothing," he said. "We can't raise it."[8]

Yet despite doubts like Whites Swan's, the hype merchants of western settlement were making fantastical meteorological claims to push more rapid settlement of the plains. A Nebraska writer and land speculator named Charles Wilber had proclaimed in 1881 that "rain follows the plow," promising that as settlers moved west and broke up the prairie with deep plowing, that the climate would adapt to civilization and more ample rains would follow. The "Great American Desert" would soon enough turn into a lush garden of crops—if the sod could be simultaneously busted from Texas to Canada.

"Suppose an army of frontier farmers 50 miles, in width, from Manitoba to Texas, could acting in concert, turn over the prairie sod, and after deep plowing and receiving the rain and moisture, present a new surface of green growing crops instead of dry, hard-baked earth covered with sparse buffalo grass," Wilber wrote in *The Great Valleys and Prairies of Nebraska and the Northwest*. "No one can question or doubt the inevitable effect of this cooling condensing surface upon the moisture in the atmosphere at it moves over by the Western winds. A reduction of temperature must at once occur, accompanied by the usual phenomena of showers. The chief agency in this transformation is agriculture. To be more concise: Rain follows the plow."[9]

Never mind that such claims were preposterous, or that various government policies since then (including the construction of massive dams on the Missouri River in the mid-twentieth century) have not turned the entire Great Plains into the lush green gardens of Wilber's dreams. Boosterism on that delusional scale, led by railroads and land speculators, exerted immense pressure to open Sioux land ostensibly protected by treaty. The military was having trouble holding off white settlers from taking Native land in the new states of South and North Dakota, which had been granted statehood in November of 1889.

"We know the anxiety of the people of South Dakota for the early opening of the ceded territory, and we would be glad to advance their wishes in all proper ways, yet the duty of the Government lies in the direction of the protection of the Indians in the full enjoyment of every right accorded to them in the new law," the three commissioners reported.[10]

Even though she had made no known public or private declarations on the Dawes Act, Corabelle was reported to have visited the Indian Affairs office in Washington, DC, and convinced her husband to sign and claim an allotment. The St. Paul *Daily Globe* further alleged that Corabelle had lobbied Sioux leaders to do the same.

"Chaska would surely sign, and, since she has just returned from Washington and learned the full merits at the Indian department, and the Indian Rights association, she felt that it was in the Indians' interest to sign," the paper reported, referring to Sam and Corabelle's visit to the Indian Affairs office. "Should they refuse, it was very probable that a repetition of the Black Hills treaty might follow, where the whites rushed in and made a treaty to suit themselves."

The article claimed that Corabelle had told the mysterious "ex-lover" that she had talked with Hump, Crow Eagle, Charger, and other Sioux leaders, and that "all are satisfied with the Dawes bill, and unless something happens within the next two days these Indians will sign without parley."[11]

Yet nowhere in *Blue Star* or in her handwritten memoirs does Corabelle come across as remotely that political. And, as we shall later discover, her husband would resist pressure to take sides on one of the biggest moments of the Dakota frontier: Support for Sitting Bull.

Chapter 18

A Three-Pronged Assault on the Power Order

Why did newspapers so sensationalize the marriage between this rebellious young woman and quiet Native man? In retrospect three things combined to create the conditions that turned love into a national sensation.

First, prior to their marriage, Sam and Corabelle were unknown, mere blank canvases upon which to lay all the social, racial, and cultural conflicts of the age. Second, her family vehemently disapproved, privately and publicly, providing juicy grist for headline-seeking yellow pressers for which fealty to fact wasn't a priority. And finally, the Fellows-Campbell marriage was an assault on the accepted power order of race, gender, and class in the late nineteenth century. Ridiculing and sensationalizing them was a way of defending that accepted order. The marriage was a threat, especially when Native men married white women.

As the historian Margaret D. Jacobs put it: "White men would lose their patriarchal power over a white woman who married an Indian, and, in the process, Indian men would gain a power and a prerogative that many white men believed should be theirs alone."[1]

Although interracial marriage was illegal in many states in 1888, and would be until the 1960s in some, marriage between whites and Indigenous people was not banned in Dakota Territory.

The anti-miscegenation laws of the era, like in many of the more than forty states that eventually passed them, were mainly aimed at preventing marriage between Blacks and whites. Yet the reaction to individual marriages between Natives and whites were not always the same. Fame and connections had much to do with it.

Even while Sam and Corabelle were being scorched in the press, famous white women were marrying famous Native men without any public scorn. Reporting on the Fellows-Campbell nuptials, the Cincinnati *Enquirer* pointed out that a Miss Ida Belle Richards, whose lineage traced directly to the Mayflower, and who was "said to be a distant cousin of the late Ex-President [Chester A.] Arthur, a beautiful brunette of St. Louis, was married not long since to Dr. Eliphalet Nott Wright, a full-blooded Choctaw, son of an Ex-Governor of the Choctaw Nation."

It noted that other famous Native people had also married white spouses, including Ely Parker, a top Civil War aide to Ulysses S. Grant and a Seneca Indian, who served as commissioner of Indian Affairs when Grant was president. "Instead of being exterminated," the paper reported, "it may be better for the red man to be assimilated by intermarriage to the whites."[2]

But even if marriages between whites and Natives were legally permissible, even despite the celebrity intermarriages, many whites looked harshly on the practice. The opposition dated back to Colonial laws banning interracial marriages in the seventeenth century. The taboos were complex. Historian John M. Coward observed that in newspapers and in literature, Indigenous people were often simultaneously identified as both "savage" and "romantic," and both views conspired to identify Natives as "an enemy of the new American civilization."[3]

"In the colonial era in American history there was widespread opposition to marriage between white women and Native American men," the historian Jacobs observed.[4] Early American newspapers often blared scandalous headlines of white women marrying Indigenous men.[5]

While Sam and Corabelle's marriage was celebrated and blessed by the Native people in her home community of Swift Bird, the take of their time in the press and within Corabelle's family was swift, brutal, and unforgiving. The couple may not have violated the law, but they had flaunted unwritten race and gender codes of the late nineteenth century. Newspapers and literature were imbued with the scare scenario of "damsel-in-distress"; a white woman's vulnerability to being captured by "wild" Native men drove many story and plot lines in the dime novels and, later, movies depicting the American West.

Or, as the historian Brian Dippie put it in Jacobs's book, "The white woman would ordinarily be the unwilling victim in a union consummated through force—that is, as the captive ravished by her Indian captor, her body defiled, her spirit still pure."[6]

Sam Campbell's father, a mixed-race man, had married a Native woman. But Antoine Joseph Campbell's union with Sam's mother had not been seen nearly as scandalous as how their son's marriage to a white woman was received a half century later. Bluntly put, license was given to the intrepid frontier scouts, fur traders, and explorers to "take" a Native wife. It was lonely on the frontier, the rationale went, and a man had understandable desires.

"In contrast, white American attitudes toward white men who took Indian concubines or wives in the period before the Civil War were much more lenient," the historian Jacobs wrote. "The attitude toward such men was a sense of mild disapproval and sympathetic understanding; since these men lived in remote frontier outposts where there were few white women, they simply had to take Indian women as last resorts. According to [historian] Richard Slotkin, white Americans gradually transformed the white frontiersman who consorted with Indian women into a 'hero rather than a racial traitor.' Because these frontiersmen were so integral to English colonization of the North American continent eventually their liaisons with Indian women were excused and even largely ignored."

Marriages between white women and Native men were seen as more of a threat to whites' presumed racial superiority. Jacobs observed that "by the 1820s a notion had emerged that there was an essential biological difference between Indians and whites, and it made many whites recoil in disgust and dismay from such marriages. A woman who preferred a 'savage' over one of her own 'blood' upset the supposedly natural racial order, that the 'civilized' white conqueror maintained superiority over the 'savage red-skinned Indian.'"[7]

Jacobs also hypothesized that a white woman seen as subservient to a Native man was too much for late nineteenth century whites to accept.

"Interracial relationships between white women and Indian men also threatened predominant nineteenth-century American views of gender relations. America still operated under the notion of the femme couvert; when a woman married, she became entirely 'covered' by her husband. Any property she brought to the marriage as well as her legal identity became subsumed under her mate's."[8]

Adding more context to the disparities between races and sexes in 1888, Corabelle and Sam were married thirty-two years before women could vote, and thirty-six years before Indigenous Americans were given blanket citizenship. In a pure political sense, neither was permitted full participation in American democracy.

Then, there was the element of the children. If such marriages broke up, societal norms usually meant the children would remain with the mother. A white woman with children of mixed-race status presented a new target for derision and disapproval, and those biases would soon enough be exposed in the coverage of the eventual breakup between Sam and Corabelle.

Stigmas of being different or lesser placed on children of Black and white parents had traumatized entire generations in the South; now that same harsh stigma was being placed on children of mixed marriages between Natives and whites on the western frontier.

"The status of any children born to such interracial couples also troubled white Americans," Jacobs wrote. "As with the children of white masters and their black slave women, it was assumed that the children of white men and Indian women were Indian. But what of the children of white women and Indian men?" These children, Jacobs wrote, "made a mockery of racial categories, revealing their instability and impermanence."[9]

But class and familial reactions also played a part. As Ely Parker's marriage to a white woman illustrated, not all marriages between Native men and white women were treated the way Sam and Corabelle's was. In fact, some were celebrated.

In an 1891 dispatch from Washington, DC, about alleged troubles between Sam and Corabelle, the San Francisco *Examiner*, apparently without irony, closed out its article noting that just the previous week a prominent Dakota Sioux doctor, Charles Eastman, had married the famous white author and activist Elaine Goodale at the Church of the Ascension, an Episcopal Church at Fifth Avenue and Tenth Street in New York City. This is the same Elaine Goodale we first met waxing philosophic over the raw beauty of the Plains and the Charles Eastman who had been mentioned as one of the stars of an eastern boarding education in the *Word Carrier*.

"Mrs. Eastman, like Mrs. Campbell, is to continue her work among the Sioux Indians," the paper reported. "She will be with her husband at Pine Ridge Agency, where the Doctor holds the position of governmental medical inspector."[10]

The Goodale-Eastman wedding, in contrast to Sam and Corabelle's, was attended by high-society New Yorkers, and it was treated far more gently in the press than the Fellows-Campbell union had been scarcely three years earlier. An estimated two hundred newspapers covered the Eastman-Goodale wedding. The union was described as "poetry wedded to science."[11]

The St. Paul *Daily Globe*, brutal in its coverage of the Fellows-Campbell marriage, stressed Eastman's education at Dartmouth and Boston College, and called Goodale "a woman of attractive person and highly cultivated mind."[12]

Elaine Goodale's hometown newspaper, the *Berkshire County Eagle*, described a "wedding of exceptional interest," going into detail describing the support of the Goodale family. The bride was escorted down the aisle by her father, Henry Sterling Goodale, followed by her bridesmaid sisters, Dora and Rose. The *Eagle* predicted that Eastman-Goodale would be a "a center of civilizing influence for the Sioux" at Pine Ridge.[13]

By contrast, Corabelle's family disowned her, sent her disapproving letters, and she and Sam were ridiculed in the press as freaks and poseurs. In Elaine Goodale Eastman's memoirs, written the same decade as Corabelle's, Goodale Eastman said she had not believed marrying a Native man would present any serious problems. Having lived six years with the Dakota and Lakota, she had forged many interracial friendships, she had lobbied politicians and bureaucrats on behalf of her Native friends, and she had traveled thousands of miles helping to set up and inspect schools for Native children.

"Though I had not consciously considered marriage with a Dakota, I had closely observed several such marriages which appeared successful," she wrote. "The idea certainly did not repel me in any way."[14]

That is an interesting take. Although she did not mention the Fellows-Campbell marriage, it is very difficult to believe Goodale Eastman was not aware of the sensational press coverage that Sam and Corabelle had endured over the previous three years. Tolerance from the masses and the newspapers could not have advanced that far in such a short time. But again, there were significant differences between the two marriages reflective of class and fame in the 1890s. Fame and familiarity in the press were in the Goodale-Eastman favor. So were political connections.

Goodale and Eastman were both well known before they met in 1890. If not comfortable with their fame, they were at least practiced in how to maneuver through its advantages and around its traps. Prior to coming to Dakota Territory, Goodale had become famous as an author of children's books and, like Corabelle, had gone west to teach Sioux children. Like Corabelle, Goodale had become fluent in Sioux languages and often accompanied Native families on long trips. But Goodale was not only a well-known author prior to arriving in Dakota Territory, she was also known and respected in the government's Indian policy bureaucracy. She had written extensively for eastern newspapers on issues related to the Lakota and Dakota.

Her husband, Charles Eastman, like Sam, was a Santee Dakota and had been born in Redwood, Minnesota, three years before Corabelle. His mother had died giving birth, and he was raised, until about fifteen, by his maternal grandmother. He was a Dartmouth University graduate with a medical degree from Boston University. He was prominent in his medical practice at Pine Ridge before their marriage, and his exploits were known to eastern audiences. Goodale said her love for Eastman became complete after she learned he had stayed up all night with a sick Lakota child. Eastman had also been among the first to rush to the site of Wounded Knee to search for any wounded who had been overlooked.[15]

"The fact that the marriage brought together Eastman, who was rapidly becoming the most celebrated educated American Indian in the United States, and Goodale, a non-Indian recognized as an important reformer in Indian education, contributed to the significance of the event," wrote Theodore D. Sargent and Raymond Wilson.[16]

"The fascination with them came not only from a rare union of a white woman and a Native American man; not only because they both achieved early fame—she, as a poet and he, as a Sioux educated in Euro-American universities; and not only because the pair were writers, public speakers and active in the Indian reform movements of the late nineteenth and early twentieth centuries," the author Julie Dobrow observed. "The fascination with the Eastmans came about also because they were part of a larger American story of change."[17]

Sam and Corabelle also represented change, but not of the accepted kind, and not by the right people. Corabelle's only attachment to the eastern establishment was through a social-climbing mother who had disowned her for marrying a Native man. Sam, who aspired to a quiet life raising crops and cattle, had had no opportunity to define himself before his marriage to Corabelle. Like Eastman, he had received education in the east, but he was not known outside a relatively small circle prior to meeting his wife.

By attacking Corabelle's marriage and making her both transgressor and victim, by focusing on the horror her family supposedly felt, the press also was assaulting government policy aimed, eventually, at equality through assimilation.

"By mocking their marriage, the press offered a critique of assimilation policy as a whole," the scholar Cathleen Cahill has observed.

"The notion that young, idealistic white women could purge Native men of their savagery, the articles implied, was laughable. While public reactions to these marriages were not nearly as vicious and murderous as contemporary reactions to even the merest rumor of a relationship between a black man and white woman in the American South, the press clearly sought to discourage these racial crossings through ridicule.

"The press also attacked Samuel Campbell's efforts to live up to assimilation's manly ideals as provider for his family. Try as he might, he could not escape public emphasis on his race despite his 'civilized' behavior."

As Cahill astutely pointed out, newspaper articles depicting the couple buying equipment and other goods "essential for a middle-class household" also cast the marriage in a negative racial caste. "To the press, an Indian buying these things was striving for a respectability that he could never achieve."

Besides his race, Sam's very manhood was under attack. "In these reports the press interpreted Campbell's behavior through a racialized lens which denied that Native men could legitimately make good economic decisions or that Campbell could support his wife in a manly fashion," Cahill wrote.[18]

There was another important difference between why the press treated the Eastman-Goodale marriage and the Campbell-Fellows union so radically differently.

Goodale and Eastman had become familiar with the newspaper reporters who routinely traversed Dakota Territory. In the late 1880s, fresh waves of correspondents flooded into the Dakotas and other Native lands to cover the Ghost Dance movement. Many were at Pine Ridge, where Goodale and Eastman lived, in the days before Wounded Knee.

Goodale Eastman adamantly maintained in her memoirs that there was little threat of violence and anti-government activity from the Ghost Dance followers themselves. But she also acknowledged that the heightened press attention and military buildup in the territory had fed the tensions, although she defended her reporter friends, who she said were under pressure to produce frontier copy for big-city editors.

"Swarms of 'war correspondents' from New York, Chicago, and western cities could hardly be blamed for inventing sensational stories in default of news," Goodale Eastman wrote in her memoirs. "Yet their highly colored dispatches increased alarm and deepened prejudice against the Sioux. Army officers frankly admitted that 'the army doesn't know what it is here for' and even asserted that 'these Indians don't deserve punishment,' but we heard that the men were bored with inaction and spoiling for a fight."[19]

Goodale and Eastman became engaged days before the massacre at Wounded Knee. They heard the repeat of Hotchkiss artillery guns booming eighteen miles away while filling bags of Christmas treats for children at Pine Ridge. Their accounts published in newspapers or made to government officials in ensuing months would provide powerful counternarratives to the official US military reports that initially depicted the massacre as a legitimate military victory. Wounded Knee's aftermath hung heavily over the Eastman-Goodale wedding six months later.

In one dispatch to New York newspapers, Goodale claimed that while a single shot from a follower of Spotted Tail's (also known as Big Foot) encamped at Wounded Knee lit the tinderbox, the Lakota leader and his followers "did not deliberately plan a resistance." Goodale reported that soldiers fired on largely unarmed men, women, and children, and maintained that many of approximately sixty soldiers killed or wounded were shot by other soldiers amid the confusion and chaos. Meanwhile, Eastman was among the first to arrive on the site to administer medical aid, and his descriptions of witnessing dead women as far as two miles away from the encampment supported claims that soldiers had pursued noncombatants for long distances through the cold and snow before killing them.

"The irresponsible action of one hot-headed youth should not be the signal for a general and indiscriminate slaughter of the unarmed and the helpless," Goodale Eastman wrote.[20]

So, in the end, Goodale and Eastman were frontier actors on their own terms. Sam Campbell and Corabelle Fellows Campbell never had that chance, even though Corabelle had thought that by going on tour, they could finally get the story of their love and life to the public. That may be one of the reasons why what the press described as "freak show" participants were described only as "stereopticon" lecturers in *Blue Star*. Their sordid treatment was too much for a 1939 audience.

Like the Fellows-Campbell marriage, the Goodale-Eastman marriage also eventually broke up. Unlike Sam and Corabelle, who made a sizeable amount of money touring, the Eastmans struggled with meager salaries and the cost of raising five children over their first decade of marriage at Pine Ridge, then later in St. Paul. Eventually, capitalizing on the fame they had acquired before and after their marriage, they moved to Massachusetts, where "Charles authored seven books and became a popular and successful public lecturer," Sargent and Wilson wrote. "Elaine, in addition to her homemaking and child-rearing duties, handled all of the editorial and scheduling details for Charles' career and somehow managed to write three books of her own during this period."[21]

In her memoirs, Goodale Eastman said she had reluctantly accepted the role of a woman in an interracial marriage under late nineteenth-century conventions. Her consternation reflected Corabelle's observation about Native women's roles in traditional Dakota and Lakota society as well as the overall struggle for suffrage and equal rights for women in general.

"I won't say that the adjustment was easy or that I was never lonely, restless, and haunted by a secret sense of frustration," Goodale Eastman wrote. "Every woman who has surrendered a congenial task and financial independence will understand."[22]

Chapter 19

A Tragedy of Shakespearean Proportions

For years after their marriage, throughout their two summers on tour and beyond, Sam and Corabelle were hounded as newspapers kept percolating new developments or feigned outrages over their marriage. From the Alabama *Enquirer* to the *Cain City* (Kansas) *Razzooper*, from the Manitoba *Weekly Free Press* in Canada to the papers in all of America's big coastal cities, any rumor, fact, or speculation made it into print. The lengths to which some so-called journalists stretched the truth or speculated would have been comical if it wasn't so dehumanizing and irresponsible.

As the marriage began fracturing, Sam's character and reputation—actually, his very humanity—took a battering. The *Daily Huronite* in Huron, South Dakota, described him as a "worthless thieving Santee without any white blood in his veins, and not the Indian missionary which recent reports have announced."[1] (Where those reports of Sam as a missionary came from are unclear.)

Some declared that the marriage was a sham because Corabelle, who had just turned twenty-seven, was actually decades older than Sam, who was twenty-one. "As it becomes generally known that Mrs. Chaska, nee Fellows, was a maiden forty-five years of age, and her husband is a young, untutored savage, popular pity will be transferred from the bride to the groom, and his taste, instead of hers, will be criticized," the Galveston *Daily News* in Texas proclaimed.[2]

A few newspapers ostensibly were thrilled with the marriage, or at least with its potential for public spectacle and as a museum draw. The

Bismarck *Daily Tribune* reported on the initial St. Paul Kohl & Middleton appearance with a headline: "The Museum Thronged to See Mrs. Chaska and 'Sam-u-el.'"

> *The dime museum where Mr. and Mrs. Campbell (Chaska) began to receive the public was thronged this afternoon. Mrs. Campbell don't [sic] like the Indian name. She calls him 'Sam-u-el.' Chaska is 6 feet 8 inches tall and as straight as an arrow. He is a rather good looking fellow when he talks but usually he is sullen. He can speak excellent English if he will, having spent two years in the Lincoln Institute in Philadelphia. He has rather fine features, but small pox has left its mark upon his face and he has the high cheek bone and straight black hair of the Indian. He is 23 years old. Mrs. Campbell is a mite of humanity being just 5 feet 1 inch in height. She is rather slender, not pretty until she begins to talk and then she is bright and interesting.*[3]

Six feet eight? Sam was growing into giant stature in the newspapers. Just like Kohl & Middleton's world's tallest woman. What could they possibly think of next? Sam wrestling bears? Declaring him the strongest man on earth?

Some papers described the new couple as characters out of Shakespeare. A Montana newspaper called Sam a "dark skinned Othello" and a "very worthless redskin, without either ability or learning." Corabelle was "his pale-faced Desdemona." Shakespeare's tale of interracial love, lies, and loss in ancient Venice had come to the Wild West, at least according to that newspaper.[4]

Was the newspaper predicting that the marriage would not only collapse, but that Corabelle would eventually kill her husband? The literary corollary had apparently been too juicy to ignore. Shakespeare's Othello was about a Moorish war hero who married the Venetian beauty Desdemona against the wishes of her father, a prominent politician. In the end, Othello kills Desdemona after being told lies about her adultery. The Yellowstone *Journal* seemed to be predicting the homicidal end of a marriage right as it began.

The same paper also claimed that "Chaska hung about the home of Rev. Pay Pay, an Indian preacher, till he, the preacher, discarded him." It also said that Corabelle, who knew that the name "Chaska" was a fraud made up by a reporter, had given Sam a gold ring at their wedding ceremony engraved, "Cora to Chaska." The account of the Rev. Pay Pay disassociating from Sam was almost certainly false on top of its crude depiction of a "discarded human being." Less than a decade later Sam would name a son from another relationship George Pay Pay Campbell.[5]

The paper cited as its source a "post trader" named J. C. Robb, of Fort Bennett, who was an "invited guest at the reception given in honor of the contracting parties." Even if this trader Robb did indeed attend the wedding, and there is no known evidence he did, he either participated in the lie about "Chaska" or was used by the paper as a dupe to advance the overall fraud of the young couple embracing the name the newspapers had given Samuel Campbell.

Once Corabelle and Sam returned from the dime museum circuit that first summer, the coverage narrative pivoted from forbidden love on display to a marriage doomed to fail, to a couple struggling to handle its fame and wealth.

In a "special to the *Globe*" story purported to be from Fort Bennett and the Cheyenne River Agency, the St. Paul *Daily Globe* headlined its article "Among the Tawnies." A subhead read: "The Freaks Return from Their Flush and Drive a Festive Rig." Another subhead, referring to the Dawes Act, predicted that "Chaska Will Sign and Draw Rations as Fluently as of Yore."

The article, in an edition that also reported the lynching of a horse thief in the Turtle Mountains of Dakota Territory, began: "Cheyenne agency is the home of Mrs. Chaska, nee Corabelle Fellows, who threw her blue-blooded Washington relatives into convulsions by marrying the Sioux Indian. Mr. and Mrs. Chaska have returned home from their starring engagement as freaks, and among them have an excellent bank account on which she draws like a bloated bondholder. Her husband since doing Washington, comes back a perfect dude. He has donned a black suit and looks quite gallant. The two are very loving, and an elegant buggy purchased in the East and drawn by two spanking horses attracts great attention as they dash up and down the agency thoroughfares."[6]

The idea of a "thoroughfare" anywhere within many miles of Fort Bennett or the Cheyenne River Agency would certainly have been laughable to anyone familiar with those locales. It certainly would have been to a young couple who a few months earlier were late to their own wedding because they had gotten stuck in the prairie gumbo.

The newspapers' criticism shifted evermore toward Corabelle's alleged profligate spending, of which there was little evidence. In her memoirs, Corabelle comes across just the opposite, describing herself by that time as an adherent of the make-use-of-everything ethos of Native culture, and writing of her desire to live a quiet life on a Dakota farm.

The *New York Times*, in a story datelined out of St. Paul, declared that the couple, flush with their $500-a-week salary on the dime museum circuit, had spent beyond their means. The reporter claimed to have based his information on an interview with "Manager McFadden" of the dime museum that had hosted them in the summer of 1888. It alleged that the museum, besides paying Sam and Corabelle a salary, had also bought a farm on which Sam and Corabelle were living, a claim that appears nowhere in Corabelle's memoirs.

"Chaska and His Bride Wasting the Money They Earned on the Museum," blared the headline.

Quoting McFadden, the paper reported: "Oh, they are back on their farm in Swift Bird's camp. You remember we had to buy the farm and then we made them a present of it. But they didn't stock it as intended with the salary they got. We paid them $500 a week and expenses, and as they were engaged for 10 weeks they got a tidy little sum. After the second week she bought herself some diamond earrings and paid $600 for them. This contented the bride for awhile, but in Chicago she wanted some dresses and they were the best she could buy. She bought an outfit, including a sealskin sacque, although it was midsummer, that cost her $1,200."

But the *Times* didn't stop there. The article continued, "Then Mrs. Chaska began to fit out Sammy. She went to a swell tailor and had three suits of clothes made for him, one of which is a full dress suit. Then she bought him a gold watch and chain. The watch was a horse timer. Even then she was not satisfied, and she further adorned her redskin with a huge diamond ring and stud. Then the heart of Cora seemed happy, but her purse was empty. I don't believe they had $500 when they got back home. What in the world they will do with all their diamonds and finery on the reservation is more than I can imagine."[7]

Not to be outdone, the *Daily Huronite* ran a poem entitled "Poetic War-whoop." It read, in part:

So the preacher he united
Them in holy matrimony
Chaska straightaway then endowed her
With the sum of his possessions
Which they were a pair of mocc'sins
And a chaw of plug tobacco
Then they hied to the east-land
With a contract in his pocket,
Contract fat for him and Cora,
In dime museum to exhibit.
We will win the filthy lucre
Filthy lucre of the jays
Come to see us in the museum
When we've finished we will toodly
Toodly back to far Dakota,
And upon the reservation
We will open up a ranch where
Braves can purchase for a dollar
All the whiskey they can swallow.[8]

The Detroit *Free Press* reported that after returning from that first tour Sam and Corabelle's money was all gone—something the paper said should not be a surprise.

"It is just as difficult a matter to change the nature of a woman as it is to change the skin of an Ethiop," the paper wrote. "Take the case of

Miss Cora Fellows, the woman who married the half-breed Sioux Indian Chaska."

Confronted with "practical life" after marriage, the *Free Press* reported, Corabelle and Sam soon realized that "practical life demands money." Hence, the dime museum circuit. The paper declared: "Here is where the remark about the nature of a woman—not all women, because that would be unjust, but some women—comes in."

It then went on to list alleged purchases Corabelle had made before running out of money and returning to Dakota Territory. "The question is what will Mr. and Mrs. Chaska do there with their diamonds and seal skin cloaks and full-dress suits?"[9]

Newspapers competed to tell tales of Corabelle's alleged spending. The racism and sexism used to describe it were astounding. "One may readily understand Mrs. C.'s vanity, as it was the first time she had had an opportunity of gratifying it, but she might have at least spared poor Chaska from the adoption of a rig which will make him the sport of the bucks and is not adapted to the exigencies of Indian farming. The money might better have been saved. It would have gone a long way towards accumulation of a stock of ponies and firewater."[10]

There is no surviving evidence of any of these gaudy purchases, or any of these traits ascribed to the young couple. Corabelle's handwritten memoirs seldom mentioned material things she may have accumulated except for a few items. She held especially precious a homemade doll given to her during her mission/teaching years. She passed it onto her grandchildren, and it stayed in family possession into the twenty-first century. In her handwritten memoirs, Corabelle almost always focused on relationships and on her wonder at how Native people made do, had adapted, and had appreciated simple gifts and the practical things they made for themselves.

In retrospect, the press treatment of the Campbell-Fellows marriage stands out as an early episode of the "yellow journalism" that inflamed American newspapers in the late nineteenth and early twentieth centuries. Its sensationalist, jingoistic tones, its tendency to create enemies where they may not have existed, a decade later drummed up support for America's entry into the Spanish-American War of 1898.

"Led by newspaper owners William Randolph Hearst and Joseph Pulitzer, journalism of the 1890s used melodrama, romance, and hyperbole to sell millions of newspapers—a style that became known as yellow journalism," a writer for PBS explained.

Hearst was publisher of the *New York Journal*, Pulitzer of the *New York World*. The "yellow journalism" term came from a popular comic printed in Pulitzer's *World* called Hogan's Alley. The fictional main character was an Irish-American street urchin named Mickey Dugan who dressed in yellow and lived and roamed in the tenements that were home to the thousands of first- and second-generation Americans congregating in the boroughs of New York. A rival editor, appalled at the sensationalism of the Hearst and Pulitzer papers, labeled it "yellow journalism" after the cartoon.[11]

William Randolph Hearst was the only son of George Hearst, who himself had a Dakota Territory connection simultaneous with Corabelle's time there. George Hearst's Homestake Gold Mine in the Black Hills town of Lead, a wild west town adjacent to the famed Deadwood, was churning out tons of gold by the time Corabelle arrived in Dakota Territory.

Newspapers were also adding color to the daily paper product to hype the sensationalism, but the yellow journalism view of the world was also starkly black-and-white, a world of outsized heroes and villains, with little room in between. The coverage of the Campbell-Fellows marriage was one of the first examples of its national reach. Splashed all over the country, rarely was Corabelle and Sam's marriage described as love between two people. Articles rarely pondered the effect on two people just trying to make love work in a hostile world. Their marriage was thrust on the public as a melodrama of race and class and the supposed superiority of white civilization.

Newspapers kept reaching for the literature of fable and allegory to describe the couple. Typical was that *Daily Globe* article of September 15, 1888, which climaxed with this purported conversation between Corabelle and what it described as an "old lover":

"'Will you remain here this winter?'" asked the "old lover," according to the newspaper.

"'Oh, no I shall not,'" Corabelle allegedly responded. "'I have received so many flattering offers to again make an engagement that I cannot resist. I shall probably go to England, as I am very fond of sightseeing, I have a splendid opportunity.'"

Despite the bitter letters Corabelle had received from home, the paper falsely portrayed her family as finally coming around to accepting her marriage.

"Mrs. Chaska stated that her parents were fully reconciled to the match and treated her husband while in Washington with the greatest respect. This lady is looking excellent and the many who predicted divorce inside of two months must extend the time, and from present indications it looks as if the wedding was one of honest love, a realization of Ingomar and Parthenia."[12]

In a matter of months, Corabelle and Sam had been transformed on the pages of that St. Paul newspaper from the Othello of Shakespearean tragedy into Ingomar and Parthenia, characters in a popular nineteenth century play written by a German baron, Friedrich Halm. *Ingomar the Barbarian* told of how the unrefined Ingomar was civilized after falling in love with a young woman, Parthenia.

Despite the *Daily Globe*'s claim, nowhere in Corabelle's memoirs or in *Blue Star* was a trip to England mentioned. The reconciliation never happened. But in that made-up world, it didn't matter.

Chapter 20

Winyan Is Dead

The most egregious error of all in *Blue Star* was its treatment of Elizabeth Winyan.

Years before Corabelle spent the winter of 1885–1886 with her, Winyan had established herself as a legend among the Dakota, the white teachers and missionaries who came to serve with her, and the wealthy people in big cities in the Midwest and East Coast who financially supported them. Isley/Duncan's depiction in *Blue Star* of Winyan as a hapless, overweight "old-maid Indian" who snored through a crisis couldn't have been more incorrect. She was the mother and mother-in-law of two of the most active Native teachers and missionaries among the Dakota, Edwin and Ellen Phelps. She ran her own Riggs out-stations. *Blue Star* mentions nothing of the incredible tales of her survival of a massacre under the kettle as a toddler, of the swim to help the Riggs party survive the 1862 Minnesota violence, of her tender mercies to the sick and dying, of her fearless willingness to tackle the most physical challenges of the frontier.

She was so familiar in the missionary world by the end of her life that she was generally known by one name, Winyan. By the time of her death, she had expanded that world: She attended conferences and went on fund-raising tours to Chicago and other cities with members of the Riggs family. She often accompanied either Thomas Riggs or Louisa Riggs to help conduct off-reservation Christian services in white communities nearby.[1]

Elizabeth died of pneumonia on February 20, 1890, at age fifty-nine (or sixty-five, according to other sources on her birth year). She had ridden the forty miles from her outstation to Fort Bennett for supplies, and while there became very sick and was put to bed at the home of the Episcopal rector. As her condition worsened, her son, Edwin, was summoned but arrived after his mother died.[2]

Corabelle Fellows made no mention of Winyan's death in her handwritten memoirs, although they are filled with kind memories of their time together, and Corabelle called her "Ina," or mother. Corabelle was embroiled in the public furor over her marriage at the time Winyan died, so that may have been why.

They had had their differences, their moments of cross-cultural confusion. In *Blue Star,* the relationship had been told exclusively from the white woman's perspective, and it had mis-portrayed Winyan to the point of denigrating her intellect and physical characteristics. Had Corabelle not just died before the book came out, her reception of the Winyan portrayal in *Blue Star* could have made the book a lot more controversial than it was. This will always be an unanswered question in this story. But in her handwritten biography's description of Winyan, Corabelle made it clear that she saw their relationship as mother-daughter, and that their time together had provided moments of deep insight.

That moment in the cabin when the unwanted suitor tried to carry Corabelle away, after which Winyan had treated her with the natural herbs, had led to both women breaking the age's cultural conventions of physical contact. That happened when Corabelle impulsively threw her arms around Winyan's neck and kissed her, and when Winyan returned the kiss. In her memoirs and in the memories laid out in *Blue Star*, Corabelle connected that night in the cabin, when Winyan had saved her, to another seminal event in her life.

That tender moment between mother and daughter had pushed Corabelle's thoughts a decade back to her father stepping in to stop her secret relationship with the Captain. Safe and sound, yet shaken, in Ina's cabin, she had realized her adoptive mother had just done the same thing to save her from a relationship for which she was not prepared.

Those connections between Corabelle's past and present significantly illustrated how her experiences among the Dakota had changed her outlook on family, relationships, and the customs surrounding them. She and Winyan had come to a quiet understanding. Corabelle wrote in her handwritten memoirs that Winyan had done "the work in her own Christian Native way," while "my work was similar, though to be taught in a white woman's ways."

Blue Star made that point as well in one of Isely/Duncan's most memorable and touching passages. Long talks in Winyan's cabin or beneath a sparkling canopy of stars had forged an enduring peace—genuine love—between two women from very, very different places.

"How we talked!" Corabelle remembered. "Really talked, there in that rude cabin, shut away from the rest of the world. She asked and answered, and I asked and answered until that day with its closeness of spiritual touch became a highlight of my whole life."[3]

Winyan's very presence as a lead Native missionary was itself trailblazing. Her leadership defied both the gender roles of her people and challenged the male hierarchy of Christian missions. She had run a no-nonsense mission. She set rules, and she enforced them, and she did it together and equally with a white woman as *her* associate.

"Singlehanded, and against tradition as old as her race," Corabelle remembered, she "was bossing a camp. She had decided she would have neither gambling nor stealing."[4]

The two women had seen that their complementary skills strengthened their relationship and thus, their value in service to the Dakota people. It hadn't been easy. Corabelle, the school-educated teacher, toggled between taking the predominant position of forcing assimilation against her acquired desire to understand and hold onto Dakota language and customs. Winyan, practitioner of those customs and language, had converted to Christianity and in the spirit of both was the ready servant for virtually any physical task on the chaotic frontier. "Did I not have the wisdom she lacked?" Corabelle asked. "Did she not have the strong body I did not have? The two, together, could do it."

Corabelle hoped her family back in Washington, DC, would be proud of how she and Winyan had worked together, that they would overlook their biases to see two women just trying to do good, together. She hoped they would understand why this bold Winyan often teased Corabelle about the faux glamour of their lives. Once, as they hauled heavy jugs of water from the river to their cabin, Corabelle "suddenly wondered what Marian [her sister] and Mother would say could they see me now, bare-headed, bareback and astride a lean pony, swathed in an Indian blanket, balancing my jar of water on my shoulder and trailing behind fat old Ina, astride, also, and balancing her two great jars on either hip.

"She always looked me over skeptically when we reached the house. Invariably, when she found me unbroken, she would put her hands on her hips and laugh so hard that I was obliged to join her."[5]

Upon her death, Winyan was widely mourned in the public and religious press. The *Word Carrier* began its account simply: "Winyan is dead."

"When the news of the death of some great, public man goes flashing over the country, the whole nation is saddened," the article's author opined. "The news of the death of this consecrated Christian Indian woman comes to the Dakota mission with the same force. The white missionaries had no truer friend, her own people no more powerful example of what Christ can do for them."[6]

"There is no one to fill her place," lamented the fellow missionary Mary Collins. "God help our poor bereaved Dakotas."[7]

Speaking twenty-eight years later after a national conference on Native affairs at Harvard that included the Supreme Court Justice Oliver Wendell Holmes, Jr. and the authors James Russell Lowell and Julia Ward Howe (who wrote "The Battle Hymn of the Republic"), Collins recounted Winyan's childhood memories with her grandfather on the banks of the Minnesota River offering tributes to the Great Spirit.

Collins quoted the Sioux Leader Fire Chief: "When the white man wants to plant wheat, he plants wheat; when he wants to raise corn, he plants corn, but he says he wants to raise good Indians but he plants bad white men among us who plant bad seed."

Winyan, Collins said, had been that good Native seed.[8]

American Missionary called Winyan an "exemplary mother" and recounted a story she had once told about the day her son had wanted "English clothes." She had only the money and material to make a shirt and trousers. "I told him to pray for them; in the meantime, I worked as well as prayed, and on Saturday, when my work was done, the missionary's wife gave me a hat and a pair of shoes for Edwin. He was delighted and so was I. Since that time, he has never doubted that God would answer prayer."[9]

Newspapers around the country printed obituaries. The *Vermont Chronicle* in Bellows Falls, Vermont, placed on page one a detailed account of her life that included the claim that a young Elizabeth had been sold twice to men who had mistreated her before meeting Edwin's father. The second man, the story read, would beat Elizabeth after finding out she had secreted away to the Riggs's services.

"She was a devoted friend to the missionaries and their families," the newspaper reported, in an account whose familiarity with Winyan's acts and habits indicated it was written by a Riggs family member or by a fellow missionary. "She has had her day school and her Sunday school. She has had her Bible-reading services. She doctored to her people as well as she could; not in the old superstitious way, but with roots and herbs. When she was at our house, she would be out upon the neighboring wooded land looking for her favorite remedies. We delighted in her as a guest. She had the qualities of a refined Christian woman."[10]

Winyan may have bristled at the "refined" observation, and she may have had something to say about its suggestion she had assimilated. She had adapted to the inevitable change being forced upon her people, but she was independent of spirit and respectful of her people's traditions enough to desire a future as including both. She would not have seen as incongruous leading Christian Bible study while foraging in the wilds for medicinal plants, as her ancestors had done. She would have been happiest to hear herself being described first and foremost as a "devoted friend."

The American Missionary Association printed a brochure of addresses Winyan had given to religious and benefactor audiences. Winyan comes across as a defiant servant, a Christian convert willing to confront power if it got in the way of the work.

Not long before her death, Winyan and Louisa Riggs had traveled to Chicago for meetings with that city's minister's association, and to meet with churches in Glencoe and Oak Park. The two women also spoke to classes at the Chicago Theological Seminary. Her address to the latter was impromptu, and it was transcribed for posterity.

In that speech, Winyan recounted how she first came to the Cheyenne River missions roughly five years after the Battle of the Greasy Grass/Little Bighorn. The refugees that Sitting Bull had led into Canada had just surrendered and returned to the United States. Sitting Bull and some of his followers were held as prisoners of war for twenty months at Fort Randall, on the Missouri River, and they eventually settled at Standing Rock and Cheyenne River.

Thomas Riggs had seen that surrender as an important opening for mission work, and Winyan was a crucial early ally in the expansion of schools and missions at Cheyenne River and Standing Rock. "Our opportunities have never been better than now," Riggs had written when she arrived. "The recent gathering in of Sitting Bull's people opens a wide field. At Standing Rock, we should be ready to preach and teach salvation; not only ready afar off, but ready on the ground, and doing our Lord's work. Then with the increased number of Indians at Cheyenne River Agency comes larger opportunity than heretofore."[11]

Winyan had challenged authority in two directions.

"I was sent to a village where a good many of Sitting Bull's people had just come from British America [Canada], had been settled," Winyan told that Chicago audience not long before she died. She recalled how she immediately clashed with the white male teacher who was serving with her. He wanted to ask permission of the leaders of the bands of Dakota; she wanted to dive right into the work of teaching, feeding, and healing. She saw her way as a marriage of Christ's teachings of selflessly serving the poor and her culture's communal customs of helping those who needed it the most, of the two spiritual paths that focused on people in need over power seekers. She told the Chicago seminary students they did not need the approval of political powers to do the right things.

"I told [her fellow teacher] I did not think that was the right way; that when the Lord Jesus came to the earth, he did not seek the great men and the rich—those who were the chiefs—but He began at once among the poor and the sick and the ignorant and the little children and those who needed to have the Gospel told to them. So, I think it would be with you . . . in your work of ministry. You should begin at once to work among the poor and the needy, and those that really desire to have the love of Christ told to them. You will always find those who will oppose you, but though you may meet with many discouragements, you must remember that it is the Lord's work and that he will bless it if you undertake it in his strength."

Speaking another time to about fifty Dakota and Lakota women at a missionary conference in Oahe, a Riggs missionary station near present-day Pierre, Winyan said that leading by example is a powerful teaching tool. "If you keep your house well, others will learn from you," she said. "If you keep your children well, others learn from you. If you pray, so will others learn to pray."

Like Corabelle, she espoused a frontier feminism. "We are 'only women,'" she said, "but women can give the light to those in darkness, and the command to go into all the world means for you to help. You, and you, and me—everyone. No one has the right to say: 'Let others work; I will be good myself but cannot help. . . . Pray, depend upon God and do as He teaches, and though now you may not understand all He teaches, your mind will open and you will become wise."

At a conference at the Santee agency in October of 1887, about the time Corabelle was beginning her last posting at Swift Bird, many of Winyan's associates were trying to convince her to come in from the hard life at her remote station. She was then approaching her late fifties. While visiting homes of wealthy donors on big-city fundraising tours, Winyan had often expressed surprise that people would leave such luxury to teach and preach in Dakota Territory. But that would never be her life, or Corabelle's. When Winyan's friends kept gently reminding her that she was getting older, that it may be time to retire from hauling water up steep banks or splitting cords of wood to keep fireplaces burning in her log cabin, she "was much disturbed by the proposition," according to the excerpts of her speeches produced by the American Missionary Association.

Winyan told the friends trying to get her to slow down that she had felt stronger than ever "the voice of God" for her to continue her work.

She was motivated after seeing some Sioux leaders "lay aside war paint" after developing relationships with her, and that "I have seen the church at Oahe grow up and send out its own missionaries who are yet wild." She pleaded for an army of Dakota and Lakota to follow that same path among their people.

"Our church has grown because we have sent out missionaries as fast as we could into the darker parts of our country," Winyan proclaimed. "We must continue to send these Native missionaries from our church."[12]

She had openly challenged government edict. At the end of Grover Cleveland's first term in office, his administration was pushing hard to ban Native language in schools and to stop distribution of the Dakota Bible. A group of Methodist Episcopal Church leaders wrote the president to protest the policy. "The line of the power travels with the human heart, and the heart of the Indian is in his language," they wrote. "That it is in harmony with the genius of our country, a free church in a free state, that the operations of all missionary societies should be untrammeled by state interferences."

Cleveland responded that he was "greatly surprised and disappointed" at the opposition, and said the government mandates would stand, although he did leave open occasional use of the language and of the Bible if teaching or preaching could not be accomplished in English. But the arc of change was undeniable, Cleveland said. The language of the Dakota and Lakota going forward would be English.

"The government seeks in its management of the Indians to civilize them," he wrote back, "and to prepare them for that contact for the world which necessarily accompanies that civilization. Manifestly nothing is more important from this point of view than a knowledge of the English language."

Cleveland then declared: "It will not do to permit these wards of the nation in their preparation to become their own masters, to indulge in their Native language because it is easier for them or it pleases them."

The *Word Carrier* editors had seen Cleveland leaving daylight in the policy as an election-year move to head off "the rising indignation of Protestant Christians in this country." [13]

Winyan did not care about the politics. In a second address to missionaries at Santee, she vowed to defy any government rules banning the language and the Dakota Bible. "I shall go back and resume my work," she said. "If they send me to prison, I am ready to go. Did they not send the Apostle, Paul, to prison?"

At that conference, a quilt made by Caroline Scarlet Horse, one of the Riggs's earliest and oldest converts to Christianity at ninety-seven years old, had been sold for $4 to support missions. To "love each other," Winyan proclaimed, "we give gladly of the little that we have."[14]

In her handwritten memoirs, Corabelle said the most fulfilling days of her life had come with Winyan. "I was young. Elizabeth Winyan was a religious woman, and I was a happy convert myself. There seemed nothing too difficult for me to do. We often visited the sick, old and lonely. I had no fear, but felt God would protect us if we kept His commandments. But people without experience are at times venturesome, and so it proved with me. I was told by the missionary to do anything that might be helpful to the Sioux. They were proud and intelligent, desiring more knowledge of our ways, but often not willing to give up their customs or traditions."

Winyan had compromised, as had she. "Here," she wrote in her memoirs of the days with Winyan, "seemed the avenue for my loved vocation, and I was very happy."

"Mother held her Native services every Sunday but there were young men who wished to learn from books but had refused to attend the Govt. school because they would have to adopt our customs, have their long hair cut off, wear English clothing and shoes or boots, and stop painting their faces and bodies," Corabelle recalled. "So I compromised with them."

They could keep their hair and clothing, she had decided, but she asked them to "not paint their face when they came to school," to which they agreed.

In 1894, Congregational Church clergy and parishioners dedicated a chapel to Winyan at the Two Kettle Village overlooking the Cheyenne River. Her son Edwin was ordained as a minister at the same memorial. However pulled she was between two cultures and her yearnings of her home along the Minnesota River, Winyan had never strayed from her central mission of caring for the least she encountered, wherever that might be. A large crowd attended the ceremony in a gathering that would have delighted her, although the big fuss might also have embarrassed her.

Corabelle had left Dakota by then, and she makes no mention of attending the dedication. For those who were there, the day was memorable. The prairie was covered with wildflowers. Led by Frederick Riggs, the grandson of Stephen Riggs, missionaries attended from distant schools and churches. On the way, two white women missionaries were rescued by a group of Native people as they tried to cross the Cheyenne River in a wagon and were thrown overboard. "They were soon taken in another conveyance, but not before getting thoroughly drenched and gaining the admiration of the Indians for their courage," wrote one missionary, a Miss M. Likorish.

Tepees were scattered about the new church grounds; dozens of Native residents had come for the dedication. Ellen Phelps, Elizabeth's daughter-in-law, had prepared a supper for the missionaries, white and Native. "Our white ladies could but express their admiration for the composure and quiet dignity with which this Indian woman, who could not speak or understand English, entertained, from Saturday until Monday, about thirty-five white people and Natives at her table, and in a house of one room," Miss Likorish extolled.

On the Sunday of the dedication, she wrote, "Indians came from far and near, and filled the church till some had to sit on the floor for lack of seats, but this they did not mind, for, judging by the long hair and Dakota dress, we know many were but little used to the customs of civilized life."

That night, in "the long twilight that lingers so late here," Louisa Riggs led a service for about forty white and Native women. They, like Winyan, sang songs in Dakota. Several of the white women spoke in English; Louisa Riggs, who had been taught Dakota by Winyan, interpreted.

"We were glad to sit in the circle with these Indian mothers and speak to them of their children, our love for them, and how we were trying to help them," Miss Likorish went on. "One could not be in such a typical gathering of Indians without noting the intelligent faces and strength of character depicted in them. One is continually surprised, not at the depravity of these people, but with their many good traits, and the progress they are making in the face of so many obstacles."[15]

One reporter wrote that Winyan had been "born an apostle, died a saint, surviving as a positive force in world history. She became a bishop of souls, a humble but diversified 'faculty of instruction' in letters, in sewing and cooking, in nursing and organizing, in theology."[16] Another described her the way war heroes who died in battle were often described: "She labored among the Sioux fourteen years and died on her field."[17]

Chapter 21

It All Falls Apart

Winyan's death at the beginning of 1890 was a harbinger of a year of tumult on the plains, a year in which the Ghost Dance movement stirred followers on the reservations and raised political ruckus across the land, a year that ended with the killing of Sitting Bull and the Wounded Knee massacre. The Great Sioux Nation was being carved into smaller reservations and individually held land parcels. In the midst of all of this, while word of Winyan's death would no doubt have come to her, Corabelle's marriage was starting to break apart.

The Riggs's *Word Carrier* that had so mourned Winyan's death earlier in the year was far less charitable to men, women, and children gunned down in the ice and snow at Wounded Knee. Assimilation meant surrender; of that there was no doubt. In a front-page, unsigned report, the *Word Carrier* declared: "The slaughter of a whole tribe of Indians at Wounded Knee was an affair which looks worse the more it is investigated. But aside from the question of human culpability there is a providential aspect which demands notice. Taking it in its bearings on the whole condition of things among the rebellious Titon [sic] Sioux, it was a blessing. It was needful that these people should feel in some sharp terrible way the just consequences of their actions and be held in wholesome fear from further folly."

"The way in which this punishment came about is also significant. It was like an explosion in a powder magazine. No man planned it. But it was better that two hundred should die than that a nation should perish."[1]

What "nation" was the author referring to? The defeated Sioux, the last starving ranks of whom were being forced onto reservations by the US military? Of course not. It was the United States, whose history of broken treaties and forced assimilation was building a shameful legacy of deceit and failure. But what threat was posed to an entire nation by displaced people, many of them women and children, cornered in a bitter-cold ravine at Christmas time, clinging to fantastical promises of a religious revival and restored glorious past?

Would Winyan have agreed with this brutal take? Never, given her legacy of seeking a humane path through the Christian theology she adopted and the Native customs and beliefs she inherited. She would never have blessed killing to teach a lesson. Had she been at Wounded Knee she would have tried to be a peacemaker. Had she survived, she would have been the first to come to the rescue of the wounded and dying after the guns went silent, the first to speak against the killing.

Would Corabelle have agreed with that harsh *Word Carrier* declaration? No chance. In her memoirs she had blamed soldiers' "faint and fearful hearts" for sparking much of the conflicts in Dakota Territory.

To be fair, there was not solidarity in thought in Riggs's publication with that harsh *Word Carrier* denunciation of Spotted Tail and his massacred followers. That same edition included a more sympathetic take. "The Indians have again exhibited their desperate bravery," an article headlined "One Point of View" began. It praised those who fought back against the Seventh Cavalry and "a battery of machine guns."

"That those Indians have been crowded out of their lands, oppressed, swindled, starved, outlawed and that they have risen up against such wrongs and sold their lives in resenting them, are facts which give them the sympathy of brave men everywhere," the article concluded.[2]

Corabelle would have understood that desperate bravery. But the courage she had exhibited in following her heart and marrying Sam, and the two of them sticking together through appalling treatment, had not been enough. By the time of the Wounded Knee massacre, Corabelle and Sam's attempts to piece together a life after the dime museum tours were failing. Every hint or suggestion of trouble was seemingly news.

The press that had sensationalized their marriage in 1888 was now routinely trotting out stories of inevitable breakup. Some went into high we-told-you-so dudgeon. Of course, an interracial marriage under these circumstances couldn't work, the papers moralized. There was scant acknowledgment that any marriage would have been severely strained under such relentlessly harsh public scrutiny. An *Indianapolis Journal* headline in early 1891 was oblivious to the irony of its own words: "Pretty Indian Romance, Tinged With Sensationalism, Shattered At Last." The paper did not acknowledge it had played any role in the sensationalism, but it was certainly ready to cover the shattering.

Talk of a split had begun before Corabelle was pregnant with their daughter, who would be named Flora. In a story bylined out of Washington, DC, that *Indianapolis Journal* article portrayed Corabelle as a victim of misguided love and said a reporter had interviewed her father about rumors of the divorce.

"A very pretty romance has been shattered by the news telegraphed here a few days ago that Cora Belle Fellows Chaska [sic] will apply for a divorce from her Indian husband, Sam Chaska. Mrs. Chaska is a Washington girl," the paper reported. "Her father, Homer Fellows, is a veteran clerk in the War Department, and although the family has always lived modestly in a neat little house on Capitol Hill, Cora Belle was a great favorite of society here, where she was received by the best people of Washington. She is remembered as a remarkably pretty girl, and she might have had her own choice of husbands from among the most eligible of the young men of the capital city without going to the wilds of Dakota for a helpmate."

The paper quoted Homer Fellows saying that he had had no communication with Corabelle since right after the marriage three years earlier. That was likely a reference to that fleeting meeting in the Washington, DC, hotel while Corabelle and Sam were on their first tour, the scene described in the storybook conclusion of *Blue Star*.

"I have heard nothing about it," Homer reportedly said of the possible divorce. He called it an "unfortunate marriage," and, according to the *Journal*, "didn't care to say whether Mrs. Chaska would be again received at her home. She hadn't asked to be taken back, and this question need not be settled before it should arise."[3]

The newspapers now focused on blame for the breakup. The assaults on Sam's character and race would not let up. Once again, the couple's marriage—now, its failure—was portrayed as a morality play about interracial marriage and social norms.

A Wisconsin newspaper proclaimed that Corabelle left the marriage because she was "sick of her bargain," and it attacked Sam as "a fair sample of his race and . . . too lazy to work." Reports of a divorce, the *Wisconsin State Journal* in Madison piously proclaimed, was "the natural sequel of a marriage that shocked her society friends and brought sorrow to the home of her parents."

Corabelle had turned a "deaf ear" to pre-marriage opposition from family and friends, the *State Journal* reporter wrote, and "believed that her mission in life was to elevate and instruct the aborigines." She "would have prospered had not Cupid entered and caused his usual discord," the paper said.[4]

The newspaper hypothesized that Corabelle had not married Sam because she loved him, but because she had "allowed her enthusiasm in the Indian work to overcome her." It speculated that her family's expressions of shame, the pressures between two people of far different backgrounds, and the stress of marriage between races had all contributed to an inevitable bad ending.

"The causes which have led to this [divorce] are not given, but they can surely be traced to dissimilarity of race, temperament and education," the paper reported. Either way, a divorce was portrayed as another layer of shame for Corabelle's socially connected family back in Washington, DC. Homer Fellows "was very much agitated when speaking about his daughter and said that he and his family felt most keenly the disgrace that had come upon them."[5] Some papers reported that Sam had run off with a "buxom squaw."[6]

Records of the Santee Sioux show that a son, Gabriel, was born to Sam and Lucy Red Owl in June of 1895, at the Santee Agency. Another son, Owen followed in 1897, and a daughter, Grace, was born in 1900. Then, in 1903, Sam and Julia Frazier were recorded having a son enrolled at Santee. They named him George Pay Pay after the Native man who had raised Sam. A 1902 register of Santee families included Sam and his three children with Corabelle: Claude, Wilbur, and Flora.[7]

Some still alleged without proof that Corabelle had orchestrated the whole marriage for fame and fortune. The *Indianapolis Journal* ran that lengthy report out of Washington, DC, that depicted the once "great favorite of society" in a free fall of her own doing, a victim of her own love of romance and attention.

"Cora Belle was nothing if not romantic," the newspaper declared, incorrectly dividing her first name. "It is said of her here that, though she bore an unblemished reputation, she had planned more than one elopement during her girlhood. She always declared that her marriage would be a sensational one, and she kept her word."

The paper claimed that Homer Fellows "shared General Phil Sheridan's opinion that the only good Indian is a dead Indian, and so Cora Belle didn't care to tell him that she proposed to marry one." It was that supposed deception, not her relatives' racism, that had permanently estranged Corabelle from her family and friends, at least according to the newspapers.[8]

In her handwritten memoirs, Corabelle's general reference to mistakes she had made in her life might have been the closest she came to addressing the breakup and what followed. But she tempered even that admission by writing that she had had few regrets. It may be that she simply rationalized that no marriage could have survived what she and Sam had confronted.

Chapter 22

Storms All Around

In August of 1891, Sam decided to move to Nebraska. In her memoirs, Corabelle matter-of-factly mentioned the relocation without explanation. It was unclear if the marriage had totally broken apart by that time, or if Sam simply wanted to move and was establishing a home at Santee for the family there. But the timing—eight months after Wounded Knee and the killing of Sitting Bull, amid the breakup of the Great Sioux Reservation, and nearing the end of summer—may be significant.

Perhaps the weather was the culprit. Drought had wiped out a lot of early farmers trying to make a go of it on the notoriously fickle rainfall of the Great Plains. Severe drought hit the northern Plains in the late 1880s and early 1890s; there may not have been enough grass, or crop growth, to sustain a farm. Perhaps, like White Swan told the Crook Commission, Sam and Corabelle had learned after three years that it was impossible to successfully farm on the semi-arid grasslands, that it would have been best to leave it to the millions of roaming buffalo.

Then again, Sam's unwillingness to take sides for or against Sitting Bull might have created too much pressure for him to remain at Chargers Camp. Corabelle mentioned in her memoirs that he had refused to take sides when the Lakota leader was being blamed for stoking support for the banned Ghost Dance. In one terse passage in those memoirs, Corabelle wrote that Sam "was asked to [turn] against Sitting Bull, but would not go, prefer[ring] to remain neutral."

Perhaps Sam's decision two years earlier to sign for the Dawes allotment had become too controversial for a man of mixed heritage. A "Samuel Campbell" was recorded signing at Cheyenne River in 1889.[1] Two of the big sticking points for the Crook-led commissioners sent west in 1889 directly related to Sam's ancestry.

One was that he was Santee. Some members of eastern Sioux, like the Santee, had already individually received land from earlier treaties, although there is no record this affected Sam. But given this history, western Sioux, particularly those on the Cheyenne River and Standing Rock agencies, wanted to exclude the Santee from the newest agreement with the government because, it was thought, they had advanced further in establishing farms and in assimilation with white culture.

"The Eastern Sioux already held lands in severalty and showed marked progress over the Tetons," the author and historian Jerome A. Greene observed.[2]

Secondly, Sam may also have felt the tension over the Dawes Act between full-blood Sioux and those of mixed race. "Certain mixed bloods understood and favored the measure, but opposition emanated from the more populous full bloods, who could not shake suspicions of deceit," Greene wrote. "As time passed, the schism between progressive and traditionalist Sioux deepened. Even those Indians who liked the Bill were reluctant to sign for fear of reprisal by their tribesmen."[3]

Many of these concerns had been laid bare when the commission met with attendees at Cheyenne River Agency in July of 1889. The commission was made up of General Crook, the frontier military officer who would die five weeks after the commission's report was released; William Warner, a Missouri congressman who had just left office and later would serve as a senator from that state; and Charles Foster, a former Ohio governor and member of the US House of Representatives from the state.

Foster had opened the proceedings at Cheyenne River Agency on July 12, 1889, with a stark challenge.

"You can not live as you once lived—the buffalo are gone," Foster told an estimated five hundred to seven hundred people who attended the multi-day gathering with the commissioners. "Like the white man you must get a living out of the soil. We need not discuss how this thing came about—it is a fact and you understand it as well as I. The white man is increasing in numbers, in wealth and power, because he is an educated man. There is no doubt but what the Indian with education will equal the white man."[4]

But there was doubt, and there was distrust. One particularly poignant exchange between Crook and the Lakota leader Hump illustrated that point. Hump, of the Miniconjou band, had been wounded and had a horse shot out from under him at Little Bighorn. He was in no mood to be forced into anything, even as Crook goaded the multitudes assembled with the declaration that "you have come to the forks of the road."

"Take the right road and it will head you to prosperity and good times in the future and make provisions for your families," Crook told the large audience. "If you take the wrong one, there will be trouble all the time."

In response, Hump rose and referred to previous treaties which had not been honored by the government. "I don't see any of the payment," Hump said, adding, "I am going to say what I think about this bill. . . . I am not going to sign it."

The official proceedings of the commission noted that "great cheering and applause" followed Hump's remarks, and on that crescendo the day's proceedings were gaveled closed.[5]

Whatever the cause for Sam's decision to move cattle and household items to Nebraska in late summer of 1891, it came at a tenuous time for Corabelle, who was pregnant with the family's third child.

"It was before my little girl was born, so he took a load of household furniture and had men go with him to drive his stock," Corabelle wrote in her memoirs. "And I moved near the agency in a cottage until he came back." It was a fortuitous move into the agency village. Dakota weather was about to assert itself once again. On August 19, a "sultry day" in her memory, Corabelle took her two little boys and walked down to the Missouri River near the Cheyenne River Agency.

"I noticed some low-hanging clouds near the earth in the south east, but not like rain clouds. They lay long and dark." It was about 3 p.m. The clouds "slowly rose" on the western horizon, "but there was no wind or rain," she remembered.

Preparing supper in the temporary quarters at the agency, Corabelle noticed the clouds were "darker and more ominous looking, and were rising much higher and higher, a green color, indicating high wind.

"About midnight, the wind storm broke upon us with such violence that our little cottage was lifted on the side of the house where the porch was. And as the wind rushed upon it, it lifted that end four times and every time I expected the house to turn over. But God was with us and spared us."

Her two young boys slept through much of the storm, and "never knew how close we came to being all blown away." By her description, it could have been a tornado or a straight-wind derecho. Her description of fierce winds interspersed with calm leans toward tornado.

"It did not thunder much, if any, and between the puffs of wind, it was very still," she recalled. Then rain began falling "in torrents. I was obliged to get my broom and sweep out the water from the dining room." The storm had blown out the windows on one side the house and water was gushing in. What furniture and household items left there were blown to the wall opposite the blown-out windows.

"As soon as the storm had ceased," Corabelle remembered, "a neighbor who was spared came to see if we were all safe, and finding us bodily safe, asked if I would let some of the neighbors come in till morning, for their homes had been destroyed or roofs had blown off."

For the rest of that long night, women and children arrived and took shelter in the tiny cottage until every available space of her relatively intact structure was covered. Men "were around helping the ones who were hurt. It surely was a terrible sight to see," she said of the devastation that came into focus at the first sunlight. Entire buildings had been blown away. A Catholic church was destroyed, its statues of Madonna and Joseph lying in a pile of wreckage. An Episcopal Church had been blown two feet off its foundation A gigantic piece of lumber had pierced the roof of the Indian agent's house and, arrow-like, was embedded in a piano.

But amidst that destruction, there was reason to rejoice. "No one was hurt in any manner," Corabelle remembered, "only badly frightened."

It was one of many blessings she'd had surviving Great Plains storms. She hadn't done it alone. A young boy had helped lead her to safety in that blizzard of 1888. Now, three years later, she was taking in neighbors devastated by the summer storm. All along her journey, she had depended upon the goodwill of Native friends, and they had leaned upon her. She decided it was the way of Christ *and* of Wakan Tanka, the Great Spirit.

Chapter 23

"No More to Do with His White Wife"

By the mid-1890s, newspapers reported that Corabelle and her children Claude, Wilbur, and Flora had moved to a "small town in southern Nebraska," after leaving the reservation. Sam, who Corabelle had said had moved his livestock back to Nebraska three years before, was reported to be living back on the Cheyenne River Reservation. "He is happy and wants no more to do with his white wife," one newspaper reported.[1] But by the turn of the century, Santee records described Sam living back in Nebraska.

In 1896, newspapers reported that Corabelle had moved to Carthage, Missouri, where the "former belle of Washington society" was "a deserted and destitute woman, with three children dependent upon her for care and support."[2] Carthage, a town in southwest Missouri had endured not one, but two, battles during the Civil War. At the turn of the twentieth century, it had fewer than ten thousand people. Corabelle says nothing in her memoirs about her time there, or how she ended up in either Carthage, or later in Wichita.

One newspaper account said she had married George Tillman, a Civil War veteran with a pension, in Ashley, Illinois, on August 20, 1897.[3]

By 1905 Corabelle was living with Tillman in Jasper, Missouri.[4] They eventually settled in Wichita about 1907, where some of her children and, later, grandchildren and great-grandchildren also congregated.

Tillman was roughly seventeen years older than Corabelle, and he would have been in his early fifties when he was reported to have married her. He was an active member of the Grand Army of the Republic, a fraternal organization of Civil War veterans of the Union Army and Navy.[5] Although modern descendants are unsure if they ever married, US Census records from 1900 described them as married. Corabelle had two daughters with Tillman, Cora and Rose. The 1900 US Census listed Tillman as a farmer and said that he and Corabelle were renting a home in Jasper County, Missouri. That census report said Tillman had been born in Tennessee, and it incorrectly spelled his last name with one "l."[6]

A granddaughter remembered him as a "man with a long white beard lying in bed."[7] His Civil War pension records recorded him receiving it beginning with his release from service in March of 1864; it described him as an "invalid," meaning either he had been wounded in battle or had suffered an illness serious enough to be discharged.[8]

The 110th Illinois in which Private Tillman served was engaged in the Western Theater for much of the war, fighting in several battles, including the brutal carnage at Chickamauga in Tennessee, second only to Gettysburg in the number of lives lost. Throughout the war, the 110th lost more men through disease—154—than the ninety-five men who were killed in battle.[9]

Upon Tillman's death in 1926, Corabelle applied for a Civil War pension. Government pension records are unclear whether it was granted, suggesting the couple may either have never married, or had gotten a divorce, although there is no known record of the latter.[10]

When Tillman died in January of 1926, the *Daily Eagle* in Wichita said that "his wife" survived him, though it did not name Corabelle. It did, however, also name as survivors five children—including the two he raised with Corabelle.[11] Prior to his death, there certainly was public evidence of discord in the relationship.

In 1912 the Wichita *Eagle* reported that Corabelle had filed for divorce in the city's district court. It cited Tillman's "wicked temper," and alleged he "curses his wife, children, and stepchildren, threatens to kill them, and occasionally draws a large knife to add force to his remarks about home government." The suit alleged that Tillman had drawn a knife on one of her two sons with Sam when that son came to visit. The paper did not name which one.

If they did divorce, it was not chronicled in Corabelle's memoirs or other keepsake materials handed down to family. Some evidence beyond Tillman's obituary suggests it did not happen; granddaughter Rose, who remembered Tillman in bed with the long beard, was not born until 1918, six years after the explosive allegations were reported in the *Eagle*.[12]

Chapter 24

Samuel Campbell, Prisoner 3222

Sam Campbell could not escape the harsh spotlight, even after he and Corabelle split. In May of 1898, a paper in Nebraska reported that Sam had committed suicide. Like so much that had been written about him and Corabelle, it was false.

The widely printed story erroneously called him a "full-blooded Sioux Indian" who had "become famous by marrying Cora Belle Fellows of Washington, DC." The racist descriptions, the factual errors, continued unabated. "Neither the beauty nor wealth of his fashionable society wife, nor his learning, acquired by years of study at Carlisle could eradicate the Sioux traits that generations had left in his blood," the paper reported. "In a few years he drifted back to the reservation and sunk to the level of a common blanket Indian again. His wife left him some years ago."

The article claimed that "Chaska was in jail at the time of his death charged with stealing horses. This is the first instance in which a full-blooded Sioux ever committed suicide. By marriage the man was related to one of the most prominent families in the east."[1]

Sam had been convicted of theft, but not of horses. Reports indicated he'd gotten entangled with a group that had trafficked in stolen goods. Despondent, he may have attempted suicide in jail, but newspapers all over the country had to backtrack on reports of his death. But even then, they heaped on the ridicule. Sam was "alive and well, his attempt at ending his life having proved a failure," one reported.[2]

Other aspects of the initial reports of the suicide were true, however. Sam, identified in state records as "Prisoner 3322," had been convicted of theft, and he had been sentenced to one year in Nebraska's state prison. He was listed as just under six feet tall; hardly the six-foot-eight claims of his dime museum days.[3] Some newspapers reported that Sam had cooperated with authorities and helped to convict other men he had become involved with who had found "a ready market for stolen goods among the residents of both the Nebraska and South Dakota sides of the Missouri River in the vicinity of its operations."[4]

Sam began serving this sentence in May of 1898, almost exactly ten years after he and Corabelle had begun their first post-marriage tour. Simultaneously, a paper back in Washington, DC, still thinking Sam was dead (he had "ended it all by snuffing out his miserable life," the paper reported), printed an unusually harsh assessment of Sam's life even for newspapers of that era.

"There are those so uncharitable as to assert that the only good Indian is a dead Indian," the Washington *Evening Times* reported. "And, according to their point of view, Chaska, despite his many misdeeds—not the least of which is embodied in the shattered life of a once beautiful woman—is now wearing a halo in that portion of the Celestial Kingdom reserved for the red men who have to die before they can be good."

How the author had determined that heaven was segregated was not made clear in the article, but at least the newspaper was charitable enough to determine that Sam would find a home there.

The article claimed that Corabelle had recognized her mistake, and her friends were reported to have begun an "I told you so" campaign that was too much for Sam to bear. Sam's friends had taunted him for being subservient to Corabelle, the paper said, and nicknamed him "squaw man," and he supposedly retaliated by oppressing her.

"That was more than Chaska could stand," the *Evening Times* reported. "He was an Indian and he was proud. The indignity rankled in his breast. His veneering of civilization wore off. The true Indian nature asserted itself and the condition of affairs was reversed. Chaska's wife was no longer his pet. She became his slave."

The article ended with a question: "There is the family of half-breed children. What about them? Figure it out in your own mind, if you are able."[5]

Other reports of Sam's imprisonment hinted that fame, itself, may have been the cause for the marital breakup and his alleged suicide attempt. It was a fame they didn't seek, but one that had attracted people attempting to capitalize on it.

"Chaska has received a great deal of notoriety over his marriage with a white woman," the Nebraska *State Journal* reported. "He has been represented as a finely educated lawyer, but those who know of his marriage say he has never followed any business except the show business." Where the "finely educated lawyer" claim came from is anyone's guess; Sam had aspirations to be a farmer.

Some blamed people posing as relatives after seeing the couple's fame. The breakup occurred, the *State Journal* said, because Corabelle could no longer tolerate "a single line" of people "that seemed to be continually pigeon toeing to their house to visit, each one claiming to be a dear relative of Chaska. She drew the line at his relatives and then the divorce."[6]

Sam died on June 2, 1915, according to Santee records. There is no notation in the tribe's 1915 Census of where he was buried. He was described then as fifty-two years old, although other birth records indicated he may have been forty-eight.[7]

There is no mention in Corabelle's handwritten memoirs of Sam's death, just as there is scant mention of their breakup. Nor is there anything in her scrawled reminisces that touch on a down-and-out Sam described by the newspapers. She either had lost contact with him or, as with her estrangement from her family, chose not to dwell on it as she wrote down the story of her life. The one nod to the marriage came when she wrote that she believed her parents would be proud of their grandchildren.

It's as if Corabelle had lived separate lives that were never to intersect in her memory: The life leading to and including Dakota Territory, and the one beyond it. The life she wanted to remember was the former. It's the life Isely/Duncan wrote about. That life had adventure, purpose, love—even if it was a love ultimately scorned and demeaned. Despite all the hardships of her life, Corabelle may truly have had no regrets. Her eyes had been opened to greater challenges of the Natives of the plains, to their struggles to deal with the powerful forces of assimilation, to a people whose songs she would sing to her grandchildren.

Chapter 25

A Family Forever Apart

Corabelle's mother and father lived the rest of their lives in Washington, DC, the last few years on North Carolina Avenue, not far from the Capitol upon whose steps she had played as a young girl. Corabelle's sister, Marian, was married in 1897 to John Webster Davison, a librarian at the Naval Observatory in Washington. It was a little more than three months after Corabelle's reported marriage to George Tillman.

Newspaper reports of Marian's wedding, which took place in Alabama, buttressed evidence of the family's permanent split. There was no mention of Corabelle in the wedding accounts of attendants and attendees.[1] Marian died September 25, 1936, at her home in Arlington, Virginia.[2]

Homer Fellows died in March 1898, roughly three months after Marian's wedding, at the family home on North Carolina Avenue on Capitol Hill. He was buried at the Congressional Cemetery with Masonic honors. He had been a past master of Myron M. Parker Lodge.[3]

In 1893, while employed at the US War Office, Homer survived a collapse of the building housing five hundred government employees. It happened to be the Ford's Theater where John Wilkes Boothe assassinated Abraham Lincoln. The government had taken over the building three months after the assassination. On the day of the collapse twenty-eight years later, workmen had removed concrete supports while trying to establish electric lines in the old structure. Twenty-three people died, and scores others were injured when floors crashed down on one another. "A Death Trap" is how one newspaper described it.[4] The Washington *Evening Star* called it a "frightful disaster" and said many clerks had to be dug out of the rubble.[5]

Fourteen months later, in the wake of a financial panic and due to civil service reform during Grover Cleveland's second stint in office, Homer was among scores who lost their jobs.[6]

Cornelia Haight Fellows died eleven years after Homer in October of 1909, and she, too, was buried in the prestigious Congressional Cemetery. The vast expanse of historic graves overlooks the Anacostia River 1.7 miles southeast of the Capitol where Homer once worked. Homer and Cornelia lie among politicians, leading Washington figures, and other dignitaries and people of notoriety in American history, ranging from the pioneering photographer Matthew Brady to former FBI Director J. Edgar Hoover.

Washington, DC, newspapers noted the sudden passing of a well-known socialite. "She was in bed only two days before she died, surrounded by members of her family and a few friends who had called, not thinking that her illness was of a serious nature," one reported. "That she had many friends among the people of the District, where she had lived for thirty years, was shown by those who attended her funeral and by the floral tributes offered."[7]

The *Washington Herald* called her "one of the old residents of Washington and widely known in the southeast" quarter of the city.[8] The obituaries did not mention her surviving oldest daughter.

By the twenty-first century, Cornelia's and Homer's headstones had toppled over and had not been re-set, a situation not uncommon in the centuries-old cemetery. Visitors can stand at the site where Cornelia and Homer are buried but not see the names of those lying beneath.

Chapter 26

The Blue Star Fades

Why did the book, *Blue Star*, which was tethered accurately to other parts of Corabelle Fellows's written memories, end when it did? Why did it unfairly portray Elizabeth Winyan? In hindsight, it looks simply like a mid-twentieth century American writer fitting a narrative to the dominant biases of the times. In the 1930s, missionaries were frequently still seen as coming from positions of dominance and cultural superiority. With the notable exceptions of a few books, such as John Neihardt's 1931 *Black Elk Speaks*, the predominant image of Natives—in literature, film, and the press—remained warlike, primitive, and obstinate, the ultimate enemies of civilization and progress.

Winyan had been dead for nearly fifty years when *Blue Star* came out, but she had also left a trail of speeches and actions that might have more fully informed readers of her significance, telling the struggles of assimilation from a Native's viewpoint. Portraying Winyan in the more loving, equal-in-status-and-work way that Corabelle had remembered her in her handwritten memoirs would have challenged the biases that lingered in the culture. They were embedded deeply into what Americans read and watched. Often, Hollywood led the way.

It is notable that the movie *Geronimo: The Story of a Great Enemy* came out within months of *Blue Star*'s publication. This epic theatrical depiction of the Apache leader was a full-on racist trope, massively hyped. "Ruthless . . . Savage!" the movie's promotional posters screamed. "The most feared Apache that ever ravaged the West. . . . Leading his

10,000 yelling demons into a roaring battle against a whole regiment of the United States Army!"[1]

"Demons" who roared and ravaged. "Savages" so brave and ruthless they'd attack entire regiments of the mighty US Army. Much made up, all sensationalized. Moviegoers were reminded that the makers of this film had produced such grandiose Manifest Destiny classics as *Union Pacific*, *Wells Fargo*, and *The Plainsman*—all big-screen celebrations of the unstoppable, westward tide.

In truth, Geronimo was an Apache leader who, in revenge and trying to hold onto territory his ancestors traversed for generations, had led bands of no more than a few hundred men—not "10,000 yelling demons"—against Mexican and American targets until he eventually surrendered in 1886. He had become radicalized after his wife, mother, and three children had been killed by Mexican soldiers. Geronimo spent much of the latter years of his life as a prisoner of war, some of it in a hard-labor prison in Florida, where he became a tourist attraction. The children of many Native captives imprisoned there had been sent to the Carlisle Indian School, where a third of them died from tuberculosis.

Near the end of his life, a decade after Sam and Corabelle's breakup, Geronimo would go on a tour similar to Sam and Corabelle's circuit. He was featured at the 1904 World's Fair in St. Louis, where he was depicted as a "monument to the progress of civilization." As spectators passed by, he made bows and arrows while under guard. For a time he appeared in Pawnee Bill's Wild West Show, where Indians were depicted as "lying, thieving, treacherous, murderous" and, according to a *Smithsonian Magazine* account of the show, "would think nothing of taking a scalp from any member of the audience." Geronimo rode in full paint and feathered headgear in President Teddy Roosevelt's inaugural parade in 1905, for what one newspaper described as an illustration of how he had "buried the hatchet forever."[2]

After *Blue Star* was published, after Corabelle had died, Margaret Louisa Irvine Riggs, Thomas Riggs's widow, wrote Isely/Duncan from Riggs's home at Oahe. By then in her eighties, Louisa Riggs had spent a lifetime in missions, and in her thirties had spent a winter on the Cheyenne River outstation with Winyan, just as Corabelle had. In addition,

Winyan had taught Louisa Riggs the Dakota language. Louisa, a Native of Minnesota, had attended the New England Conservatory of Music in Boston after an initial decade of mission work in Dakota Territory. In 1885, she married Thomas Riggs, whose first wife, Nina Foster Riggs, had died seven years before.

Louisa quarreled with Isely/Duncan's spelling of Dakota words and took issue with other descriptions in the book. But Louisa was most distraught at the depiction of Winyan in *Blue Star*. She had apparently not seen Corabelle's handwritten memoirs and was dependent wholly on how Corabelle was depicted as somewhat dismissively referring to Winyan in the book.

"What I object to most is the very erroneous impression Miss Fellows gives of her companion on the Cheyenne River," Louisa Riggs wrote. "Elizabeth Winyan was a very superior Indian woman—the only Indian woman to have entire charge of a missionary out station; a woman of great force, character and discretion. She was not 'an old maid,' but had been married twice that I know of. Her second husband was the father of her son who was educated in our schools and later was for many years a valued worker among our Western Dakotas. . . . Although she did not speak English, she understood it very well. She was not 'educated' in our higher schools, but life in a family such as that of Dr. and Mrs. Stephen R. Riggs in Minnesota had given her full insight into the culture and refinements of a Christian home. She traveled with me in the interest of Oahe School in Illinois and Michigan; we were entertained in many wealthy homes. Elizabeth never made a 'faux pax' or a social error."

Continuing in flowing longhand, Louisa further described Winyan as "cheerful and full of fun, seeing the humorous side of life. But never letting that interfere with her fine sense of the 'eternal fitness of things.'

"It seems strange that Miss Fellows should have given the impression of Winyan that she did in the book," Louisa Riggs wrote. She ended the letter with "kind regards," however, and invited Isely/Duncan to visit if she was ever in central South Dakota.[3]

Isely/Duncan responded ten days later. She attributed the disagreement, in part, to Corabelle's faulty memory in old age.

"As to her veracity, I am sure, if my experience of aging persons may count at all, that, as most grow older they tend to glamorize their youth, their memory fails, and they tell of the past, enhanced," Isely/Duncan wrote to Riggs. She said she verified everything in the book from letters and other materials supplied by Corabelle. But it is also clear, in reading the difference between what Corabelle wrote in her handwritten memoirs and what appeared in the book, that Isely/Duncan had taken license to depict Winyan as sullen, subordinate, and crude. Was it appropriation of stereotypes of Native women to build up the white missionary? Did Isely/Duncan simply intend to portray the Native woman in a subordinate position? Or did she simply misunderstand Corabelle's memories of the woman she called mother?

Isely/Duncan tried to patch over the contretemps with Louisa Riggs by praising Corabelle as she knew her in her seventies.

"Whatever she may have been as a girl, I cannot say, but, in defense of a most admirable soul who cannot speak for herself, I must declare in her defense that a braver, more patient, more kindly-souled person I have never met," Duncan/Isely wrote.

Corabelle "died an heroic death" in 1938, she continued in the letter to Louisa, "smiling to the last, courteous, grateful for the least attention, after what seems to have been a very difficult life." Isely/Duncan said the Corabelle she knew was "hungry most of the time, and always cold in winter. I found her in undesirably pitiable misery—yet she was courteous, alert of mind, and very remarkably aware of the times. During her last two years, in the midst of that degradation, she mastered Braille and was reading [playwright John] Drinkwater's play, 'Lincoln,' shortly before her death."[4]

Corabelle's descendants took umbrage with that description of her final years. Surviving descendants drew a more complex picture of a woman surrounded in the Depression's hard times by a family that loved and helped her.

"She was seventy-six-years-old when she wrote this book," her granddaughter, Rose, wrote Forbes, the Morningside professor. "And she did write it herself, working on it for many years before she ever met Kunigunde Duncan."

In that 1992 letter to Bruce Forbes, Corabelle's granddaughter Rose went on: "When the book came out the family was very angry with Duncan. She obviously misled Blue Star in claiming authorship, and neither Blue Star nor her family ever received a penny for all the years of labor she so lovingly and hopefully put into her book.

"The family, not confrontational, engaged George Powers, a well-known attorney, to check into the legality of the situation. We do not know what he may have reported to our parents, but nothing ever came from the lawsuit."

The granddaughter said that Corabelle "would have been devastated that the author was listed as Duncan and the book presented 'as told to,' without showing grandma's authorship. We, her three granddaughters, still have the original manuscript she so laboriously wrote."

Corabelle, Rose wrote, "had great plans for the book and spoke of the money she would receive for it." But she also suspected it may have not been a big seller, a supposition borne out by the publisher's records.[5]

As Rose suspected, *Blue Star* had only modest sales. It may have been required reading for Girl Scouts in Wichita, but it did not catch on nationally. Amazingly, the publisher, Caxton Printers in Caldwell, Idaho, still had sales records on the book more than eighty years after it was first published. By October of 1939, only 113 of the 1,530 books in the first run had been sold. As of February 1946, sales had reached only 1,806. Isely/Duncan had received less than $300 in royalties, and in 1947, she assumed copyright of the book from the publisher for reasons unknown to the company's twenty-first century president.[6]

Shortly after publication, Corabelle's oldest son, Claude Campbell, who as an infant had been vilified as a half-breed in the press, also wrote the publisher. Then living in Long Beach, California, he wondered about the arrangement for the book's proceeds. "Up to date we have heard nothing of the amount of books pub [published] or sold or the amount pd [paid] Mrs. Isely, as I think she claims so much for expenses of re-writing the manuscript," Claude wrote. "I will greatly appreciate you telling me when we can look for our share of benefits, and who will they be paid to, and also would I be entitled to a complimentary issue of the book, being her oldest son, whose name and picture is in the book."

The then-publisher, J.H. Gipson, responded five days later, telling Claude that sales had been "exceedingly slow," and that the contract "which we have for the publication of this book provides for the submission of royalty reports and the sending of all moneys in settlement of royalties earned to Mrs. Bliss Isely."[7]

If Isely/Duncan did share some of the book's modest proceeds with any surviving members of Corabelle's family, and she may very well have without other descendants' knowledge, there was no known record of that in Corabelle's surviving papers.

In one respect, Isely/Duncan was correct in her assessment that Corabelle had led a "hard" life. As Corabelle remembered in the handwritten account in the 1930s, and as she had depicted when her memory was fresh in the *Word Carrier* stories, she willingly took on challenges that would have defeated many. But she had chosen that life. She had chosen to meet and serve Native people in their homes and communities. Hard? Most certainly. But "pitiable?" Hardly. And *Blue Star* did not touch even half of her life story.

Chapter 27

Missionary Spirit to the End

THOUGH BLIND, THE SEPTUAGENARIAN CORABELLE WAS ABLE TO LOOK back at her time in Dakota Territory with clear vision. For whatever reason, or reasons, she bleached out the harder times with Sam Campbell and George Tillman. Her troubled relationship with Tillman may simply have been a marriage of convenience for a woman who had three small children to raise and little money with which to do it.

Corabelle Fellows Campbell Tillman died on June 30, 1938, believing to the end that her greatest purpose had been in service to others. "I am getting old now and am blind, but my missionary spirit is as strong as ever, and whenever opportunity presents itself, I will do my best," she wrote in her memoirs.

Her obituary said she was survived by three daughters, two sons, eight grandchildren, and one great-grandchild.[1] It did not mention Sam Campbell.

The city where Corabelle spent the last thirty years of her life itself had a robust history of Native occupation and displacement, a mirror to her own life. It is named for the Native Kitkiti'sh, or Wichita, who roamed and settled in an area spanning modern-day Kansas to Texas. White traders in 1864 established a fort at the confluence of the Arkansas and Little Arkansas Rivers. More than three hundred years earlier, the Wichita had first encountered the Spanish explorer, Coronado. The Wichita raised corn and pumpkins and hunted buffalo. Historians believe they were the first group of Plains Indians to encounter Christian missionaries.

The Wichita Indians had been forced north by Confederates during the Civil War; after the war they were pushed onto reservations in Oklahoma. By the 1880s, the city of Wichita was growing along the Chisolm Trail and transcontinental railroad lines.[2] The city later became a center for aviation, and by the twenty-first century its metro area surpassed a half million in population. It erected statues and built a museum to honor the traditions of those who had come first. But less than 1 percent of the population identified as "American Indian or Alaska Native alone."[3]

Among its modern attractions: a forty-four-foot-tall steel statue called "Keeper of the Plains," which, according to a promotional description, "pays tribute to the Native Americans who lived here long before settlers arrived." Steps away, the Mid-America All Indian Center "educates and preserves the heritage of the American Indian."[4]

Corabelle had been civically involved in Wichita for more than three decades. She joined a flower club.[5] She signed petitions for political candidates that appeared in the newspapers.[6] As she was going blind, she reveled in giving "lively accounts of her experiences living with the Indians" in talks arranged by the Wichita Association for the Blind.[7] Her granddaughter recalled that she wrote articles for various publications. She taught her grandchildren to sing songs in Dakota, and to dance the way she had observed on the hard-packed dirt dance floors of the Rosebud and Cheyenne River reservations.

One of *Blue Star*'s biggest contributions may have been its pairing of Corabelle with a renowned composer and Native music preservationist named Thurlow Lieurance. *Blue Star* reprinted the words and melodies of Sioux songs Corabelle would sing to her children and grandchildren. Lieurance, who was then the director of fine arts at what was then known as Wichita University, had helped Corabelle put the melody and lyrics to paper. Lieurance, who later had a library named after him at the university, was by then quite famous in the music world. His most famous Native composition, "By the Waters of Minnetonka," was based on a Sioux love song he had heard sung by a man named Sitting Eagle on the Crow Reservation in Montana in 1911.[8]

Corabelle lived her final years in a house on Water Street about five blocks from the Wichita River. Her granddaughter remembered it as a "pleasant home where she was given board and room that she could afford." The house was in a working-class neighborhood south of downtown. In the blistering summer heat of the 1930s, it would have been a tough environment. Suffering from cancer as well as blindness, she lived her last days with her son Wilbur and his wife Lena. Daughters Cora and Rose lived within a block of them.[9]

Like many in the 1930s, Corabelle had had to turn to public assistance, receiving $15 a month from the county at various times. The newspapers' lists of people on public assistance filled long columns in local newspapers.[10] Her granddaughter, Rose Staunton Kirkbright, acknowledged that Corabelle's oldest son, Claude, had trouble with alcohol and, at times made her life "miserable."

"She was a proud woman and may not have communicated to the rest of the family in the same city how bad the situation was," Rose wrote. "But we were always and often in touch, and she was determined to make a home for Claude when she could. But for most of the time she lived with one of her other children, including my family."[11]

Fittingly, one reviewer of *Blue Star* was Elaine Goodale Eastman, the famous author whose marriage to a Native man had been accepted and praised. "Since the present reviewer happens to have been familiar with this same aspect of Indian life between 1886 and 1903, it is possible to testify to its essential truth as well as to detect a few errors," Goodale Eastman wrote for the Springfield, Massachusetts *Republican*. She said the book's first-person format was "simple and naïve," but that she had also determined that "life on an Indian reservation a generation or more ago was realistically portrayed."

Goodale Eastman wrote that Sam "was far from the 'savage' he was represented to be." Corabelle "was warm-hearted and much in earnest, finding the people lovable on the whole in spite of much that was sordid and depressing in the environment, and she withstood the many hardships with determination."[12]

On that point, Corabelle would have agreed. "I have never regretted a moment of the time I marked to help lift others and the little joys and comforts I gave these Sioux Indians to lift and brighten their lives and

Corabelle and her grandson
COURTESY OF CARRIE LINDSEY

surroundings," she reminisced in her handwritten memoirs. "God made them a noble people."

In retrospect, she said, "there were dangers as well as good, and there were powers through my work in God's plan for saving and teaching His people."

Through it all, through being disowned by her family and humiliated and exploited across the country, it was the memory of Dakota Territory's remote challenges and the hearts of the struggling, once-wandering people of its plains, that had sustained her.

"There were so many delightful and happy experiences," she said in her final years, "that now as I look back I know God was with me." She said she believed that "God has a great work yet for his Indians. The Sioux Indian is proud and intellectual; he sees the good and beautiful in nature."

In the mid-1920s, Corabelle traveled to South Dakota to seek out old friends and see old places. In her memoirs, she wrote of being struck by how log homes and tepees had been replaced by frame houses, by how sewing machines and other modern inventions occupied prominent places in Native homes. Many of the people she had encountered, like Winyan, had died, but the rekindling of one friendship was memorable.

Almost forty years after she had fallen out of the back of Nancy Dupre's runaway mule-driven wagon, Corabelle discovered the old lady living in Santee, across the Missouri River from Springfield, the place in which the young teacher and missionary had first stepped off the train that Thanksgiving week of 1884. As Corabelle described it in her memoirs, a widowed Nancy was supporting herself by selling dolls and moccasins she'd made by hand. The two women had a fleeting moment in which they tried to place the other until, Corabelle wrote, "she recognized my smile."

When Nancy smiled back, "I recognized the same merry woman, with the deep dimples. She also brought out some pictures I had given her to prove she was Nancy, and said, 'Blue Star,' the name they gave me."

In that passage of her handwritten memories, Corabelle marveled at how paved roads and motor cars and modern household conveniences had made life so much easier even in the most remote places. But it was that memory of the rugged ride in the wagon with Nancy Dupre, the one that ended with the Native woman laughing so hard at the white woman trying to catch up, that connected them through time. They had remembered one another through their smiles.

Epilogue

This tale comes home to where it began, in Swift Bird, where Sam and Corabelle had courted and planned a life together. It seems a fine place from which to tell the history that has followed.

Swift Bird's very survival is a testament to the transient, yet permanent, nature of this land and the people who dwell upon it. The village was once called Marksville, and it was located just across US Highway 212 from the current-day Swift Bird. Gregg Bourland, the former chair of the Cheyenne River Sioux Indian Tribe, told me the Marksville community was also called Swift Bird to honor the chief. Its present location is where the federal government in the late-twentieth century built "cluster housing" for people displaced from the Missouri River bottomlands when the Oahe Dam was built. Bourland told me that residents who lived in and around the old agency village along the river—the one where Corabelle survived the summer storm with her two young sons—were relocated to Swift Bird or other communities higher above the river. Some were relocated as far away as the reservation's headquarters in Eagle Butte, sixty miles west. Some dispersed far away from the reservation.

The federal government eventually determined that the Cheyenne River Reservation lost about one hundred thousand acres of bottomland to the permanent flooding from the dams. Dissatisfied with the original $10 million in payment for that loss, Bourland's tribal government lobbied Congress for more, and received an additional $290 million, plus interest.[1]

In building their case for the compensation, Cheyenne River tribal leaders held meetings in every community on the reservation. Elder after elder came with stories. Some talked of sitting on the banks watching the river rise slowly over their homes and remains of their ancestors. Some recalled raising vegetables and hay for cattle and horses in the bottomland. Some remembered swimming in the unpredictable, untamed Missouri, using willow poles to mark the drop-offs.

Lanniko Lee, a Lakota writer and citizen of the Cheyenne River Indian Reservation who was educated in a Bureau of Indians affairs boarding school, remembered what life was like along the river as a young child before the dams came.

> *I see a river shoreline of men and women, young and old, carrying water, picking berries, gathering firewood, fishing from the shore, wading in the sloughs for cattail root, gathering teas of so many kinds, making toys for children from the fallen leaves and branches, telling stories of how we came to be a people, making furniture, women telling river stories to their grandchildren, children learning the gifts of the river. I hear men singing; I hear women, old and young, singing as they work and live among the trees. I hear children's laughter, too.*[2]

Corabelle, who once crossed the Missouri River alone, would not recognize it today. Lake Oahe now is wide and deep and stretches 231 miles, from one state capital (Pierre) to another (Bismarck), and its meandering and tentacled shape adds up to 2,250 miles of shoreline.[3] But one can still hear children's laughter on its shores. Lake Oahe and other Missouri River reservoirs in the twenty-first century attract fishers, hunters, boaters, swimmers, and other recreation seekers, Native and non-Native. New family stories are being made on its waters and the shores. The dams' hydropower feeds homes, farms, and businesses in many states. It may or may not be progress depending upon the vantage point, but it is life.

But, as in Corabelle's time here, conflicts persist. In the 1970s and 1980s, white farmers protested and rejected giant government irrigation projects from the Oahe Reservoir. Disputes persist between states over flood-control policies. Tribal and state governments fight over water rights.

One story from those many meetings about the compensation claim stood out for Bourland more than two decades later. He remembered one old woman describing how she gathered "mouse berries" from plants that proliferated primarily in the river bottom. The old lady's description of seeking mouse caches was very similar to Corabelle's "beans" tale—with one addition. The old lady assured the politicians that the act was a tradeoff; the gleaners would take only a portion of the berries, she said, and they would always leave something in return. Perhaps a dried cherry or another food in abundance would be left, so diets of human and animal would be sufficient and balanced. "And so it was a tradeoff between the Lakota and these little animals," Bourland told me. Now prime "mouse berry" habitat along the river is gone, he lamented, "under 100 feet of water."

The Riggs missions are gone, too. Oahe, which means "foundation" in Sioux, has an entirely different context today. In 1940 Thomas Riggs was buried at the Riggs Family Cemetery at Oahe Mission astride the Missouri. His first wife, Nina Foster Riggs, had been buried there sixty-two years before. Two of Thomas's children from his second marriage, two grandchildren, and a daughter-in-law also lie in the cemetery. In 1951 Thomas's second wife, Louisa Riggs, the woman who had served with Winyan and Corabelle, who had protested Isely/Duncan's depiction of Winyan in *Blue Star*, was the last to be buried in the Riggs family cemetery.

Later that decade, when the Oahe Dam was under construction and the river began rising, the Riggs chapel was moved and preserved. The rest of the mission buildings at Oahe were left behind. The family graves were left undisturbed, eventually submerged in fresh history. Now, the spirits of white missionaries and Indigenous people from millenniums past lie together under the same waters.[4]

Acknowledgments

This book would not have been possible without the discovery of Corabelle Fellows's handwritten memoirs, which had been handed down through the family for generations, into the hands of a great-great granddaughter, Carrie Lindsey, from the Tillman side of the family. Throughout the process of researching and writing this book, Carrie was a selfless, compassionate source of information and inspiration, and to her I am eternally grateful.

Lora Meinzer, a descendant of Elizabeth Winyan and lifelong member of Ascension Presbyterian Church in Spring Grove Township, South Dakota, was a great help in supplying photos of Elizabeth and the family. Ascension Presbyterian was founded by Elizabeth's son, Edwin Phelps. The legacy of this family is rich and deep. Lora is a member of the Sisseton Wahpeton Oyate Tribe of northeastern South Dakota.

Elizabeth Cisar, research assistant at the Center for Western Studies at Augustana University in Sioux Falls, guided me through their valuable collections and was especially accommodating as we maneuvered through the challenges of COVID-19. The staff at Wichita State University Libraries' Special Collection and University Archives was very helpful and accommodating.

Many thanks to researcher Jason Miller, whose passion and knowledge was indispensable and of especially good help when travel was rough during the early days of COVID-19. My agent, Victoria Skurnick, was instrumental in getting this work to print. Books can still civilize us in a callous, mistrusting world.

This book was not intended as a critique of *Blue Star*. Flora Isely, nee Kunigunde Duncan, recognized a fantastic and important story, and she told it in a hopeful, spirited way. She advanced understanding of women, Native and non-Native, on the American frontier. My intentions were solely to tell the rest of Corabelle's story.

Finally, and forever, my friend Jeff Stinson was a great help in understanding Wichita and the neighborhood where Corabelle spent her last years. Jeff, a lifelong friend who grew up in Wichita, died suddenly, scant weeks after he had visited Corabelle's gravesite at my behest. We so miss this Wichita boy, and this book is dedicated to his memory.

Notes

Preface

1. Elaine Goodale Eastman, *Sister to the Sioux: The Memoirs of Elaine Goodale Eastman, 1885–1891* (Lincoln: University of Nebraska Press, 1978), 131.

2. US Census Bureau (2021), American Community Survey 5-year estimates. Retrieved from Census Reporter Profile page for Cheyenne River Reservation, censusreporter.org/profiles/25200US0605R-cheyenne-river-reservation, accessed September 4, 2022.

3. "South Dakota Reservations by the Numbers," keloland.com, keloland.com/keloland-com-original/south-dakota-reservations-by-the-numbers.

4. Atlanta *Constitution*, April 5, 1888, 4.

5. Mead Gruver, "US Changes Names of Places with Racist Term for Native Women," AP News, September 8, 2022, https://apnews.com/article/Native-americans-climate-and-environment-government-politics-004fa29f3967ae7ab74958a61fda02d2.

6. Darren Thompson, "Christian Mission Ousted from Pine Ridge Indian Reservation after Distribution of Hate Materials," Yahoo! News, July 25, 2022, https://news.yahoo.com/christian-mission-ousted-pine-ridge-222306684.html?fr=sycsrp_catchall.

7. Nick Estes, *Our History Is the Future, Standing Rock versus the Dakota Access Pipeline, and the Long Tradition of Indigenous Resistance* (New York: Verso, 2019), 8.

8. Virginia Driving Hawk Sneve, That They May Have Life: The Episcopal Church in South Dakota, 1859–1976 (New York: Seabury Press, 1977), 3.

9. "Explore The Seven Council Fires," Minnesota Historical Society, accessed October 3, 2022, mnhs.org/sevencouncilfires.

10. "Tim Giago, Native American Newspaperman, Is Dead at 88," *New York Times*, accessed July 29, 2022, nytimes.com/2022/07/28/us/tim-giago-dead.html.

Chapter 1

1. Kunigunde Duncan (pen name for Flora Isely), Letters to I. Louisa M. Riggs, 1899–1950 (archives of the Center for Western Studies, Augustana University, May 20, 1939).

2. Kenneth Sauer, "Life Story of Former Wichita Woman Told in New Book," Wichita *Eagle*, December 4, 1938, 50.

3. Letters from Rose Staunton Kirkbright to Bruce D. Forbes (Minnesota Historical Society, December 28, 1992).

4. Ibid.

5. Kunigunde, Letters to I. Louisa M. Riggs.

6. J. A. T., "Girl Teacher is Heroine of Indian Book," Ogden, Utah, *Standard-Examiner*, November 6, 1938, 25.

7. "Scanning New Books," Sioux Falls *Argus Leader*, January 29, 1939, 14.

Chapter 2

1. Kunigunde Duncan (pen name for Flora Isely), *Blue Star: The Story of Corabelle Fellows, Teacher at Dakota Missions 1884–1888* (St. Paul: Minnesota Historical Society Press, 1990), 64.

2. Duncan, *Blue Star,* 64–68.

3. Anthony M. Richter, *A Heritage of Faith: Religion and the German Settlers of South Dakota* (Pierre: South Dakota Historical Society, 1991).

4. "New Helpers," *Word Carrier*, November 1884, 1.

5. Fellows, Corabelle, "Views of a New Teacher," *Word Carrier*, January 1885, 3.

6. *Word Carrier*, April 1884, 1.

7. *Word Carrier*, January 1891, 1.

8. *Word Carrier*, September 1884, 1.

9. Roger Holtzmann, "Apostles on the Plains," *South Dakota Magazine*, November–December 2010, accessed October 3, 2022, southdakotamagazine.com/apostles-on-the-plains.

10. Nick Estes, *Our History is the Future, Standing Rock Versus the Dakota Pipeline, and the Long History of Indigenous Resistance* (New York: Verso, 2022), 140.

11. *Word Carrier,* November 1884, 1.

12. Beth A. Twiss Houting, "Indian Rights Associations," the *Encyclopedia of Greater Philadelphia*, 2014, philadelphiaencyclopedia.org/essays/indian-rights-associations.

13. Duncan, *Blue Star*, xiv.

14. Charles Howard, "Two Presbyterian Elders," *Word Carrier*, May 1884, 3.

15. Alfred L. Riggs, "The Last of the Sun Dance," *Word Carrier*, June 1884, 1.

16. Duncan, *Blue Star*, 114–117.

17. "Message from the President of the United States, transmitting reports relative to the proposed division of the Great Sioux Reservation, and recommending certain legislation" (University of Oklahoma College of Law, February 10, 1890), 28, accessed September 1, 2022, https://digitalcommons.law.ou.edu/cgi/viewcontent.cgi?article=8728&context=indianserialset.

18. Nancy Hunter, *Word Carrier*, April 1884, 1.

19. Claire Giangravé, "In Canada, Pope Francis Apologizes to Indigenous Peoples, Says It's Only 'First Step,'" Religion News Service, July 25, 2022, accessed November 20, 2022, https://religionnews.com/2022/07/25/in-canada-pope-francis-apologizes-to-indigenous-peoples-says-its-only-first-step.

20. Bryan Newland, "Federal Indian Boarding School Initiative Investigative Report," (US Department of the Interior, May 2022).

21. Santee Normal Trading School and American Missionary Association, "Santee Normal Training School, Santee Agency, Nebraska, report for the year ending

June 30, 1885" (University of Nebraska-Omaha digital commons archives), https://digitalcommons.unomaha.edu/santee_school, accessed November 20, 2022.

22. Ibid.

23. "Soap and Syntax," *Word Carrier*, April 15, 1884, 1.

24. Alfred L. Riggs, "To Our Friends," *Word Carrier*, October–November 1888, 35.

25. Alfred L. Riggs, "A Missionary School," *Word Carrier*, October–November 1888, 351.

26. Alfred L. Riggs, "Phantom Missions," *Word Carrier*, March 1886, 2.

27. "Discreditable Marriages," *Word Carrier*, March 1, 1884, 3.

28. Mary Buel Hatch Riggs, "A Letter to Eastern Friends," *Word Carrier*, April 1, 1884, 2.

29. Corabelle Fellows, "Views of a New Teacher," *Word Carrier*, January 1885, 3.

30. Corabelle Fellows, "Among the Wild Indians," *Word Carrier*, January 1886, 4.

31. Ibid.

Chapter 3

1. Kunigunde Duncan (pen name for Flora Isely), *Blue Star: The Story of Corabelle Fellows, Teacher at Dakota Missions 1884–1888* (St. Paul: Minnesota Historical Society Press, 1990), 120.

2. Duncan, *Blue Star*, 10.

3. Duncan, *Blue Star*, 36.

4. Duncan, *Blue Star*, 18.

5. Duncan, *Blue Star*, 50.

6. Duncan, *Blue Star*, 33.

7. Duncan, *Blue Star*, 31.

8. Duncan, *Blue Star*, 32.

9. Ibid.

10. Duncan, *Blue Star*, 35.

11. Duncan, *Blue Star*, 38.

12. Ibid.

13. Duncan, *Blue Star*, 41.

14. Ibid.

15. Duncan, *Blue Star,* 47–50.

Chapter 4

1. "Indian Civilization," St. Paul *Daily Globe*, November 6, 1884, 4.

2. "Dakota & Montana: Northwestern Notes," St. Paul *Daily Globe*, November 25, 1884, 3.

3. "Crook's Campaign," *Black Hills Daily Times*, June 5, 1883, 2.

4. George Crook, *General George Crook–His Autobiography* (Norman: University of Oklahoma Press, 1946).

5. Henry M. Teller, "Interior Department: Secretary Teller's Annual Report—The Indians and Manual-Labor Schools," *Chicago Tribune*, November 28, 1884, 6.

CHAPTER 5

1. Fellows, Corabelle, "Views of a New Teacher," *Word Carrier*, January 1885, 3.

2. Kunigunde Duncan (pen name for Flora Isely), *Blue Star: The Story of Corabelle Fellows, Teacher at Dakota Missions 1884–1888* (St. Paul: Minnesota Historical Society Press, 1990), 52

3. *Word Carrier,* August–September 1887, 1.

4. Fellows, "Views of a New Teacher," 3.

5. A.S. Quinton to Corabelle Fellows, September 14, 1885, Kenneth Isely Collection of Bliss Isely and Flora Isely Papers, Wichita State University Libraries Special Collection and University Archives.

6. Duncan, *Blue Star*, xxiii.

CHAPTER 6

1. Thomas Hughes. *Old Traverse des Sioux, A History of Early Exploration, Trading Posts, Mission Station, Treaties and Pioneer Village* (St. Peter: Herald Publishing Company, 1929), 10–11.

2. Dennis Wagner, *State of the Union History*, www.stateoftheunionhistory.com/2017/12/1824-james-monroe-voluntary-indian.html, accessed September 19, 2022.

3. Mary Lethert Wingerd, *North Country: The Making of Minnesota* (Minneapolis: University of Minnesota Press, 2010), 186–189.

4. Minnesota Indian Affairs Council, *Relations: Dakota and Ojibwe Treaties*, treatiesmatter.org/treaties/land/1851-Dakota, accessed September 12, 2022.

5. Stephen Riggs, "Dakota Portraits," *Minnesota History Magazine*, 485, http://collections.mnhs.org/MNHistoryMagazine/articles/2/v02i08p481-568.pdf?__hstc=206163532.2798172561f57be7554f30baf429eedc.1681418291686.1681418291686.1681418291686.1&__hssc=206163532.1.1681418291686&__hsfp=2003037740

6. Hughes, *Old Traverse des Sioux*, 10.

7. *American Missionary* (Minnesota State Historical Society archives of Elizabeth Winyan, Edwin Phelps, Elias Gilbert, April 1890), 121.

8. Hughes, *Old Traverse des Sioux*, 11.

9. Ibid.

10. Thomas Hughes, *Indian Chiefs of Southern Minnesota, Containing Sketches of the Prominent Chieftains of the Dakota and Winnebago Tribes from 1825–1865* (Minnesota State Historical Society archives of Elizabeth Winyan, Edwin Phelps, Elias Gilbert), 51.

11. Stephen Return Riggs. *Mary and I—Forty Years with the Sioux* (Williamstown: Corner House Publishers, 1971), 155.

12. Riggs, *Mary and I,* 178.

13. Hughes, *Indian Chiefs of Southern Minnesota,* 71.

14. *The Northwestern Congregationalist* (Minnesota State Historical Society archives of Elizabeth Winyan, Edwin Phelps, Elias Gilbert, March 28, 1890), 5.

15. Autobiography of Mary C. Collins (South Dakota Historical Society Archives), 15, 44, 65, 114, https://sddigitalarchives.contentdm.oclc.org/digital/collection/manuscript/id/4956/rec/2, accessed September 12, 2002.

Chapter 7

1. Corabelle Fellows, "The Indian Problem," *Word Carrier*, October–December 1885, 4.
2. *Word Carrier*, October–December 1885, 1.
3. *Word Carrier*, October–December, 1885, 4.
4. Kunigunde Duncan (pen name for Flora Isely), *Blue Star: The Story of Corabelle Fellows, Teacher at Dakota Missions 1884–1888* (St. Paul: Minnesota Historical Society Press, 1990), xxiv.
5. Fellows, "The Indian Problem," 4.
6. Corabelle Fellows, "Among the Wild Indians," *Word Carrier*, January 1886, 4.
7. Duncan, *Blue Star*, 133.
8. Duncan, *Blue Star*, 134.

Chapter 8

1. Kunigunde Duncan (pen name for Flora Isely), *Blue Star: The Story of Corabelle Fellows, Teacher at Dakota Missions 1884–1888* (St. Paul: Minnesota Historical Society Press, 1990), 147–154.
2. *Blue Star*, 174–178.

Chapter 10

1. Corabelle Fellows, "Among the Wild Indians," *Word Carrier*, January 1886, 4.
2. Kunigunde Duncan (pen name for Flora Isely), *Blue Star: The Story of Corabelle Fellows, Teacher at Dakota Missions 1884–1888* (St. Paul: Minnesota Historical Society Press, 1990), 192.

Chapter 11

1. Charles McChesney to Corabelle Fellows, January 2, 1886, Kenneth Isely Collection of Bliss Isely and Flora Isely Papers, Wichita State University Libraries Special Collection and University Archives, Series One.
2. Kunigunde Duncan (pen name for Flora Isely), *Blue Star: The Story of Corabelle Fellows, Teacher at Dakota Missions 1884–1888* (St. Paul: Minnesota Historical Society Press, 1990), 196.
3. Candice Millard, *Destiny of the Republic: A Tale of Madness, Medicine and the Murder of a President* (Random House, 2011).
4. *Blue Star*, 150.
5. *Blue Star*, 186–187.
6. American Bison Association, *Bison by the Numbers*, https://bisoncentral.com/bison-by-the-numbers, accessed October 3, 2022.
7. *Blue Star*, 195–196.
8. *Blue Star*, 199–200.

Chapter 12

1. Kunigunde Duncan (pen name for Flora Isely), *Blue Star: The Story of Corabelle Fellows, Teacher at Dakota Missions 1884–1888* (St. Paul: Minnesota Historical Society Press, 1990), 183.

2. Vicky Valenta, "Santee Sioux Genealogy," facebook.com/Santee.Sioux.Genealogy.

3. Valenta, "Santee Sioux Genealogy."

4. Baptiste Scott Campbell, findagrave.com/memorial/47617886/baptiste-scott-campbell, accessed September 14, 2022.

5. Lawrence J. Barkwell, "Antoine Scott Campbell," scribd.com/document/53676354/Campbell-Antoine-Scott, accessed September 12, 2022.

6. Gary Clayton Anderson and Allan R. Woolworth, eds., *Through Dakota Eyes: Narrative Accounts of the Minnesota Indian War of 1862* (St. Paul: Minnesota Historical Society Press, 1988), 287.

7. "Chaska and His Bride: The Curiously Mated Pair from the Cheyenne Reservation," *Atlanta Constitution,* May 11, 1888, 5.

8. "The Museum Thronged to See Mrs. Chaska and 'Sam-u-el,'" Bismarck *Daily Tribune*, May 8, 1888, 1.

9. "Chaska and His Bride: The Curiously Mated Pair from the Cheyenne Reservation," *Chicago Tribune*, May 9, 1888, 9.

10. *Blue Star*, 200.

11. *Blue Star*, 202.

12. Ibid.

13. "A Red Man's Bride: Chaska, the Cheyenne Brave, and Miss Fellows will Wed on March 16," St. Paul *Daily Globe*, March 2, 1888, 6.

14. Ibid.

15. Ibid.

16. "Will Prevent His Daughter's Marriage," reprinted in the Alton, Ill., *Evening Telegraph,* March 8, 1888, 2.

17. "She Marries Poor Lo: Miss Cora Belle Fellows United to Chaska, the Sioux Buck," *Cain City Razzooper*, March 29, 1888, 1.

18. "Miss Cora Fellows and Chaska to be Married To-day," *Bismarck Tribune*, March 24, 1888, 1.

19. "A Letter from Miss Fellows," *Evening Star*, March 27, 1888, 6.

20. Aunt May to Corabelle Fellows, February 26, 1888, Kenneth Isely Collection of Bliss Isely and Flora Isely Papers, Wichita State University Libraries Special Collection and University Archives, Series One.

21. Marian Fellows to Corabelle Fellows Campbell, March 24, 1888, Kenneth Isely Collection of Bliss Isely and Flora Isely Papers, Wichita State University Libraries Special Collection and University Archives, Series One.

Chapter 13

1. Kunigunde Duncan (pen name for Flora Isely), *Blue Star: The Story of Corabelle Fellows, Teacher at Dakota Missions 1884–1888* (St. Paul: Minnesota Historical Society Press, 1990), 202–203.

2. Marlys Fratzke, administrator at Episcopal Diocese of South Dakota, email to Chuck Raasch (author), July 7, 2022.

3. "Rev. J. W. Hanford Dead," *Daily Commercial Herald*, August 8, 1888, 2.

4. *Blue Star*, 202.

5. *Blue Star*, 204.

6. Ibid.

Chapter 14

1. Kunigunde Duncan (pen name for Flora Isely), *Blue Star: The Story of Corabelle Fellows, Teacher at Dakota Missions 1884–1888* (St. Paul: Minnesota Historical Society Press, 1990), 204.

2. Power of Attorney document, June 14, 1888, Hamilton County Ohio; Kenneth Isely Collection of Bliss Isely and Flora Isely Papers, Wichita State University Library Special Collection and University Archives. Series One.

3. Cheyenne River Sioux Tribe Historic Marker, Highway 212 and Missouri River Bridge.

4. *Blue Star*, 205.

5. Ibid.

6. "She Loves a Savage," St. Paul *Daily Globe*, May 6, 1888, 5.

7. "Full Fledged Freaks: Mr. and Mrs. Chaska Will Appear at the Dime Museum," St. Paul *Daily Globe*, May 6, 1888, 2.

8. Neil Gale, "The History of Dime Museums in Early 20th Century Chicago," Illinois History Journal, https://drloihjournal.blogspot.com/2017/05/kohl-middletons-dime-museums-chicago.html, accessed September 8, 2022.

9. Andrea Stulman Dennett, *Weird and Wonderful: The Dime Museum America* (New York: New York University Press, 1997), xi.

10. "Dime Musium," Minneapolis *Star Tribune*, May 13, 1888, 9.

11. "Cora and Chaska Again," *Sioux City Journal*, April 11, 1888, 2.

12. "Will Be Represented," Black Hills *Weekly Journa*l, March 8, 1889, 1.

13. Louis S. Warren, *Buffalo Bill's America: William Cody and the Wild West Show* (New York: Vintage Books, 2006), 286.

14. Warren, *Buffalo Bill's America*, 404.

15. Warren, *Buffalo Bill's America*, ix.

16. Warren, *Buffalo Bill's America*, xv.

17. Frederick Jackson Turner, *The Frontier in American History*, paper read to the American Historical Association on July 12, and first published by the State Historical Society of Wisconsin, December 14, 1893, http://xroads.virginia.edu/~Hyper/TURNER/home.html, accessed September 22, 2022.

18. John DeFerrari, "The St. James Hotel on Pennsylvania Avenue," *Streets of Washington*, streetsofwashington.com/2012/06/st-james-hotel-on-pennsylvania-avenue.html, accessed September 21, 2022.

19. Duncan, *Blue Star*, 205.

20. Duncan, *Blue Star*, 205–206.

Chapter 15

1. *Atlanta Constitution*, April 5, 1888, 4.

2. "Saintly City Doings: Six Feet of Indian and a White Woman Not at All Pretty," St. Paul *Daily Globe*, May 7, 1888, 2.

3. Ibid.

4. Larry Millett, "Lost Twin Cities: St. Paul's Ryan Hotel Was a Victorian Masterpiece," Minneapolis *Star Tribune*, January 4, 2019, startribune.com/lost-twin-cities-st-paul-s-ryan-hotel-was-a-victorian-masterpiece/503905672.

5. Dave Kenney, The *Grain Merchants: An Illustrated History of the Minneapolis Grain Exchange* (Edina: Afton Historical Society Press, 2006), N1.

6. "History," National Presbyterian Church, https://nationalpres.org/welcome/history-archives, accessed October 5, 2022.

7. "Saintly City Doings," 2.

8. "Whoopla There, Chaska," *Chicago Tribune*, May 22, 1888, 5.

9. Ibid.

10. "Don't Like Cora's Actions," St. Paul *Daily Globe*, May 10, 1888, 3.

11. Death records of Dewitt C. Haight, ancestry.com, accessed September 22, 2022.

12. St. Paul *Daily Globe*, May 10, 1888, 3, https://www.newspapers.com/image/87819897.

Chapter 16

1. Half Injun: Chaska and Cora Belle are Dad and Mom," *Daily Huronite (Daily Plainsman)*, December 26, 1888, 1.

2. "One Little Injin," St. Paul *Daily Globe*, December 25, 1888, 1.

3. *Sioux City Journal*, December 26, 1888, 6.

4. "Cora and Chaska: A Romance Set Forth in Something Worse Than Blank Verse," *Minneapolis Tribune*, June 3, 1894, 5.

5. "Chaska Receiving His Spotless Angel Bride," *Chicago Tribune*, May 27, 1888, 15.

6. "Chaska and His High-Born Bride," St. Paul *Daily Globe*, May 13, 1888, 13.

7. "Indian Chaska and His White Wife," St. Paul *Daily Globe*, May 5, 1889, 8.

8. "One Little Injun: Chaska Will Have Her Pappoose at Yankton to Please the Firemen," *Daily Huronite* (the *Daily Plainsman)*, June 11, 1889, 2.

9. "Cora and Chaska: A Romance Set Forth in Something Worse Than Black Verse," *Newark Advocate*, April 23, 1894, 4.

Chapter 17

1. Henry F. Graff, "Grover Cleveland: Domestic Affairs" (University of Virginia: Miller Center), https://millercenter.org/president/cleveland/domestic-affairs, accessed September 12, 2022, and The American Presidency Project, "Republican Party Platform of 1888," presidency.ucsb.edu/documents/republican-party-platform-1888, accessed September 12, 2022.

2. National Park Service, "The Dawes Act," nps.gov/articles/000/dawes-act.htm, accessed September 21, 2022.

3. Graff, "Grover Cleveland."

4. Editors of *Encyclopaedia Britannica*, "Dawes General Allotment Act," britannica.com/topic/Dawes-General-Allotment-Act, accessed October 4, 2022.

5. "Among the Tawnies: Chaska Will Sign and Draw Rations as Fluently as of Yore," St. Paul *Daily Globe*, September 15, 1888, 12.

6. Gene Demby, "The Ugly, Fascinating History of the Word 'Racism,'" National Public Radio, September 6, 2014, npr.org/sections/codeswitch, accessed October 8, 2022.

7. Smithsonian Institution National Anthropological Archives, "Delegation to Washington, October 14, 1888, under James McLaughlin," Negative 436563, primeau.org/1888, accessed October 8, 2022.

8. "Message from the President of the United States, transmitting reports relative to the proposed division of the Sioux Reservation, and recommending certain legislation," (University of Oklahoma College of Law, February 1890), 28, accessed September 1, 2022, https://digitalcommons.law.ou.edu/cgi/viewcontent.cgi?article=8728&context=indianserialset.

9. Charles D. Wilber, The *Great Valleys and Prairies of Nebraska and the Northwest*" (Daily Republican Print Press, 1881), 68, https://archive.org/details/cu31924083881155/page/n5/mode/2up?q=inevitable.

10. "Message from the President," 28.

11. "Among the Tawnies," St. Paul *Daily Globe*, 12.

CHAPTER 18

1. Margaret D. Jacobs, "The Eastmans and the Luhans: Interracial Marriage between White Women and Native American Men, 1875–1935," (Lincoln: University of Nebraska-Lincoln, 2002) 7, https://docplayer.net/215055709-October-margaret-d-jacobs-university-of-nebraska-lincoln.html, accessed September 22, 2022.

2. "Squaw Men of the West: Indians with White Wives," Cincinnati *Enquirer*, May 19, 1888, 14.

3. John M. Coward, *The Newspaper Indian: Native American Identity in the Press, 1820–90* (Champaign: University of Illinois Press, 1999), 36.

4. Jacobs, "The Eastmans and the Luhans."

5. Coward, *The Newspaper Indian*, 36.

6. Jacobs, "The Eastmans and the Luhan," 6.

7. Ibid.

8. Jacobs, "The Eastmans and the Luhans," 7.

9. Ibid.

10. "Weary of Her Dusky Brave: The Wife of Chaska Said to Want a Divorce," *San Francisco Examiner*, June 24, 1891, 1.

11. Julie Dobrow, "'Poetry Wedded to Science.' On the Love and legacy of Elaine Goodale and Charles Eastman," Literary Hub, January 20, 2022, lithub.com/poetry-wedded-to-science-on-the-love-and-legacy-of-elaine-goodale-and-charles-eastman, accessed September 22, 2022.

12. "Eastman-Goodale: The Lady Poet-Philanthropist Weds an Indian Physician," St. Paul *Daily Globe*, June 19, 1891, 8.

13. *Berkshire County Eagle*, Pittsfield, MA, June 25, 1891, 2.

14. Elaine Goodale Eastman, *Sister to the Sioux: The Memoirs of Elaine Goodale Eastman, 1885–1891* (Lincoln and London: University of Nebraska Press, 1978), 169.

15. Ibid.

16. Theodore Sargent and Raymond Wilson, "The Estrangement of Charles Eastman and Elaine Goodale Eastman," South Dakota State Historical Society, 2010, sdhspress.com/journal/south-dakota-history-40-3/the-estrangement-of-charles-eastman-and-elaine-goodale-eastman-the-mystery-of-the-other-woman-solved/vol-40-no-3-the-estrangement-of-charles-eastman-and-elaine-goodale-eastman.pdf. Accessed September 22, 2022.

17. Dobrow, *Poetry Wedded to Science*.

18. Cathleen Cahill, "You Think It Strange That I Can Love An Indian: Native Men White Women, and Marriage in the Indian Service," Frontiers: A Journal of Women's Studies, June 1, 2008, 13, www.thefreelibrary.com/%22You+think+it+strange+that+I+can+love+an+Indian%22%3b+Native+men%2c+white...-a0187482598, accessed September 22, 2022.

19. Eastman, *Sister to the Sioux*, 153.

20. Eastman, *Sister to the Sioux*, 164.

21. Sargent and Wilson, "The Estrangement."

22. Eastman, *Sister to the Sioux*, 173.

Chapter 19

1. "Sneaking Sam Campbell," *Daily Huronite*, April 3, 1888, 1.

2. "One Indian Civilized," *The Galveston Daily News*, April 25, 1888, 8.

3. "The Museum Thronged to See Mrs. Chaska and 'Sam-u-el,'" Bismarck *Daily Tribune*, May 8, 1888, 1.

4. "Chaska Married for Sure," *Yellowstone Journal*, April 4, 1888, 1.

5. Vicky Valenta, "Santee Sioux Genealogy," facebook.com/Santee.Sioux.Genealogy.

6. "Among the Tawnies," St. Paul *Daily Globe*, September 15, 1888, 12.

7. "Chaska and His Bride Wasting the Money They Earned in the Museum," *New York Times*, October 6, 1888, 2.

8. "Chaska and Cora Expected Friday!—Poetic War-whoop," *Daily Huronite (Daily Plainsman)*, June 5, 1888, 2.

9. Detroit *Free Press*, October 9, 1888, 4.

10. *Daily Wamegan*, Wamego, Kansas, November 28, 1888, 2.

11. "Yellow Journalism," Public Broadcasting System, pbs.org/crucible/journalism.html, accessed October 3, 2022.

12. "Among the Tawnies," St. Paul *Daily Globe*, September 15, 1888, 12.

Chapter 20

1. *Daily Huronite*, April 6, 1887, 3.

2. "Died—at Fort Bennett, Dakota, on Thursday, February 20, of pneumonia, Elizabeth Winyan," *Word Carrier*, February 1, 1890, 1.

3. Kunigunde Duncan (pen name for Flora Isely), *Blue Star: The Story of Corabelle Fellows, Teacher at Dakota Missions 1884–1888* (St. Paul: Minnesota Historical Society Press, 1990), 128.

4. *Blue Star*, 124.

5. *Blue Star*, 126.

6. "Died—at Fort Bennett" *Word Carrier*.

7. *American Missionary* vol. 4, no. 4 (April 1890), gutenberg.org/files/15609/15609-h/15609-h.htm, accessed September 12, 2022.

8. "The Religious Nature of the Indian," *Word Carrier*, July–August–September 1918, 2.

9. *American Missionary*, vol. 4, no. 4 (April 1890), accessed Sept. 12, 2022, online at gutenberg.org/files/15609/15609-h/15609-h.htm.

10. *Vermont Chronicle*, April 18, 1890, 1.

11. *Annual Report of the American Board of Commissioners for Foreign Missions* (Cambridge: Riverside Press, October 3–4, 1882).

12. American Missionary Association, *Elizabeth Winyan's Addresses* (reprinted by the Chippewa County Historical Society, Mary Collins Collection, Center for Western Studies, Augustana University).

13. *Word Carrier*, April 1888, 1.

14. American Missionary Association, *Elizabeth Winyan's Addresses.*

15. M. M. Likorish, *The American Missionary,* October 1894, 363–364.

16. "Elizabeth Winyan," *Word Carrier*, January 1895, 2.

17. "State News," *Reporter and Farmer*, June 7, 1894, 2.

Chapter 21

1. *Word Carrier*, January 1891, 1.

2. "One Point of View," *Word Carrier*, January 1891, 2.

3. "The Chaska Divorce Suit: Pretty Indian Romance, Tinged with Sensationalism, Chattered at Last," *Indianapolis Journal*, June 26, 1891, 5.

4. "Sick of Her Bargain: Last Chapter in the Chaska Indian Love Affair," *Wisconsin State Journal,* June 25, 1881, 1.

5. "Caused a Sensation: The Dramatic History of Mrs. Cora Chaska," *Altoona Tribune,* June 25, 1891, 1.

6. "End of a Romance: Mrs. Chaska Deserted by Her Indian Husband for a More Buxom Squaw," *Boonville Standard*, Boonville, Indiana, March 2, 1894, 2.

7. Vicky Valenta, "Santee Sioux Genealogy," facebook.com/Santee.Sioux.Genealogy.

8. "The Chaska Divorce Suit," 5.

Chapter 22

1. "Message from the President of the United States, transmitting reports relative to the proposed division of the Sioux Reservation, and recommending certain legislation," (University of Oklahoma College of Law, February 1890), 288, accessed September 1, 2022, https://digitalcommons.law.ou.edu/cgi/viewcontent.cgi?article=8728&context=indianserialset.

2. Jerome A. Greene, The *Sioux Land Commission of 1889: Prelude to Wounded Knee* (South Dakota Historical Society, 1970), 50, sdhspress.com/journal/south-dakota-history-1-1/the-sioux-land-commission-of-1889-prelude-to-wounded-knee/vol-01-no-1-the-sioux-land-commission-of-1889.pdf, accessed September 2, 2022.

3. Greene, *The Sioux Land Commission*, 50.

4. "Message from the President," 152.

5. "Message from the President," 172.

Chapter 23

1. "Tired of His White Wife: Miss Fellows' Friends Not Surprised at the Sequel of Her Marriage to Chaska," *St. Louis Post-Dispatch*, February 21, 1894, 2.

2. "Cora Fellows in Want: Woman Who Married Chaska, the Sioux, in Penury at Carthage, Mo.," *Douglas County Herald*, Ava, Missouri, May 14, 1896, 1.

3. "Met Guest with Knife," *Wichita Daily Eagle*, August 18, 1912, 23.

4. A.P. Darling to Corabelle Tillman, December 19, 1905, Kenneth Isely Collection of Bliss Isely and Flora Isely Papers, Wichita State University Library Special Collection and University Archives, Series One.

5. "George Tillman Dies," Wichita *Eagle*, January 8, 1926, 4.

6. US Census, 1900, ancestry.com/discoveryui-content/view/79280924:7602?_phsrc=mzf505&_phstart=successSource&gsfn=George+&gsln=Tillman&ml_rpos=2&queryId=6592419ccd180769956733c047ecdcca, accessed September 29, 2022.

7. Rose Staunton Kirkbright to Carrie Lindsey, undated, private collection.

8. US Civil War Index, General Index to Pension files, ancestry.com/discoveryui-content/view/10678207:4654, accessed September 29, 2022.

9. Union Regimental Histories, Civil War Archive, civilwararchive.com/Unreghst/unilinf9.htm#110th, accessed September 19, 2022.

10. United States General Index to Pension Files, 1861–1864, image supplied by researcher Jason Miller.

11. "George Tillman Dies," 4.

12. "Met Guest with Knife," Wichita *Eagle*, August 18, 1912, 23.

Chapter 24

1. "Suicide of a High-Flying Sioux," *Evening World-Herald*, May 3, 1898, 2.

2. "Chaska Didn't Kill Himself," *Blackfoot News*, August 6, 1898, 7.

3. Kathleen Kokensparger, public records manager, Nebraska Department of Correctional Services, email to Chuck Raasch (author), August 9, 2022.

4. "Chaska Didn't Kill Himself," *Blackfoot News*, 7.

5. "An Indian's Suicide: Leaves a Beautiful White Widow in Weeds," Washington *Evening Times,* May 10, 1898, 6.

6. Cora Belle's Red Husband: Chaska Goes to the Penitentiary to Close His Career," Nebraska *State Journal*, June 1, 1898, 4.

7. Vicky Valenta, "Santee Sioux Genealogy," 1915 Santee Census, facebook.com/Santee.Sioux.Genealogy.

Chapter 25

1. *Pine Belt News,* Newton, Alabama, December 2, 1897, 6.

2. Virginia death records of Marian Fellows Davison, ancestry.com, accessed September 9, 2022.

3. Washington *Evening Star,* March 26, 1898, 3.

4. "A Death Trap: Collapse of the Old Ford Theater Building in Washington," St. Joseph *Weekly Herald,* June 15, 1893, 8.

5. "Frightful Disaster: Hundreds of Clerks Buried in an [sic] Ruined Building," Washington *Evening Star,* June 9, 1893, 1.

6. "Clerks Discharged: Names of those Dropped from War Department Rolls," Washington *Evening Star*, August 15, 1894, 3.

7. "Funeral of Mrs. Fellows: Venerable Lady is Buried in the Congressional Cemetery," Washington *Evening Star*, October 26, 1909, 12.

8. *Washington Herald*, October 26, 1909, 2.

Chapter 26

1. Advertisement in the Allentown, Pennsylvania *Morning Call,* January 25, 1940, 11.

2. Gilbert King, "Geronimo's Appeal to Theodore Roosevelt," *Smithsonian Magazine*, November 9, 2012, smithsonianmag.com/history/geronimos-appeal-to-theodore-roosevelt-117859516, accessed September 14, 2022.

3. Louisa Riggs to Kunigunde Duncan, May 10, 1939, Kenneth Isely Collection of Bliss Isely and Flora Isely Papers, Wichita State University Libraries Special Collection and University Archives.

4. Kunigunde Duncan (pen name for Flora Isely), Letters to I. Louisa M. Riggs, 1899–1950 (archives of the Center for Western Studies, Augustana University, May 20, 1939).

5. Rose Staunton Kirkbright to Bruce D. Forbes, December 28, 1992, Minnesota Historical Society.

6. Scott Gipson, president and publisher of Caxton Printers, Ltd., email correspondence to Chuck Raasch (the author), February 2, 2021.

7. Claude Campbell to Caxton Publishing Company, October 20, 1939, and Caxton Printers to Claude Campbell, October 25, 1939; both letters provided to author by Scott Gipson, president and publisher of Caxton Printers, February 2, 2021.

Chapter 27

1. "A Wichitan 31 Years," *Wichita Eagle,* July 1, 1938, 5.

2. *Wichita People*, Encyclopedia Britannica, britannica.com/topic/Wichita-people, accessed September 30, 2022.

3. US Census Bureau, Population Estimates, July 1, 2021, census.gov/quickfacts/wichitacitykansas.

4. "Wichita: A City with Culture and History," *Visit Wichita*, visitwichita.com/articles/post/wichita-a-city-with-culture-and-history, accessed September 30, 2022.

5. Ruth Keller, "In Society: Carnation Club," *Wichita Daily Eagle*, April 4, 1911, 4.

6. "Endorsements of A. E. Jacques for Clerk of the District Court," *Wichita Citizen,* October 31, 1930, 9.

7. Kenneth Sauer, "Life Story of Former Wichita Woman Told in New Book," Wichita *Eagle*, December 4, 1938, 50.

8. Ibid.

9. Rose Staunton Kirkbright to Bruce D. Forbes, December 28, 1992, Minnesota Historical Society.

10. *Wichita Evening Eagle*, February 28, 1935, 10.

11. Rose Staunton Kirkbright to Bruce D. Forbes, December 28, 1992, Minnesota Historical Society.

12. Handwritten copy of a review of *Blue Star* by Elaine Goodale Eastman, Springfield, MA, *Republican*, winter 1939, Center for Western Studies, Augustana University.

EPILOGUE

1. "Cheyenne River Sioux Tribe's Additional Compensation Claim for the Oahe Dam," US General Accounting Office, January 1998, gao.gov/assets/rced-98-39.pdf, accessed November 20, 2022.

2. Lanniko L. Lee, "Ways of River Wisdom," *Shaping Survival; Essays by Four American Indian Tribal Women*, eds. Charles L. Woodard and Jack L. Marken (Lanham and London: Scarecrow Press, Inc., 2001), 25.

3. *Lake Oahe*, recreation.gov/camping/gateways/292, accessed October 15, 2022.

4. *Oahe Chapel*, South Dakota Historical Society, history.sd.gov/preservation/docs/BROCHUREOaheChapel2013Color.pdf, accessed October 15, 2022.

Index

About the Author

Chuck Raasch is a journalist and author and leads tours for the Smithsonian Institution. He was one of the five original long-form writers for *USA Today* when it began in 1982 and later was a columnist and national correspondent for Gannett News Service for twenty-five years. He retired in 2017 after a stint as the Washington correspondent for the *St. Louis Post-Dispatch*. He has reported from forty-nine states and five continents. A graduate of South Dakota State University, Raasch completed a journalism fellowship at Stanford University and is a member of the National Press Club and the Gridiron Club. He lives in the Washington, DC, metro area.